*Practice* ~~GJ~~
*and the*
*Ministry of the Church,*
*1952–1984*

*Edmund P. Clowney*

# Practical Theology and the Ministry of the Church,

## 1952–1984

## Essays in Honor of Edmund P. Clowney

*Edited by*
Harvie M. Conn

**Presbyterian and Reformed Publishing Company**
**Phillipsburg, New Jersey**

Copy editing by Edward W. Ojarovsky.
General editing and page design by Thom E. Notaro.
Typesetting by BookMasters, Inc., Ashland, Ohio.
Manufactured in the United States of America.

**Library of Congress Cataloging-in-Publication Data**

Practical theology and the ministry of the church, 1952–1984 : essays
   in honor of Edmund P. Clowney / edited by Harvie M. Conn.
      p.    cm.
   Includes bibliographical references.
   ISBN 0-87552-207-6
   1. Theology, Practical.   2. Clergy—Office.   3. Evangelicalism—
United States.   4. Reformed Church—United States.   5. Clowney,
Edmund P.   I. Clowney, Edmund P.   II. Conn, Harvie M.
BV3.P693   1990
253—dc20                                  90-34698

*To*
*Jean and Ed,*
*with many thanks*

# Contents

# PART THREE: PROJECTIONS

# Foreword

## Harvie M. Conn

$P$roducing a festschrift to honor someone like Edmund P. Clowney does not require a lengthy defense. But there are those who may wonder what we are doing as we turn it also into yet another book on practical theology.

Edward Farley, professor of theology at the Divinity School of Vanderbilt University, is more than quizzical in this area. He suggests that " 'practical theology' may prove not to be a salvagable term." The prevailing consensus of past definitions, he contends, can no longer be assumed. The term now functions, he continues, "more as a rubric for self-interpretation and location on the curricular map than a name for a discrete phenomenon."[1]

Farley has many provocative suggestions for why that is so. One reason is especially pertinent to this book. It is what others have called the "crisis of cognitive claims."[2] Ever since the Enlightenment, academic theology has been increasingly separated from the practice of faith; theology now questions its own possibility. It talks less about God and more about the possibility of talking about God. Theological talk is perceived as more a metaphor, and less a mirror, of reality.

This crisis has grown to epic proportions in the last three decades. The most recent titles on practical theology resemble more apologetic

1. Edward Farley, "Interpreting Situations: An Inquiry into the Nature of Practical Theology," in *Formation and Reflection: The Promise of Practical Theology*, ed. Lewis S. Mudge and James N. Poling (Philadelphia: Fortress, 1987), 1.

2. Ibid., xxiii.

documents for the legitimacy of the discipline than expositions of its traditional concerns. One writer puts it this way:

> What is the relation between "theology" as an academic discipline and living, worshiping, serving communities of faith? Despite good intentions that it should be otherwise, many today would say that little relationship exists. On the one hand, the academic theological world seems preoccupied with its own problems of methodological coherence and reality reference. On the other, faith communities—whether oriented to the center, the left, or the right—function with scant attention to theology of the scholarly, critical kind. Nuances and qualifications aside, traditional Western assumptions about the relation between church and theology, between faith lived and faith thought-through, seem by and large to be evaporating before our eyes.[3]

The agenda raised by this kind of analysis suggests much more than that practical theology has been neglected or sold short. Nor is it simply that practical theology has disappeared into a wide-ranging plethora of specialty studies. Nor do we understand if we say the problem is that practical theology is "simple-minded theology" and "easy," while systematic and biblical theology is "hard" and therefore "intellectually respectable."

The problems are much deeper. Enlightenment skepticism has robbed practical theology of its moorings in an inerrant Word of God. The acceptance of theological pluralism in the church has left the people of God with "trajectories" and "paradigms" instead of "guidelines." Pragmatism has minimized the need for theological reflection on the life and practice of the faith.

We are left with a church that cries for relevant theology. But one side cannot find such relevance in the many contradictory theologies it claims to find in the Bible. And another side cannot find any relevant theology because of its captivation with the how-to-do-it side of theology's practice.

The achievement of Ed Clowney, whose name we seek to honor in these essays, is his rooting of the discipline of practical theology in a pre-Enlightenment mentality that sought to overcome both these problems. With his predecessor, R. B. Kuiper, who occupied virtually single-

3. Ibid., xiii.

handedly the chair of practical theology at Westminster Seminary for two decades (1933–52), Ed shared similar convictions about what that title meant.

It can be said of Ed, as it was of Kuiper:

> Of first importance was the point that Practical Theology is theology. He did not think of his work at the seminary as anything like a glorified assembly line turning out kits containing ten simple tools for becoming a successful preacher. His teaching in no way resembled a popular image of a department of Practical Theology as being little more than a place for learning the techniques of effective pastoral public relations. . . . The great biblical principles that powered the Reformation had captured the full allegiance of his mind and heart. These same principles governed all of his teaching, just as they had governed his work in the churches he served. This fact among others endeared him to his colleagues. They knew he was an able theologian and not merely a homiletical technician.[4]

No one who studied under Ed Clowney from 1952 to 1984 ever missed that commitment. He brought to every course biblical insights shaped by his studies in the history of special revelation. Whether homiletics or Christian education, missions or ecclesiology, each class moved from Genesis through Revelation, drawing together the whole of Scripture with new insights that pointed in a fresh way to Christ and His redemptive purposes.

I was reminded of this again as I reviewed Ed's writings in the preparation of this volume. Looking for appropriate quotes that might preface each of the chapters, I found all I needed and marvelled, moreover, at the depth of biblical study wherever I turned. No area of practical theology was untouched. And no discussion began or ended without being touched by the mark of Scripture.

That touch was always doxological. The doctrines of sovereign grace and God's electing love in Christ are the themes to which Ed consistently returns. His study of ecclesiology is particularly marked by this emphasis. The outlines of his papers and books on this topic are trinitarian calls to praise and thanksgiving. Calvinism's caricatures as "a cold and heartless system," "without interest in evangelism or missions," are exposed as stereotypes in his calls to Christian meditation and to the missionary calling of the church.

4. Edward Heerema, R. B.: A Prophet in the Land (Jordan Station, Ontario: Paideia, 1986), 131.

Those commitments to Reformed theology are displayed also in his service in the church and its reformation. The visible church plays no peripheral role in his thinking or practice. Out of concern for its purity, his convictions brought him into the Presbyterian renewal movement of the 1930s associated with the name of J. Gresham Machen and the church that eventually came out of it, the Orthodox Presbyterian Church.

Ordained in 1942 by that body, Ed served pastorates in Connecticut, Illinois, and New Jersey before beginning his teaching career at Westminster in 1952. As editor of the Christian Education Committee of that church from 1949 to 1954 and continuing member of that committee for years after, he wrote much of its vacation Bible school material and played an important part in shaping the church's educational program. Charles Schauffele reflects on this contribution in a delightfully personal way in his chapter in this collection.

In 1984, two years after his retirement from the presidency of Westminster (1966–82), Ed joined the Presbyterian Church in America, a denomination with historical roots similar to the Orthodox Presbyterian Church. He continues to serve as associate pastor and teacher-in-residence at Trinity Presbyterian Church, Charlottesville, Virginia.

Ed's commitments to the Reformed church have not kept him from service outside that community. They have, in fact, driven him to it. A frequent speaker for InterVarsity Christian Fellowship, he has also contributed more recently to the work of the Theological Commission of the World Evangelical Fellowship, of which he is a member. In his own words:

> We sometimes assume that the Reformed church is guarding all the fullness of God's truth like the mythical dragon coiled around its treasure in a cave. The evangelical church, on the other hand, we see travelling far and wide with no more to distribute than four spiritual laws. But Paul's goal of fulfilling the gospel does much more than add zealous propagation to zealous preservation. It transforms both. When the Reformed church coils upon itself in the dragon posture it loses more than the missionary dynamic of the gospel. It loses in significant measure the gospel itself.[5]

In recognition of Ed Clowney's service and in gratitude to God for his gifts, this book is offered in thanks. Written by colleagues and friends,

5. Edmund P. Clowney, "The Missionary Flame of Reformed Theology," in *Theological Perspectives on Church Growth*, ed. Harvie M. Conn (Phillipsburg, N.J.: Presbyterian and Reformed, 1976), 146–47.

many of them his former students, it seeks to chronicle the directions of practical theology in the Reformed and evangelical communities during the time of Ed's teaching at Westminster. It provides, in the opening chapters, something of the background against which this work was undertaken. Each essayist was also asked to offer forecasts and weather predictions for the future of practical theology.

Edward Farley, whose words began this foreword, traces the ultimate failure of practical theology to "the clerical paradigm, limiting praxis to ministerial professional activities."[6] Controlled by its satellite sciences, he concludes, this subfield of study alienates theology from practice on three levels: the personal, the societal, and the churchly.

Certainly there are missing elements in these studies that might suggest Farley has a point. The societal is most apparent to me, though William Edgar's essay goes a long way to dispelling that criticism. And obviously there is enough in these chapters to convince a Farley that the practical theology we are still talking about remains "a generic term covering a number of church leadership related studies."[7]

At the same time, there are those of us willing to suggest that Farley is confusing the task of a Christian university with the task of the theological seminary. One cannot ask apples to be oranges.

And beyond that, we see two of Farley's lost requirements for the integration of theology and practice as not lost at all within the Christian community represented by these writers. He calls for the restoration of theology as *habitus* or theological understanding and knowledge. This meaning, he says, was taken away by the Enlightenment. The other lost sense is that of theology as science. Schleiermacher, he says, took that away with his definition of religion as feeling.[8]

In this volume, you read the writings of men whose thinking about practical theology has not come through the Enlightenment and been reprocessed by Schleiermacher. Theology as wisdom and as science still functions, its Reformational roots sometimes disturbed but still intact. After all, it was not Kant or Schleiermacher who called for *sola scriptura*. It was pastoral clerics like Calvin and Luther.

Before I close these introductory words, there is one other person to be thanked. Ed Clowney would not be Ed Clowney without her. Since

6. Edward Farley, "Theology and Practice outside the Clerical Paradigm," in *Practical Theology: The Emerging Field in Theology, Church and World*, ed. Don S. Browning (San Francisco: Harper and Row, 1983), 35.

7. Ibid., 39.

8. Ibid., 25–29.

1941, Jean Wright Clowney has shared her life with Ed's. Raising five
children, producing flannelgraphs designed by Ed for a whole denomination in the basement of the manse, offering her quiet support and her
musical gifts to the church, she has stood with her husband and behind
him. She has been a "secret sharer" in this project from the beginning,
providing information and encouragement all the way. None of this, including Ed, would be complete without her.

We give thanks to God for you both.

# Contributors

*Jay E. Adams,* S.T.M., Ph.D., has served as professor of practical theology at Westminster Theological Seminary since 1963, first in Philadelphia and from 1982 at its California campus. He is also founding dean of the Christian Counseling and Educational Foundation. The author of over fifteen books on preaching and counseling, he is perhaps best known for his ground-breaking volume, *Competent to Counsel.*

*Derke P. Bergsma,* M.A., Rel.D., is professor of practical theology at Westminster Theological Seminary in California. He came to this post in 1982 after a fifteen-year teaching career at Trinity Christian College, Palos Heights, Illinois. He also holds the rank of captain in the Naval Reserve Chaplaincy.

*Harvie M. Conn,* Th.M., Litt.D., is professor of missions at Westminster Theological Seminary, Philadelphia. He joined that staff in 1972 after twelve years of foreign missions service in Korea. He is also editor of *Urban Mission.* His most recent book is *A Clarified Vision for Urban Mission.*

*William Edgar,* M.Div., Ph.D., has served for almost a decade as professor of apologetics at the Faculté Libre de Theologie Reformée in Aix-en-Provence, France. He joined the faculty of Westminster Theological Seminary, Philadelphia, in 1989. He is the author of *Taking Note of Music* (1986).

*George C. Fuller*, M.B.A., Th.D., is president of Westminster Theological Seminary, Philadelphia, an institution he has served since 1978. He came there after almost twenty years in the pastoral ministry (1956–76) and eight years as executive director of the National Presbyterian and Reformed Fellowship (1976–83).

*Arthur F. Glasser*, M.Div., D.D., has served as dean of the school of World Mission and professor of the theology of missions and East Asian studies at Fuller Theological Seminary, Pasadena. Prior to this position, he served for twelve years as the home secretary for the Overseas Missionary Fellowship. Under this same board, he had labored as a foreign missionary in western China at the end of World War II.

*Burton L. Goddard*, S.M., Th.D., is dean emeritus and professor of biblical languages and exegesis at Gordon-Conwell Theological Seminary, Wenham, Massachusetts. He is an ordained minister of the Orthodox Presbyterian Church.

*Roger S. Greenway*, Th.D., is executive director of Christian Reformed World Missions and professor of missions at Calvin Theological Seminary in Grand Rapids. He served for twelve years as a foreign missionary of his church in Sri Lanka and Mexico (1959–70). His latest book is *Cities: Missions' New Frontier*, co-authored with Timothy Monsma.

*Arthur W. Kuschke, Jr.*, Th.M., is librarian emeritus of Westminster Theological Seminary, where he served from 1940 to 1979.

*Bruce J. Nicholls*, B.D., M.Th., is pastor of a Hindi-speaking congregation of the Church of South India. A missionary laboring with Inter Serve (formerly the Bible and Medical Missionary Fellowship), he was for many years executive secretary of the Theological Commission of the World Evangelical Fellowship. He authored the 1979 title, *Contextualization: A Theology of Gospel and Culture*.

*Roger R. Nicole*, Th.D., Ph.D., is professor emeritus of theology at Gordon-Conwell Theological Seminary, Wenham, Massachusetts. He has served there since 1945. A festschrift commemorating his seventieth birthday, *Reformed Theology in America*, appeared in 1985.

*James I. Packer*, D.Phil., D.D., is professor of systematic and historical theology at Regent College, Vancouver. He joined the staff there in 1979 after ten years of continuous service at Tyndale Hall (and its successor, Trinity College), Bristol (1970–79). His book, *Knowing God*, has become an acknowledged classic.

*Robert G. Rayburn*, Th.D., D.D., served as the founding president of Covenant Theological Seminary, St. Louis (1956–77) and taught in the areas of homiletics and practical theology. His ministerial experience spanned the pastorate, active duty as a chaplain in both World War II and the Korean War, and the presidency of two Christian colleges. He went to be with the Lord while this volume was in production.

*Samuel F. Rowen*, M.Div., Ph.D., has served for over fifteen years on the staff of Missionary Internship, Farmington, Michigan, most recently as director of intercultural research. He served for six years in Jamaica with Worldteam (formerly West Indies Mission). He is the co-editor of *Missions and Theological Education in World Perspective*.

*Charles G. Schauffele*, Th.B., D.D., was professor emeritus of Christian education at Gordon-Conwell Theological Seminary, Wenham, Massachusetts, where he joined the faculty in 1964. Prior to that he served in three pastorates in the Orthodox Presbyterian Church—totaling a ministry of twenty-eight years. He too went to be with the Lord during the production of this volume.

*Geoffrey Thomas*, B.D., has pastored the Alfred Place Baptist Church, Aberystwyth, Wales, since 1965. He is an assistant editor of *The Banner of Truth* and presently the chair of the Grace Baptist Assembly Organizing Committee.

*Ted Ward*, Ed.D., holds the G. W. Aldeen Chair of International Studies at Trinity Evangelical Divinity School, Deerfield, Illinois. He has served the institution since 1985 as professor of Christian education and mission and dean of international studies. Prior to this post, he was professor of education at Michigan State University and director of programs in non-formal education of the Institute for International Studies.

# Part One
# *Backgrounds*

We cannot affirm doctrine that is less than Reformed, for we believe this is Pauline doctrine, Petrine doctrine, Johannine doctrine, Biblical doctrine. Yet we wish to be Reformed only in obedience to Scripture, and therefore with the deepest resolve not only to learn from one another, but also to reach out to all our brethren in Christ. Our conviction about Scripture encourages us to overcome the most hardened barriers that separate us from those who will acknowledge with us the Bible as the Word of God. New richness of Bible interpretation has opened the way for new discussions with Lutheran and Baptist believers. A freshly united church confessing the grace of Christ could have a fruitful ministry in calling men to consider anew the doctrinal differences that have divided the church. . . . Our fellowship is with Him; it is also with one another, with whom we have so much to share of the riches of His grace.

"By God's Grace . . . The Church" (1971)

# I

# Evangelicalism in America: A Look at Three Decades

## Burton L. Goddard

*I*t would be a big mistake to think that suddenly, at midcentury, evangelicalism appeared on the scene full-blown. The movement had been at least in low gear for a long time; and, if one is to understand in any comprehensive way its forms and spirit in the decades that followed, he or she does well to look back to its roots and expression in the several decades that preceded.

### GENERAL BACKGROUND AND DEVELOPMENT

Nineteenth-century theological liberalism with its antisupernaturalism, low view of Scripture, and attachments to the social gospel movement gradually came to dominate colleges, seminaries, and increasingly the church as a whole. But God had long ago promised that the gates of hades would not overcome His church. And, as at a time in the distant past, it could still be said that He had seven thousand whose knees had not bowed down to Baal.

Shortly after the turn of the century, numbers of Bible-believing Christians began to raise their voices in protest. In a series of small volumes entitled *The Fundamentals* issued from 1910 to 1915, concerned writers defended such doctrines as the infallibility of Scripture, the virgin birth of Christ, His substitutionary atonement, His bodily resurrection, and His second coming. Other voices were raised against the theory of naturalistic evolution.

3

Words were soon translated into action, and in the 1930s separatist movements resulted in the formation of the Independent Fundamentalist Churches of America and the General Association of Regular Baptists. At the same time, and with similar apologetic emphasis, two organizations dedicated to the defense of Bible teaching over against the views of modern science came into being—the Religion and Science Association and the Deluge Geological Association.

In the following decade, reacting to the liberal ecumenism of the Federal Council of Churches, Carl McIntire led in the formation of the American Council of Christian Churches. Because of the narrow, defensive stance of these sincere attempts to counter the liberalism of the time, the number of committed Christians jumping onto that bandwagon remained relatively small.

Who, then, would successfully spread the word about the threat to Christ's church? The response came from Christians who shared in large measure the doctrinal viewpoint of the so-called fundamentalists but who had a more positive approach and chose to call themselves "evangelicals." In short, they were Bible-believers. Described further, they were Christians who looked upon the saving work of Jesus Christ as central in the teaching of Scripture and who considered it imperative to take the Good News of Christ's salvation to the whole world.

In the providence of God, the evangelical message spread in a remarkable way through various channels. Radio broadcasters such as Charles Fuller, Walter Maier, and Donald Grey Barnhouse took the gospel into an untold number of homes. Bible conferences brought together earnest Christians from a great variety of backgrounds. *The Sunday School Times* and *Moody Monthly* were widely read. Bible institutes and Bible colleges sprang up in many places. Most of these were unrelated to denominations. In due time seminaries of evangelical persuasion opened their doors.

Scholarship was hardly the earmark of the fundamentalist movement. But in 1929 J. Gresham Machen and other professors withdrew from Princeton Theological Seminary for doctrinal reasons and established Westminster Theological Seminary, giving the evangelical cause a new respectability in academic circles. Interestingly enough, although Machen disliked the connotations of the fundamentalist label, he made it clear where his basic sympathies lay, declaring that if categories were pressed, he wanted to be known as "a fundamentalist from the word 'go.' "

The founding of the National Association of Evangelicals in 1942 brought many Christians together. In the previous year, the American Scientific Affiliation was formed, and in 1949 the Evangelical Theological Society appeared, providing fellowship and common study on the basis of full commitment to the integrity of Scripture. Evangelicals with common ties as members of the business community had founded the Christian Business Men's Committee in 1937, and 1951 saw the creation of the Full Gospel Business Men's Fellowship International.

The years 1941 to 1951 witnessed the emergence of parachurch evangelical youth movements—Young Life, Youth for Christ, Campus Crusade for Christ—all of which were to have a profound influence on American youth.

As denominationally operated foreign missionary programs became more and more infiltrated with liberalism, those who called themselves fundamentalists (with their spiritual successors) began to form independent mission organizations, commonly known as "faith missions," whose statements of faith were strongly evangelical.

In the somewhat narrower field of evangelism, the year 1949 witnessed the rise of Billy Graham to public stature as an evangelist. His ministry, as perhaps that of no other individual, gave credence and visibility to the evangelical cause and received the backing of conservative Christians around the world.

By midcentury one evangelical banner after another was raised proclaiming the authority of Scripture, crossing denominational lines, emphasizing the fundamentals of the Christian faith, and offering fellowship to conservative Christians. But twentieth-century evangelicalism was still in its infancy. In the three decades or so to follow, it would burst forth into full bloom and reach a certain degree of maturity.

## A LOOK AT THE LOCAL CHURCH

Imagine, if you will, an evangelical church worship in the middle of our century that included the following: (1) a reading of Bible passages spelled out in a bulletin insert with the pastor as one reader, a lay person standing at his pew as a second reader, and the congregation reading in unison at designated places; (2) Scripture readings taken from a modern English translation of the Bible; (3) numbers of specialized short prayers at various points; (4) a major prayer time, when prayer requests were solicited, jotted down by the pastor, and presented to the Lord by lay volunteers; (5) a lay person at the front of the auditorium describing a specific missionary project or telling about the work of a particular missionary; and (6) a guitarist standing by the front pews and leading the congregation in the singing of a modern composition, the words of which were printed in the bulletin. All these features would have been a surprise in the forties but not in the eighties. Something has happened to age-old traditions of worship—and to just about every phase of church activity.

Small groups, such as those for weekday Bible study, for fellowship, and for prayer, are more and more found in the churches. Planning sessions formulate goals and how to achieve them, evaluate progress, consider what God would be pleased to have His people be and do. Programs are targeted for singles, young adults, senior citizens, and other specialized groups within the church. There are training sessions for leadership, discipling of others, house-to-house visitation. Church offices are equipped with computers. Management techniques are studied and applied.

"Church renewal" is the umbrella term that describes what has happened, and the evangelical church is often in the forefront as changes are introduced. In the sixties and seventies books on church renewal spurred congregations to awake from their lethargy and examine themselves. Too long had churchgoers gone through forms of worship and activities without the power of God being manifest.

Over a number of years evangelical churches put new emphasis on the Sunday school—its curriculum, its effectiveness, its outreach. Sunday school conventions, once a prominent feature of churches, now increased again in number. Here and there an evangelical church came to number its Sunday school attendants in the thousands.

During the period presently being examined, some sections of the country that had been to a large extent spiritually barren felt the impact of evangelicalism. In New England, to cite but one example, community after community was confronted with biblical preaching and emphasis, and new life came to many communities as young pastors with evangelical training increasingly found places in the pastoral ministry.

## EVANGELICAL GROUPINGS

An impressive phenomenon of the period has been movements that have brought Bible-believing Christians together through organizations other than denominational ones.

Although the McIntire efforts were not very productive, the National Association of Evangelicals (NAE) had healthy growth and brought together more than forty denominations and a sizable number of individual churches from other denominations. Its name suggests its commitment to evangelicalism, and the association has an impressive record of accomplishments in the fields of missions, broadcasting, and world relief. Above all, it has given several million evangelicals a corporate identity.

Among blacks, the NAE counterpart is the National Black Evangelical Association, begun in 1963.

The Reformed Ecumenical Synod, meeting first in 1946, is distinctly evangelical but has a much narrower doctrinal basis than the NAE. International in character, its membership includes thirty-eight denominations. Later, the North American Presbyterian and Reformed Council was organized, allowing American churches of Reformed persuasion to further common causes.

The Evangelical Theological Society has grown apace, reaching a membership of about fourteen hundred. With a common commitment to the Scriptures as inerrant, it attracted scholars from many educational institutions, acquainting them with one another and giving them a sense of working together as fellow laborers in the common task of evangelical theological education. Suspicion gave way to trust and cooperation. Annual as well as regional meetings of the society have provided opportunity for theological discussion and personal fellowship. The society's quarterly journal and a monograph series give public expression to writings of its members.

Other organizations that transcend denominational lines include the Institute for Biblical Research, the North American Theological Students Fellowship, the Wesleyan Theological Society, and the Society for Pentecostal Studies.

One of the most striking phenomena of the last several decades has been the emergence of charismatic groups and individuals outside Pentecostal denominations. The new charismatics tend to identify with the theological stance of evangelicalism, holding to a high view of Scripture, an emphasis on the saving work of Christ, and winning of the lost.

Such organizations as the Presbyterian Charismatic Communion and the Episcopal Charismatic Fellowship provide fellowship within denominations, and the Full Gospel Business Men's Fellowship International brings together men from the business community. Another international rallying point was an International Conference on Charis-

matic Renewal in Christian Churches in 1977. Jesus '79 was a similar
conference.

Just as increasing numbers of individual churches include Bible study
groups, so also there are similar programs that transcend denominational
lines, typical of which is the Bible Study Fellowship. In just one year
some eighty thousand persons, mostly women, met for two and one-half
hours weekly to engage in Bible study.

Other groupings that have brought evangelical women together include the Christian Women's Clubs and the Evangelical Women's Caucus. Evangelical feminists such as Nancy Hardesty, Letha Scanzoni, and
Virginia Mollenkott, by both their writings and their speaking, have
brought the themes of the feminist movement to the attention of evangelical women, with mixed reactions. Elisabeth Elliot has defended the
more traditional views of the place of women in the home and the
church. While the voice of Anita Bryant has become silent due to personal problems, Beverly LaHaye continues to rally evangelical women
around Christian causes through Concerned Women of America.

With beginnings in 1977, the International Council on Biblical Inerrancy focused the attention of evangelicals on the importance of regarding the Bible as free from error. Its "Chicago Statement," issued the
following year, clarified the meaning to be attached to the term *inerrancy.* Then in 1981 it put forth a document relating hermeneutics to
the nature of Scripture. Conferences and printed materials are designed
to defend the inerrancy of the Bible "in a spirit of Christian love and
concern for the truth."

Evangelicals have joined in a variety of conferences: the Wenham Conference on Scripture (1966); the World Congress on Evangelism, Berlin
(1966); the Thanksgiving Workshop on Evangelical Social Concern
(1973); the International Congress on World Evangelism (1974); and
follow-up conferences; an evangelical feminist conference that set up the
Evangelical Caucus (1975); the Consultation on Future Evangelical Concerns (1977); and the Chicago Call, an appeal for Christian unity (1977).

Seminars led by Bill Gothard, James Dobson, Tim and Beverly LaHaye,
and others have attracted considerable numbers of evangelicals, stressing
the application of Christian values in a confused and frustrated world.

Both broad evangelical interests and numbers of special interests have
seen evangelicals banded together to provide fellowship, to study and
discuss common concerns, to formulate positions, and to join in concerted action. The account given above is only representative of what
has been taking place.

## EVANGELISM AND WORLD MISSIONS

Evangelists and revivals made their mark during the nineteenth century. But who could have foretold the reappearance of mass evangelism in the second half of the century that followed? At midcentury people were beginning to hear about a man named Billy Graham, and before long that name was not only a household word but one publicized by the media. This man, together with the Billy Graham Evangelistic Association, has had an effective worldwide ministry.

Developing a different type of evangelism at the Coral Ridge Presbyterian Church in Fort Lauderdale, pastor D. James Kennedy has shared that methodology in training sessions with many evangelical pastors. The procedures are now carried out through many local churches nationwide. Evangelism Explosion, as the movement is called, is centered in lay visitation in the community—the aim being to tell the Good News, win people to Christ, disciple them, and make them participants in the evangelistic ministry.

One of the most significant developments in evangelism was the founding in 1973 of Jews for Jesus, led by Moishe Rosen. The organization has enjoyed a good degree of visibility and has effectively evangelized sizable numbers of Jews, especially young people.

At the turn of the century the total number of independent foreign mission agencies was relatively small, but the *Encyclopedia of Modern Christian Missions* (1967) tells the story of hundreds of such agencies. The number of organizations, almost all evangelical in character, has continued to grow, while the foreign mission programs of most of the large denominations have been retrenching.

Cooperative effort in the program of world evangelism has proved rewarding, two associations taking the lead: the Evangelical Foreign Missions Association (affiliated with the National Association of Evangelicals) and the Interdenominational Foreign Mission Association. Together, they represent more than a hundred mission organizations. These associations have done much to facilitate the work of evangelical programs the world around, such as the promotion of missionary endeavor, relations with governments, and cooperation in purchasing and in travel arrangements.

A relatively recent development designed to foster world evangelism was the establishment at Wheaton College of the Billy Graham Center. Another was the opening of the United States Center for World Mission, founded and directed by Ralph Winter and dedicated to the task of finding ways and means for evangelizing the unreached millions cut off by cultural bonds from a knowledge of the gospel.

Of the various kinds of missionary programs that have flourished since midcentury, perhaps none is better known than Wycliffe Bible Translators. Supported and manned to a large extent from America, the work speaks in loud voice of the vitality and vision of American evangelicalism. Wycliffe is dedicated to the task of making the Scriptures available to peoples everywhere so that they may more easily hear God speaking and so respond to the call of the gospel. Its translating efforts have been fruitful, despite opposition in some of the countries where workers are stationed.

One of the most significant innovations in recent years was the development under evangelical auspices of Theological Education by Extension. TEE is a program of supervised, nonresidence learning in biblical and theological studies. Those involved in ministry remain in their ministries and work with programmed materials to further refine their skills for effective witness to the gospel.

At the University of Illinois in Urbana, InterVarsity Christian Fellowship has undertaken a series of triennial missionary conferences with special focus on interesting Christian youth in missionary service abroad, projecting a goal of a thousand volunteers at each conference. Each of the last several conferences attracted an attendance of approximately eighteen thousand, and enthusiasm for missions had a marked effect on those who attended.

Another way in which students frequently identify with home and foreign missions is by group visits to mission areas, fraternizing with the people, visiting homes, becoming acquainted with other cultures, witnessing to their faith, engaging in teaching ministries, and, more often than not, participating in such endeavors as renovation and construction projects. Such programs do much to create and heighten zeal for missions.

Oswald Smith and the People's Church in Toronto pioneered in setting goals and soliciting pledges for foreign missions. Following this pattern, Boston's Park Street Church, during the pastorate of Harold Ockenga, instituted an annual missions conference and introduced a system of pledges so that giving to missions increased amazingly. The 1984 total amounted to $1,003,055. Many churches, large and small, followed suit with conferences and "faith pledges," transforming their participation in the cause of Christian missions.

Evangelism and missions are central in modern evangelicalism, and the spiritually healthy church is a church that emphasizes this centrality.

## YOUTH MINISTRIES

For the last several decades, youths have been prime targets of evangelism. One organization after another has come into being for the purpose of winning students to Christ, teaching them the Word, and strengthening them through Christian fellowship.

Youth for Christ and Young Life operate on the high-school level. InterVarsity Christian Fellowship, Campus Crusade for Christ, and the Navigators minister primarily to college students. Teen Challenge carries on inner-city ministries designed to reach young lives marred by such devastating influences as gang warfare, prostitution, alcohol, and drugs.

Whereas denominational youth programs have proved ineffectual or have achieved only moderate success, these parachurch organizations have touched untold lives—bringing young people to Christ, transforming their outlook, turning them about, and often sending them into training for Christian service. Many of those reached have come from mainline church homes.

Founded in 1969, Youth Specialties is dedicated to the training of youth leaders, supplying them with resource materials, and challenging their thinking through seminars. Humor is widely employed, more particularly in its periodical, *The Door* (formerly *The Wittenburg Door*).

Although centered in Switzerland, l'Abri Fellowship has had a profound influence on many American young people. Through books and films and lectures, Francis and Edith Schaeffer and their son Franky Schaeffer V have helped Christians to develop an evangelical worldview. The Schaeffers have emphasized the authority of Scripture and pinpointed the awfulness of such modern sins as abortion.

On the sports scene, the Fellowship of Christian Athletes is the best known organization, but it is not alone in the effort to minister to athletes, bring them to saving faith, and encourage them to witness to the world about Jesus Christ. Even in professional sports such as football, chapel services and fellowship and study programs provide an effective ministry. And it is not unusual for athletes, like American presidents, to talk publicly about being born again.

## BROADCASTING, TELECASTING, MUSIC, FILMS

Christian radio broadcasting during the second quarter of the twentieth century paved the way for continuation and expansion in the years to follow. A random sampling of the more recent evangelical broadcasting programs reveals such corporate names as "The Back to the Bible Hour," "The Hour of Decision," "The Joyful Sound," "The Radio Bible Class," and "The Back to God Hour" and such individual names as J. Vernon McGee, James Boice, and Chuck Swindoll.

Telecasting names are perhaps more familiar to the nation at large: Billy Graham, Oral Roberts, Jerry Falwell, Robert Schuller, Pat Robertson, Jim Bakker, Jimmy Swaggart, James Robison, Rex Humbard, D. James Kennedy, and Richard DeHaan. Some represent the charismatic movement; all have evangelical characteristics.

That the "electronic church" has made considerable impact is apparent from the attacks directed against it. Financial givers number in the millions, as do the amounts given. Listeners identify with what they see and hear, and the support they provide gives them the feeling that they are participants in a corporate testimony of great proportions to what they regard as basic Christian truths.

More or less influenced by the rock music of our day, evangelicals have made a place for popular music on Christian themes, for electronic guitars and drums, for the familiar beat. Andrae Crouch, Debby Boone, B. J. Thomas, Larry Norman, Ken Miedema, John Michael Talbot, and Amy Grant caught the ear of Christian young people in the seventies and eighties. In many evangelical churches the new trends are being woven into services of worship more and more. And the sales of recordings featuring the new religious music testify to its popularity.

At the same time, musicians such as Don Wyrtzen produce contemporary compositions that are yet appreciated by those of the older generation.

Billy Graham films and those produced by a variety of Christian agencies carry the message of the gospel to many viewers, both in the United States and abroad.

It is certainly true that music and films take a distant second place to broadcasting and telecasting in getting out the message of the Good News, but they do indeed leave their mark on evangelicals, especially the young.

## CHRISTIAN EDUCATION

Although Catholics, Lutherans, and Seventh-day Adventists had for a long time operated parochial schools, by midcentury the Christian day school movement was still in its infancy. Today, this largely evangelical movement is in high gear with more than seven hundred new elementary and secondary schools being opened each year. By the mid-eighties the total number of such schools in the United States was estimated to be at least thirty-four thousand with an enrollment exceeding two million. Add to this the growing practice among conservative Christians of home schooling, and the picture is an encouraging one for the preparing of dedicated Christian young people. Many of them go on to schools of higher education, more often than not enrolling in Christian institutions.

By the year 1900 higher and theological education was largely in the hands of the secularists and those of liberal theological persuasion. Reacting to this situation, evangelicals had founded Bible training schools such as Moody Bible Institute, Northwestern Bible Training School, the Bible Institute of Los Angeles, and Nyack Missionary College.

Schools like these were essential if workers were to be prepared for missionary service, such demands being constantly on the increase. In time, the schools learned that they could service the evangelical community by expanding the curricula to include more general studies on the college level, and "Bible colleges" sprang up. They offered four-year courses with either a Bible major supplemented by arts and science courses or a double major: Bible and a liberal arts subject. It is estimated that there are now more than 250 Bible colleges in the United States and Canada, and an accrediting association continues to upgrade the academic character of these institutions.

Some schools that began as missionary training institutions or Bible schools were caught up in an evolutionary process that eventually turned them into Christian liberal arts colleges, a few of which added programs of theological training. And evangelicals started other Christian colleges.

A dozen of the larger Christian colleges have banded together as the Christian College Consortium, working together for common goals. Also, the consortium brought into being the Christian College Coalition, some seventy schools cooperating in making contacts with legislators and providing for students to study in the national capital in areas related to government.

Christian colleges have come a long way during the past thirty years. Perhaps best known are Asbury, Bethel, Calvin, Gordon, Taylor, Westmont, and Wheaton, but others are prominent regionally and are increasingly well known nationally. Most Christian colleges have seen a remarkable increase in the numbers of faculty and students. Faculty members more often than not have earned doctorates from reputable graduate schools. Majors are offered in many fields. Physical facilities are impressive. And alumni make their way with distinction through graduate programs in universities in America and abroad. Moreover, the quality of the education offered by Christian colleges is attested by accreditation from standard accrediting associations.

To cite but one example, in 1950 Gordon College had a student body of 331; a faculty of 21, of whom 6 had earned doctorates; and a handful of buildings in the heart of Boston. In 1984 there were 1,073 students; the faculty had increased to 52, of whom 42 had earned doctorates; it occupied an eight-hundred-acre campus near Boston with a pleasing array of physical facilities; and it had liberal arts accreditation.

Just as Wheaton College so long supplied a large percentage of America's leaders in evangelical enterprises, the various Christian colleges now thrust forth well-trained graduates into many professional fields as well.

When there were few evangelical theological seminaries, Dallas came into being in 1924, Eastern Baptist in 1925, and Westminster in 1929. Gordon Divinity School took distinctive form in the early thirties, and Fuller was started in 1947. Since then, more schools have been added to the list: Alliance, Bethel, Biblical, Covenant, Denver Conservative Baptist, Eastern Mennonite, Grace, Mid-America Baptist, Reformed, Talbot, Trinity (Episcopal), Trinity Evangelical, Western Conservative Baptist, and others. And there are biblical-theological departments at Bob Jones University, Columbia Bible College, Liberty University, Oral Roberts University, and Wheaton College.

Like the Christian colleges, evangelical seminaries have made great strides in the last three decades. Consider Dallas Theological Seminary. Enrollment in 1950 stood at 199 with 13 faculty members, 8 of whom had earned doctorates. Figures for 1984 showed 1,939 students and 64 faculty members, of whom 41 had earned doctorates.

Books dealing with American evangelicalism most commonly mention Asbury, Denver Conservative Baptist, Dallas, Fuller, Gordon-Conwell, Trinity Evangelical, and Westminster, but each year well-trained young people from an ever-increasing number of other evangelical seminaries enter various forms of Christian ministry.

Numbers of seminaries have felt the need for extension programs by which theological training is made available in the inner city to pastors and other Christian workers who would otherwise have to minister with limited preparation. Courses include offerings on methodology designed to reach urban residents for Christ. Fuller, Gordon-Conwell, and Westminster have pioneered in this area.

The Southern Baptist Convention is so often thought of as a community by itself rather than a body under the general banner "evangelical." But it must be noted that Southwestern Baptist Theological Seminary, conservative in theology, is by far the largest of the seminaries, boasting a total 1984 enrollment of 4,296.

The Lutheran Church-Missouri Synod represents much the same situation as that of the Southern Baptists. In 1984 its St. Louis seminary had 616 students and the seminary at Fort Wayne had an enrollment of 779.

At the half-century mark the American Association of Theological Schools had relatively few accredited members from among evangelical seminaries, but by 1984 the following had been added to the accredited list: Anderson, Ashland, Bethel, Concordia, Concordia Theological, Covenant, Denver Conservative Baptist, Eastern Baptist, Fuller, Goshen, Gordon-Conwell, Mennonite Biblical, Mennonite Brethren Biblical, Moravian, New Orleans Baptist, Northern Baptist, North American Baptist, North Park, Oral Roberts (School of Theology), Phillips University (Graduate Seminary), Reformed, Talbot, and Trinity Evangelical.

Increasingly many theological students receive their training in evangelical seminaries independent of church control and then enter ministry in mainline denominations. The evangelical presence in these churches is increasingly apparent.

Three study programs deserving mention are Regent College, New College (Berkeley), and the Institute for Christian Studies. The first two offer training on the graduate theological level, especially for lay persons, while the Toronto-based institute provides opportunity for advanced study of the implications of Christianity for the many facets of human relationships.

On all levels evangelical education is an amazing contrast to what it was at midcentury.

## BOOKS, PERIODICALS, CASSETTES

Recent years have witnessed the production of a flood of books evangelical in character. Not long ago major evangelical book publishers could be counted on the fingers of one hand, but the number has multiplied in a striking way. To Eerdmans, Zondervan, Moody, Revell, and Baker have been added such names as Word, Presbyterian and Reformed, Bethany Fellowship, Tyndale House, and many others. And

general book publishers, with religious book divisions, issue numbers of
books written by evangelicals.

Christian bookstores market evangelical literature not only in large
cities but in communities of limited size as well. Membership in the
Christian Booksellers Association has risen to around three thousand.

Evangelicals are writing books of many kinds: devotional literature,
group study guides, Christian biographies, popular and scholarly biblical
and theological works, and volumes on the church, missions, the Christian life, and so on.

Heavy teaching loads at evangelical colleges and seminaries long prevented faculty members from writing academic books on biblical and
theological themes. But several quality studies are being produced as
teaching loads have been reduced. Bible commentaries, for example, evidence careful scholarship.

Outstanding among evangelical writers have been men like Carl
Henry and Gordon Clark, although many others have authored volumes
of merit and are increasingly becoming well known.

Modern English translations of the Bible by evangelicals deserve mention at this point, for they have put the Scriptures into forms that more
readily take the message of salvation to the unchurched. *The Living Bible*
has had unusual marketing success, and the *New American Standard Bible*
has had fairly wide evangelical acceptance. Like *The Living Bible*, the
*New International Version* excels in communication, follows the most reliable textual sources, and clarifies the meanings of difficult passages.
Sales of the NIV quickly passed the ten million mark, and it continues
to be the fastest selling of all modern versions.

Leading evangelical organizations that distribute the Scriptures worldwide include the Gideons, the World Home Bible League, and the International Bible Society.

Evangelical periodicals cover a wide range of material and are widely
read. Probably best known have been *Christianity Today, Eternity, Christian Herald, Moody Monthly, Decision,* and *Charisma* (formerly *Christian
Life*). Of these, *Christianity Today*, which began publication in 1956, has
reached an audience considerably larger than narrow evangelical circles
and has widespread influence. In the academic world the Evangelical
Theological Society and the American Scientific Affiliation publish
journals, as do some conservative seminaries.

Over the course of years, Sunday school lesson guides and take-home
papers have improved markedly in format and pedagogical character.
The same is true of vacation Bible school materials. One has only to

think of the contributions of Scripture Press, Gospel Light, Standard Publishing, David C. Cook, and Great Commission Publications products to be aware of the advances that have been made. Audio tape cassettes are a relatively new but very effective means of communicating biblical and theological knowledge, both to ministers and to the laity. Theological seminaries, broadcasters and telecasters, and independent agencies supply cassettes on a variety of subjects and make possible their wide distribution. In this way the human voice adds a personal dimension of distinct value.

Evangelical communication has indeed come of age and is reaching even beyond the Bible-believing community.

## SOCIO-POLITICAL CONCERNS

Reacting to the social gospel movement that had characterized much of American Protestantism in the latter part of the nineteenth century, fundamentalists were wary of giving any major place to "social" concerns. Rather, they concentrated on "gospel" matters.

They were taken to task by Carl Henry in 1947 when he wrote *The Uneasy Conscience of Modern Fundamentalism*, followed in 1964 by his *Aspects of Christian Social Ethics*. Supporting and advancing upon Henry's thesis that conservatives were failing to face up to their social responsibilities, David Moberg, Ronald Sider, Vernon Grounds, Leighton Ford, Stephen Mott, and other evangelicals advanced the claim that the Bible calls upon Christians not only to proclaim the gospel but to press for action to meet human needs.

In 1973 a number of evangelicals issued a social action statement, the "Declaration of Evangelical Social Concern," calling upon Christians to work together for social and political justice. The following year, the International Congress on World Evangelism affirmed that "evangelism and socio-political involvement are both part of our Christian duty."

Periodicals as well as books now promote the cause of social activism. Among these are *The Other Side, Sojourners,* and *The Reformed Journal.*

Bible-believing Christians are certainly beginning to translate social action rhetoric into social action. They have rallied to the call of World Vision International as it ministers through orphanages and provides food and medical aid when natural disasters strike. They also support Food for the Hungry, Bread for the World, and similar organizations, and their churches respond with help in times of famine and other special needs. Chuck Colson's Prison Fellowship and Chaplain Ray's International Prison Ministry exemplify evangelical social concern. The World Relief Commission does an important work as an arm of the National Association of Evangelicals.

Evangelical theologians watching the rise of liberation theology in Latin America and listening to black activists in the United States may reject their proposed package solutions, but they (and rank and file evangelicals) are thinking more and more about biblical grounds for Christian social responsibility. While the Bible-believing community has been somewhat slow to participate in peace demonstrations and anti-nuclear rallies, its people show much concern over the killing of unborn children. They also discern homosexual practice and pornography as threats to Christian social values and enlist in the fight against them.

Although Paul Henry and numbers of other younger evangelicals have been calling for greater participation in the political process, conservative Christians have been cautious about getting involved in politics in an organized way to achieve Christian ends.

In broad terms, evangelicals are urged to exercise their voting rights, to consider Christian principles in their choice of candidates for public office, to get fellow Christians to register to vote, to encourage evangelicals to run for office, and to support organizations that seek through political means to turn back the tides of immorality that characterize the nation.

Without much doubt, evangelicals have been attracted to vote for professing Christians, at least for candidates for national office. The assumption would seem to be that as national leaders such candidates would use their influence to promote righteousness through both rhetoric and action.

Perhaps surprising is the fact that polling results indicate that conservative Christians, even more so than liberals, consider it important for religious organizations to express themselves publicly on matters involving Christian principles.

High on the list of organizations that call for Christians to get involved in the political process have been the Moral Majority (disbanded in 1989), Religious Roundtable, and the Christian Voice.

Recent presidents of the United States have not hesitated to identify themselves as Christians, and members of Congress such as Mark Hatfield, John Anderson, and Jesse Helms have spoken out time and again on issues in which they discern moral and Christian relevance.

There can be little question that evangelicals are manifesting new interest in seeking to gain desired ends through political process. At the same time, they do not all speak with one voice or agree on methodology to achieve desired ends.

## SPECIAL EVANGELICAL COMMUNITIES

Three evangelical communities stand somewhat by themselves—Southern Baptists, Missouri Synod Lutherans, and blacks—without any great degree of fraternization with smaller evangelical denominations and the large number of evangelicals in other mainline churches.

Traditionally, the Southern Baptists have emphasized the integrity of the Scriptures, a lifestyle that largely conforms to that of other Bible-believing Christians, and evangelism and world missions; but liberalism has infiltrated their colleges and theological seminaries to some degree. Liberal proponents, calling themselves moderates, have tried repeatedly to capture denominational posts that would give them more and more control of the various aspects of Southern Baptist endeavor. However, in the 1985 assembly the moderates failed again in that attempt. Meanwhile, the churches have thrived, and some congregations boast membership in the thousands. Total enrollment is near the eight-million mark. Life is church-centered, whether for worship or social activity, and one gets the impression that as a whole they are very dedicated and happy Christians.

Traditionally a very conservative body, the Lutheran Church, Missouri Synod found itself drifting from its biblical moorings only to be wakened by the bold action of its president, Jacob A. O. Preus, who in 1974 suspended the president of its seminary in St. Louis in view of the liberalizing trends at the school. The upshot of this action was that those sympathetic with the stand of President Tietjen left to found a new seminary and a new denomination.

But for the first time in American church history a denomination that over the years had been faithful to the Word only to find itself on the road to liberalism demonstrated an ability to purge itself and once again take its stand on the great truths of historic Christianity. Evangelicals cannot but rejoice at the courageous action that characterized this body of more than two and one-half million Christians.

The third group, Bible-believing blacks, has also found itself isolated from other evangelical churches and parachurch organizations. Evangelical churches and church leaders have felt it necessary to set up a separate evangelical association rather than becoming part of the National Association of Evangelicals. The American racial situation being what it is, this reticence on the part of black evangelicals to identify with white evangelical programs is not hard to understand. White evangelical churches have not been strong in their denunciation of racism. Nor have they vigorously pursued the path of reconciliation. Moreover, such black leaders as John Perkins, William Pannell, and Tom Skinner have espoused viewpoints associated by some whites with the evangelical left. This has increased the fellowship gap between the two groups. But it must be recognized that trust in the Bible and the importance of putting one's faith in the Son of God for salvation are key characteristics of the great majority of black Christians and their churches.

## EVANGELICALS AND OTHERS

Since theological liberalism has so largely characterized the ecumenical movement, conservative Christians have to a large extent avoided fraternization with those not in theological agreement with them. And, except in cooperative evangelism as represented by Billy Graham, mainline evangelicals have not had much contact with nonmainliners.

Over a period of time, independent fellowships have been set up within denominational structures to forward evangelical concerns: the Presbyterian Lay Committee, Presbyterians United for Biblical Concerns, Covenant Fellowship of Presbyterians, Good News (Methodist), the Fellowship of Witness (Episcopal), and several charismatic fellowships. Theoretically, the presence of such parachurch organizations should bring helpful relationships between evangelicals and denominational leaders; but it is not surprising if the latter sometimes look askance at the independent organizations, remembering how the formation of the Orthodox Presbyterian Church, the Presbyterian Church in America, the Conservative Congregational Christian Conference, and the Anglican Church of North America came into being following the establishment of similar organizations. In any case, a certain amount of tension exists between evangelicals and leaders of several of the large denominations. And many evangelicals find it difficult to remain in denominations controlled by bureaucracies unsympathetic toward Christian truths they hold most dear.

However, some dialogue is now transpiring between evangelicals and mainline denomination representatives, and conservative voices are being heard in national assemblies and the deliberations of denominational committees. Witness the voice of Richard Lovelace in the United Presbyterian Church in the U.S.A. in opposition to the ordination of practicing homosexuals.

As of 1984, an *ad hoc* group of evangelical scholars including people like John Stott, David Wells, and David Hubbard had been in dialogue with Roman Catholic scholars over a period of seven years, discussing biblical grounds for their theological agreements and differences. And, spearheaded by Marvin Wilson, conferences have been held that have brought Jews and evangelicals together for dialogue.

These and other signs point to the likelihood of increasing communication between evangelicals and those with whom they have major differences.

## AN ATTEMPT AT EVALUATION

The above sketch of evangelicalism is professedly not at all complete. Selective, it gives little attention to extremists, whether on the right or on the left. However, it is designed to provide a general picture of the movement since about 1950.

Evangelical growth in recent years has not taken place in a corner—witness the statement by Richard G. Hutcheson, Jr., "The evangelical resurgence was probably the most significant development in American Christianity in the decade of the seventies."[1] With reason, America's bicentennial was designated as "The Year of the Evangelical."

Obviously, evangelicalism is a fragmented movement, with each organization doing its own thing. There has been no great evangelical army going out to bring modern culture into captivity to Christ. J. Gresham Machen once said that we should "go forth joyfully, enthusiastically, to make the world subject to God";[2] but many evangelicals operate on the conviction that God's plans do not envisage a takeover of the world, and so we should be content just to win people one by one in order that a remnant may be saved. At the most, rank and file evangelicals tend to take the position that we should be content to try to influence a culture that is secularist and humanist. Bible-believing Christians have pecked

1. Richard C. Hutcheson, Jr., *Mainline Churches and the Evangelicals: A Challenging Crisis* (Atlanta: John Knox, 1981), 18.
2. Ned B. Stonehouse, *J. Gresham Machen: A Biographical Memoir* (Grand Rapids: Eerdmans, 1954), 187.

away here and there without mounting a united front against a culture
that is morally and spiritually decadent.

Evangelicals tend to disagree strongly with one another at many
points. So we speak of neo-evangelicals, those on the left, those on the
right, and charismatics. Since they don't always get along with one another very well, there is a certain divisiveness in the evangelical camp.

Recent writers have been quick to make much of the so-called young
evangelicals, or the evangelical left. It is true that numbers of evangelicals have adopted views on such issues as the nature of Scripture and its
interpretation, the place of women in the church, and the nature and
degree of social concern that differ from traditional positions. And dire
prophecies have been made regarding the future of evangelicalism.

In his book *The Worldly Evangelicals* Richard Quebedeaux even has a
chapter entitled "Today's Evangelicals, Tomorrow's Liberals?"[3] While he
comes short of giving a categorical answer, he prophesies that much liberalizing will take place.

Other writers have pictured evangelicals as susceptible to the pack-
aged philosophy and programs of the religious right as represented by
such evangelical leaders as Jerry Falwell. Largely through the medium of
television, certain individuals have come to positions of power and influence and in large measure control the thinking of great numbers of
the Lord's people. They speak with authority, and many evangelicals
tend to receive what they have to say without questioning whether this
or that particular thrust is consonant with the Word of God.

But "to err is human." When one examines the platforms of such
leaders, one becomes aware of the fact that they frequently give little
attention to certain all-pervasive teachings of the Scriptures and at the
same time advocate some positions not supported by the Word—or even
contrary to it. One has only to remember the saga of Jim Jones to realize
that dire consequences may result. At the very least, evangelicalism may
be brought into disrepute in the eyes of the public as the man on the
street comes to associate the evangelical cause with leaders who crusade
along questionable religious, political, economic, and social lines.

Shall we then write off evangelicalism as a losing cause despite its
manifest gains? Emphatically no! The very fact that it is not structurally
united and yet has so many units that have risen up conquering and to
conquer testifies to the grass-roots character of the movement; it also
testifies to the work of God in the hearts and minds of His children

3. Richard Quebedeaux, *The Worldly Evangelicals* (New York: Harper and Row, 1978),
163ff.

here, there, and everywhere and to His calling and preparing a varied leadership to effect His purposes. Significantly, church historian Martin Marty prophesied that "the 1980s would continue to be a time of movements rather than of denominations."[4]

Where there is much evangelical smoke, one has reasonable assurance that there is considerable fire, and such fire continues to spring up on every hand and to spread more and more. It may well be that the evangelical left will not turn out to be the transforming force it has been made out to be, and that unfortunate aspects of the religious right will be identified, unmasked, and corrected.

Without question, evangelicalism has many weaknesses. Although the Bible is strongly God-centered, too often those who call themselves Bible-believers evidence trust on the human will, even in matters pertaining to salvation. Too frequently the evangelistic call is this: All you have to do is accept Christ as personal Savior. It is altogether too easy for one to be a professing Christian. In portions of the evangelical church little in the way of a disciplined Christian life is required.

Critics point out that there is much in evangelical practice that is superficial. Many evangelicals tend to be captive to the lifestyle of the world with its emphasis upon pleasure, popularity, sexual permissiveness, and social respectability. Instead of transforming society, they embrace some of its unfortunate aspects.

Acknowledging the many weaknesses and the fact that some of their number have moved toward questionable positions on the left or the right, Christians are more and more setting themselves to strengthen the evangelical camp, standing fast on biblical values, taking the offensive in making these values known, and urging the church to cherish and preserve them.

The flood of evangelical literature, the great number of evangelical educational institutions, the renewed interest in Bible reading and study—all these bode well for the continuing health of evangelicalism.

Following significant developments in the forties, the next several decades saw phenomenal evangelical growth and visibility. Would that today's evangelical community not only rejoice in the progress made but also examine the charges of weakness leveled against it and, consequently, put its house into the kind of order that will insure inner health, numerical growth, and increasing impact upon the world.

4. Martin Marty, quoted in "The Church in the '80s: A Survey of Opinion," *Theology News and Notes* 26, no. 2 (June 1979): 17.

The authority of preaching is not heightened but lost if the preacher forsakes his place behind the Book. We are called to be Christ's but not Christs. The Incarnation is not continued in us, so that we may declare, "I say unto you." Nor are we apostles or prophets, inspired of the Spirit to lay afresh the foundations of the church for a new day. We are ministers of the Word: . . . men of God thoroughly furnished by the Holy Scriptures for every good work of our calling.

*Preaching and Biblical Theology* (1961)

## 2

# Thirty Years' War:
# The Doctrine of Holy Scripture

## James I. Packer

*I* n the story that follows, spanning the years 1955–85, I myself played a small part, of which I shall first narrate some details. I do this partly to show how it is that Edmund Clowney is today an honored friend and partly to make clear how I view the rest of the facts that I shall record. Knowing where I "come from" (as we say) should in any case help the reader in assessing my account of things. So, despite the risk of indulging unmortified egotism, I proceed as announced.

For forty years, first in Britain and then in North America, I along with many others have battled for the authority of the Bible as God's true Word, the trustworthy and sufficient rule of faith. All that time, I have known myself called to be a pastor and have sought to express that identity in my preaching and teaching. So I have fought this good fight (for such I take it to be).

I see biblical authority as methodologically the most basic of theological issues. And I have fought not just for the sake of confessional orthodoxy or theological certainty or evangelical integrity or epistemological sanity or to counter dehumanizing irrationalisms. Rather, my affirmation and defense of Holy Scripture has been first and foremost for the sake of pastoral and evangelistic ministry, lay godliness, the maturing of the church, and spiritual revival. By these things the glory of God and the good of human beings are most truly advanced.

It is no news that not all who are called to academic work have a pastoral motivation, just as not all who are called to pastoral work have academic sensitivity to questions of truth.[1] But I, for one, feel the constraint of both concerns together. So my goal in dogmatics is to find pure streams and strain out sewage; in communication, to relay tested truth for believers to embrace and feed on as their own; and in polemics, to keep such communication from being obstructed. Edmund Clowney, I believe, will empathize; for it is apparent that throughout his own career as pastor, professor, and seminary president, these have been his goals too.

My bit of the story started at Oxford University in 1944. Having been brought to faith in Jesus Christ out of empty religious formalism, I began devouring Scripture devotionally. When I had read it before, it had seemed uninteresting, but now it glowed and spoke. At the close of a Bible exposition forty-one days after my conversion, I knew that the Bible was not, as I had previously thought, a mixture of history, legend, and opinion, requiring selective treatment as other human miscellanies do. I knew now it was in its own nature a divine product and a channel of divine communication, triggering insight and praise.

Years later, when I found Calvin saying that every Christian experiences Scripture speaking authoritatively as from God,[2] I rejoiced to think that, without any prior human instruction and certainly without any prior acquaintance with Calvin, I had long known that experience. When, later still, I found Cornelius Van Til characterizing the Bible by saying that Christ, his Lord, had written him a letter,[3] my heart spoke its own "Amen" once more. The truth is that one element of the catholic Christian experience into which the Bible leads is precisely the experience of the Bible challenging thought and will with God's authority. That experience, by grace, has been mine throughout my Christian life—and is so still.

## EVANGELICAL DISCUSSIONS

In the fifties I often addressed student and church groups on biblical authority. And when I was asked to write up a talk I had given rebutting

1. See E. L. Mascall, *Theology and the Gospel of Christ* (London: SPCK, 1977), esp. chap. 1.

2. Calvin *Institutes* 1.7.5.

3. The sentence is etched on my memory: "I have never seen my Lord Jesus Christ, but He has written me a letter." The reference, alas, I cannot find. The idea of Scripture as a letter from Christ is evidently an extrapolation from the letters to the seven churches (Rev. 2–3).

a series of attacks by church leaders on what they called "our English fundamentalism" (specified by some as the religion of Inter-Varsity Fellowship reinforced by Billy Graham), what came out of the hopper was a full-length book that brought together much of what I had been saying over those years. Its title (apt enough, I think, though devised by the publisher, not me) was *"Fundamentalism" and the Word of God*,[4] a defiant echo of the title of Gabriel Hebert's critique, *Fundamentalism and the Church of God*, published the previous year.[5]

In his censuring of conservative evangelicals for obscurantist incompetence in biblical study and self-sufficient tunnel vision in religious relationships, Hebert had traversed well-worn territory. Throughout the twentieth century evangelicals on both sides of the Atlantic had been execrated as the awkward squad in God's church, for three reasons. First, they showed disrespect to the academic establishment by doubting such "assured results" of higher criticism as the post-Mosaicity of the Pentateuch, the mythical character of the early chapters of Genesis, the seventh-century date of Deuteronomy, the second-century date of Daniel, and the pseudonymity of Isaiah 40-66, the Fourth Gospel, the Pastorals, and 2 Peter. Second, evangelicals treated Jesus' demonstrable confidence in Scripture as decisive for their own, and diagnosed Christians who disbelieved the Bible as disloyal to Christ. Third, they insisted that Christianity requires personal faith in Jesus Christ as one's prophet, priest, and king—an insistence constantly misheard as a demand for a stereotyped sudden conversion. It was on these rather wearisome conventionalities that Hebert, in the style of a genial veteran instructing the foolish young, had rung the changes.

My book, which begged that the word *fundamentalism* be dropped, the infallibility of Scripture recognized, and biblical evangelicalism acknowledged as mainstream Christianity, also said nothing that had not been said before. But, appearing at a time when British evangelicals were looking for ammunition, it was kindly received and widely read. It was

4. J. I. Packer, *"Fundamentalism" and the Word of God* (London: Inter-Varsity Press; Grand Rapids: Eerdmans, 1958); currently marketed in England by Paternoster Press, Exeter.

5. Gabriel Hebert, *Fundamentalism and the Church of God* (London: SCM Press, 1957). Understandably, in view of the withdrawal of the founders of the Inter-Varsity Fellowship from the Student Christian Movement after 1919 on account of the latter's embrace of theological liberalism, SCM Press has had a continuous interest in publishing attacks on evangelical beliefs about the Bible. *The Doctrine of an Infallible Book* by Charles Gore (1924) was the first such attack, and James Barr's *Fundamentalism* (1977; 2d ed. 1981) and *Escaping from Fundamentalism* (1984) are the most recent.

published in America (though it was not addressed to the American scene, of which at that time I knew little) and remains in print there.

In the ongoing North American debate between evangelical and liberal Protestants, in which a large number of the former took the name "fundamentalists" as a badge of honor, signifying their stand for Christian fundamentals,[6] biblical inerrancy was from the first made the touchstone more directly and explicitly than was ever the case in the parallel debates in Britain.[7] This, I now think (I did not always think so), argues clearer-sightedness in the New World, for without inerrancy the structure of biblical authority as evangelicals conceive it collapses. Biblical authority means believing, affirming, applying, and obeying all biblical teaching, both informative and directive, and submitting all human opinion—worldly, churchly, and personal—to the judgment of that teaching.

This procedure assumes that all biblical teaching is trustworthy truth from God. It would, after all, be a Hitlerish negating of our rational humanity to demand total acceptance of what is not totally true. But if Jesus Christ and His apostles are trustworthy teachers, the assumption is justified. For the New Testament documents put it beyond doubt, as a matter of history, that these teachers, the founders of Christianity, viewed all Scripture, as such, as God's instruction, divinely authoritative against all human views that diverged from it.[8]

6. On the idealism and goals of American fundamentalism, see now two brilliant books by George M. Marsden: *Fundamentalism and American Culture: The Shaping of Twentieth Century Evangelicalism, 1870–1925* (New York: Oxford University Press, 1980) and *Reforming Fundamentalism: Fuller Seminary and the New Evangelicalism* (Grand Rapids: Eerdmans, 1987).

7. "Prior to 1870, inerrancy, while often assumed, was not used as a test of orthodoxy. But. . . . a pivotal episode was the debate in the 1880s and 1890s between Benjamin Warfield and Charles Briggs. . . . Warfield used the inerrancy issue to attack Briggs's moderate revisionism. Once the battle line was so drawn, there was no backing down" (Marsden, *Reforming Fundamentalism*, 214). No such battle of the giants occurred in Britain, however, where from 1880 to 1950 a pacific pietism, which lacked altogether the intellectual passion exemplified by Old Princeton, dominated evangelical life.

8. This point has been argued by, e.g., Packer, "Fundamentalism," 54–64; J. W. Wenham, *Christ and the Bible* (London: Inter-Varsity Press; Downers Grove, Ill.: InterVarsity Press, 1973), chap. 1; J. W. Wenham, "Christ's View of Scripture," in *Inerrancy*, ed. Norman L. Geisler, (Grand Rapids: Zondervan, 1979), 3–36; cf. Wayne Grudem, "Scripture's Self-attestation and the Problem of Formulating a Doctrine of Scripture," in *Scripture and Truth*, ed. D. A. Carson and John D. Woodbridge (Grand Rapids: Zondervan, 1983). Behind these and similar discussion stands Warfield's magisterial analysis, "The Real Problem of Inspiration," in *The Works of Benjamin B. Warfield* (reprint, Grand Rapids: Baker, 1981), vol. 1, *Revelation and Inspiration*, 169–226 together with the rest of the material in that volume.

Though *inerrancy*, like *trinity*, is not a biblical word, it expresses a biblical thought. Inerrancy, meaning the full truth and trustworthiness of what the Bible tells us, is entailed, that is, necessarily and inescapably implied, by the God-givenness of what is written.

Certainly, the confession of inerrancy needs to be circumscribed by precise hermeneutical guidelines. What is inerrant is the expressed sense, the meaning that can be read out of the text in its own context and not any imposed sense, any meaning that can be read into the words when they are placed in a different context. Moreover, interpreters are not inerrant, and time-honored interpretations are not always beyond criticism.

Certainly, too, the confession of inerrancy requires clarity about the extent of the biblical canon. Only God-given Scripture, as such, is to be believed inerrant and treated as a sure rule for faith and life.

Also, the confession of inerrancy assumes awareness of the radical incompetence of our fallen minds in matters theological. Only so will God's gift of the inerrant Book be properly valued, and only so will it be properly put to use as light for our path. Only so will the Adamic delusion that we can know better than the Word of God be seen for the irreverence and folly that it is, and only so shall we escape the related delusion that our right and duty to believe the Bible depends on our own ability to prove it true. The veracity of God, its primary author, is the warrant for our believing it: "it is to be received, because it is the Word of God."[9]

To disbelieve, and try to correct, any part of the Bible is always a recipe for some error about God and some ignorance of Him as well as being a real if unintended insult to Him. But those who heed the testimony of Christianity's founders to the spiritual blindness of fallen man will not lapse in this way.

Given all this, it is plain that the confession of inerrancy will, and should, function as a basic determinant of one's way of using the Bible. It prescribes harmonistic exegesis and harmonious synthesis, without remainder, of biblical material—the two procedures that together constitute the expository control called *the analogy of Scripture*. It forbids all modes of opposing Scripture to Scripture, of positing real discrepancy and self-contradiction within Scripture, and thus, as it is sometimes put, of "criticizing the Bible by the Bible." It requires that God be kept in view as the narrator of the history, the preacher of the sermons, the

9. Westminster Confession of Faith 1.4.

teacher of the wisdom, and the deviser of the worship forms that Scripture sets before us. It requires that when the harmony and coherence of biblical statements escape us, we put this down to the inadequacy of our insight rather than the incompetence of God's penmen. Inerrancy thus goes far to settle the shape of one's biblical scholarship and the content of one's eventual beliefs. North American evangelicals as a body have seen this, and they have confessed accordingly.

## THE WENHAM CONFERENCE

However, there are exceptions. And this explains why in 1966 I found myself in company with Edmund Clowney and forty-nine other scholars from ten countries at a ten-day private conference held in Wenham, Massachusetts. The conference was called in hope of healing a breach that had developed between some faculty members and trustees of Fuller Seminary and the rest of North America's evangelical academic world. [10] Fuller had been founded in 1947 with a view toward opening an era of triumphant antiliberal scholarship and standardizing a broadly Reformed theology filtered through an apologetic rationalism of a developed fundamentalist type. Fundamentalism had by now become a defensive mind-set, prone to fit God into a conceptual box and forget His incomprehensibility.

Fuller had recruited teachers who, reacting against what they saw as simplistic one-sidedness in their own fundamentalist upbringing, now declined to affirm the full truth of Scripture. Their reasons varied. Three scholars (two of whom were at Wenham) appeared to hold, on the basis of observing the "phenomena" of the text, that some statements in Scripture on matters of historical, geographical, and scientific detail are evidently "nonrevelational," and of these some are equally evidently wrong. [11] Another scholar (not at Wenham) seemed to think that

10. See Marsden, *Reforming Fundamentalism*, chaps. 11–12, and on Wenham, p. 228; Harold Lindsell, *The Battle for the Bible* (Grand Rapids: Zondervan, 1976), 106–21, and on Wenham, pp. 131f.

11. This was the position of Daniel Fuller, who summarily set it forth in "Benjamin B. Warfield's View of Faith and History," *Bulletin of the Evangelical Theological Society* 11 (1968): 80–82, and "The Nature of Biblical Inerrancy," *Journal of the American Scientific Affiliation* 24 (1972): 47, 50. Clark Pinnock criticized it in his chapter, "Limited Inerrancy," in *God's Inerrant Word*, ed. John Warwick Montgomery (Minneapolis: Bethany Fellowship, 1974), 147f. It is ironical that, traveling by a different theological route (a revised doctrine of God), Pinnock should now have come to a position that amounts to much the same thing as Fuller's. See Pinnock, *The Scripture Principle* (San Francisco: Harper and Row, 1984), chap. 4, esp. 100–105.

the conceptual inadequacies of some parts of Scripture constitute mistaken assertions. Another seemed to decline the word *inerrancy* because it was associated with an inferior style of interpretation. Those who organized and funded Wenham wanted it to be a peace conference, either resolving the differences or showing that all were already agreed deep down. But all were not agreed, and peace was impossible, although a friendly communique was issued at the end. Division continued.[12]

## THE INTERNATIONAL COUNCIL ON BIBLICAL INERRANCY

In 1977, concern over growing uncertainty among evangelicals regarding Scripture led to the formation of the International Council on Biblical Inerrancy (ICBI), on which both Edmund Clowney and I served under the vigorous chairmanship of James M. Boice. The council announced "as its purpose the defense and application of the doctine of biblical inerrancy as an essential element for the authority of Scripture and a necessity for the health of the church. It was created to counter the drift from this important doctrinal foundation by significant segments of evangelicalism and the outright denial of it by other church movements."[13]

Over its ten-year life the ICBI mounted three "summits" for scholars and leaders, dealing respectively with the meaning of inerrancy, the principles and practice of biblical hermeneutics, and the application of a trusted Bible to key problems of personal and community life. It also held two major congresses on biblical faith and life today and produced or sponsored a series of substantial books, besides its *Foundation Series* of dignified tracts.[14]

12. Marsden perceptively comments: "The doctrine of inerrancy was . . . functioning at several levels at once. At the most academic level, many conservatives saw it as simply a logically necessary doctrine of the faith. Many progressives, on the other hand, viewed it as confusing, misleading, or simply wrong. But the . . . doctrine also functioned at ecclesiastical and para-ecclesiastical institutional levels. That in turn meant that it was becoming the chief symbol for party division within institutions" (*Reforming Fundamentalism*, 227).

13. Cited from a statement prefixed to each item in ICBI's *Foundation Series* of small books.

14. The books included *The Foundation of Biblical Authority*, ed. James M. Boice (Grand Rapids: Zondervan, 1978); *Inerrancy* (Papers from Summit I), ed. Norman L. Geisler (Grand Rapids: Zondervan, 1979); *Biblical Errancy: Its Philosophical Roots*, ed. Norman L. Geisler (Grand Rapids; Zondervan, 1981); Gleason L. Archer, *An Encyclopedia of Bible Difficulties* (Grand Rapids: Zondervan, 1982); *Hermeneutics, Inerrancy, and the Bible* (Papers from Summit II), ed. Earl D. Radmacher and Robert D. Preus (Grand Rapids: Zondervan, 1984); *Inerrancy and the Church*, ed. John D. Hannah (Chicago: Moody Press,

To round off the ICBI story, I move for a moment two years beyond my announced terminus, to 1987. In that year the council closed down, believing that for the present its work was done. What had been accomplished? In the words of Dr. Boice: "The literature produced by ICBI has been disseminated round the world; similar, supportive organizations have been founded; and the three 'Affirmation and Denial' statements have achieved almost creedal stature in some quarters. The Council believes that many have been recalled to the highest standards of biblical authority by these efforts. . . ."[15] I think this is so. By God's grace, the inerrancy line was held; its strategic significance was made plain. Worthwhile new work expounding, vindicating, and applying it was done. A far higher degree of consensus than could have been anticipated was achieved on difficult questions of interpreting and applying Scripture. And the model of noninerrantist evangelicalism that remains part of Fuller Seminary's stock in trade was made to appear more than a little eccentric and unfruitful.[16] I continue to thank God as I remember ICBI.

## THE EVANGELICAL RESURGENCE

But back now to things that happened before 1985. So far from standing alone, or being a pioneer, ICBI was from the first carried along on the crest of a large-scale wave of evangelical resurgence. This in its academic expression was under way on both sides of the Atlantic well before

1984); Challenges to Inerrancy: A Theological Response, ed. Gordon Lewis and Bruce Demarest (Chicago: Moody Press, 1984); Applying the Scriptures (Papers from Summit III), ed. Kenneth S. Kantzer (Grand Rapids: Zondervan, 1987). The consensus statements from the first two summits, with exposition, were reprinted as appendixes to my own book, God Has Spoken (Grand Rapids: Baker, 1988); "A Short Statement" from Summit I (1978) is reproduced as an appendix to this essay.

15. Boice, in James M. Boice, ed., Transforming Our World (Speeches at ICBI's final activity, the 1987 Congress on the Bible in Washington, D.C.) (Portland, Ore.: Multnomah Press, 1988), 11. ICBI's initiatives have prompted some valuable seminary-sponsored symposia on the inerrancy question: Roger R. Nicole and J. Ramsey Michaels, eds., Inerrancy and Common Sense (Grand Rapids: Baker, 1980); D. A. Carson and John D. Woodbridge, eds., Scripture and Truth (Grand Rapids: Zondervan, 1983); idem, Hermeneutics, Authority and Canon (Grand Rapids: Zondervan, 1986); Harvie M. Conn, ed., Inerrancy and Hermeneutic (Grand Rapids: Baker, 1988).

16. See esp. John D. Woodbridge, Biblical Authority: A Critique of the Rogers and McKim Proposal (Grand Rapids: Zondervan, 1982). Jack Rogers—joint-author with Donald McKim of The Authority and Interpretation of the Bible: An Historical Approach (San Francisco: Harper and Row, 1979), a large and uneven special plea for a noninerrantist, functionalist view of biblical authority as warranted by the best patristic and Protestant precedents—was a leading Fuller Seminary professor. My estimate of this work is given in J. I. Packer, Beyond the Battle for the Bible (Westchester, Ill.: Crossway, 1980), 146–51.

1955, seeking not just to defend the faith but to recapture the theological initiative that had been lost through liberal capture of the major church establishments.

In Britain the resurgence effectively began with the founding in 1938 of the Biblical Research Committee, later the Tyndale Fellowship, within the network of the Inter-Varsity Christian Fellowship (now Universities and Colleges Christian Fellowship) in order to nurture evangelical scholars and foster evangelical biblical scholarship.[17] Now possessed of a superb research library (Tyndale House, Cambridge), the Tyndale Fellowship has seen more than two dozen of its members teach theology in British research universities, over and above the far larger number who have held positions in Britain's graduate theological colleges.

In the United States, B. B. Warfield (d. 1921), J. Gresham Machen (d. 1937), and his successor at Westminster Seminary, Ned B. Stonehouse (d. 1962) had maintained a pattern of constructive academic interaction at a technical level with nonevangelical specialists in their fields. But it was the founding of Fuller Seminary in 1947 that marked the moment when the thought of a crusading counterattack on entrenched liberalism effectively took hold of American evangelical minds.[18] Manpower for this new era of biblical scholarship soon emerged through the growth of the evangelical student movement in the 1950s, followed by the "Jesus movement" of the next decade. The fallout from all this remains impressive enough to lead Richard Lovelace (and latterly, it seems, John White) to allege that a revival is now in process.[19] The remarkable expansion of the evangelical seminary world during our thirty-year period has meant more posts for evangelical scholars and a corresponding increase in the output of literature elucidating the Bible as the Word of God and countering the erratic skepticism of liberal Bible work. A study of publishers' catalogs over the past generation tells the tale.

Writing in 1985, Mark Noll gave details of "the profusion of outstanding commentaries. . . . four academic series. . . . six other semi-

17. See Douglas Johnson, *Contending for the Faith* (Leicester: Inter-Varsity Press, 1979), 209–13, 297–99; Geraint Fielder, *Lord of the Years* (Leicester: Inter-Varsity Press, 1988), 82ff.

18. See Marsden, *Reforming Fundamentalism*, chaps. 1–3.

19. Richard F. Lovelace, *Dynamics of Spiritual Life: An Evangelical Theology of Renewal* (Downers Grove, Ill.: InterVarsity Press, 1979), 11f.; John White, *When the Spirit Comes with Power: Signs and Wonders Among God's People* (Downers Grove, Ill.: InterVarsity Press, 1988), esp. chap. 16.

popular series. . . . general dictionaries of theology, Christian ethics, and church history. . . . several large introductions to the discussion of criticism as applied to both the Old and New Testaments. . . . Bible translations. . . . the fruit of an academic rebirth."[20] In these enterprises, as Noll points out, British scholars led at first, but their American colleagues are currently overhauling them, and Australian and Asian contributors to the mix have also appeared.

The reality of academic recovery, consolidation, and staying power appears from many facts: the steady flow of critical[21] and elucidatory books on the Bible from sizable firms like Eerdmans, Word, Baker, Zondervan, and the InterVarsity presses of Britain and the United States; the emergence of a small fleet of evangelical technical journals, with Britain's *Tyndale Bulletin* as its flagship; the vigor of Britain's Tyndale Fellowship and America's own Evangelical Theological Society (founded in 1949, now over 2,000 strong) and Institute for Biblical Research (created in 1970 for specialists and boasting a current membership of 150); the blossoming among evangelicals of "biblical theology," understood as the unfolding of the progress of the historical-redemptive biblical message according to the analogy of faith,[22] a discipline pioneered and programmed by President Clowney himself;[23] Westminster Seminary's doctoral program in hermeneutics, which President Clowney saw into place, and parallel endeavors in other places; and the observable process whereby, while the number of veteran evangelical scholars grows steadily, leadership in the biblical fields, as elsewhere, increasingly

20. Mark Noll, *Between Faith and Criticism: Evangelicals, Scholarship, and the Bible in America* (San Francisco: Harper and Row, 1987), 131–37.

21. To avoid misunderstanding, let it be said that *criticism* and *critical*, as applied to biblical study, have become systematically ambiguous words. If *biblical criticism* is defined as answering questions about the date, place, sources, background, literary character, credentials, and purpose of each composition, all evangelicals practice it. If it is defined as affirming answers to these questions that imply untrustworthiness or fraudulence of any kind in the documents, all evangelicals oppose it. Whether particular evangelicals profess to accept or oppose biblical criticism thus depends on how they define it.

22. The phrase *analogy of faith* stands for the principle of interpreting Scripture harmoniously, letting what is basic and clear illuminate what is peripheral and obscure. The procedure assumes that, inasmuch as all Scripture proceeds ultimately from a single mind, that of God, intrinsic coherence is there to be discovered in the biblical material. Biblical exploration over two millennia has shown that this heuristic principle is every bit as viable as is the denial of it. But in non-evangelical Protestantism today the assumption of coherence is lacking, and the discipline of "biblical theology" has consequently lost its way. See, for evidence of this, Brevard S. Childs, *Biblical Theology in Crisis* (Philadelphia: Westminster Press, 1970).

23. See Edmund P. Clowney, *Preaching and Biblical Theology* (London: Inter-Varsity Press; Grand Rapids: Eerdmans, 1961).

passes to younger men. The advance since 1955 has been spectacular. Resurgent evangelical biblical scholarship has come to stay.

The purpose of academic biblical study in any age is that the Word of God may be preached and heard within the frame and mind-set of that age—challenging it, no doubt, but first tuning into it. The necessary disciplines are *linguistic*, for fixing the meaning of the Hebrew and Greek sentences; *literary* and *historical*, for focusing the message that each biblical book and each unit within each biblical book was conveying to its intended readership; *theological*, for integrating the various messages into the total frame of God's historical self-disclosure; *hermeneutical*, for transposing biblical teaching into different cultures without loss and seeing how it should shape service of God in our world today; and *homiletical*, for hammering home the awareness that God's Word to the world in Scripture is personally addressed to every individual whom it reaches.

It is by blessing the practice of these disciplines, at whatever level each Bible student operates, that the Spirit interprets the Word. The true goal of biblical scholarship is to present an adequately interpreted Bible to preachers and Bible students—and so to the whole church. At this point the resurgent evangelical biblical scholarship is essentially traditional in both its method and its findings. Its own detailed technical work leads it so to be and to take its stand on essentials in the places where conservative Protestants have been standing ever since the Reformation. Advanced academic technique has confirmed continuity rather than spawned novelty of beliefs. The militant conservationism in theology that marks mainstream evangelicals reflects their certainty that, given a trusted Bible to be expounded as a whole in its own terms, the key features of Christianity—the divine triunity; man's fallenness; incarnation; reconciliation; new creation; faith, hope, love—are found to be unambiguously plain and have, in fact, been found so for centuries.

## NONEVANGELICAL PERSPECTIVES

Among nonevangelical Protestants, however, the story is different, though the goal of giving an interpreted Bible to preachers and to the whole church is formally the same. In these circles Scripture is seen as no more than human witness to God—uneven, fallible, and sometimes wrong—and this inevitably affects theological method in drastic ways. For many years, "critical" biblical scholarship (as nonevangelical study of Scripture proudly called itself) made little of the theological, herme-

neutical, and homiletical disciplines and treated the deliverances of historical exegesis (i.e., "what it all *meant*") as the whole of biblical
interpretation. Our thirty-year period, however, saw several endeavors
against a "critical" background to recover the missing dimensions of interpretation, through which knowledge of the original significance might
be made to show how life should be lived here and now (i.e., "what it
all *means*"). The three such endeavors that seem to have been most influential will now be reviewed.


### INTERPRETATION ACCORDING TO "BIBLICAL THEOLOGY"

In 1955, the movement in the world of "critical" study that took to
itself the name "biblical theology" (not, as we shall see, in quite the
same sense in which modern inerrantists use the phrase) was riding
high. It was, however, riding for a fall. This movement had broken surface in Britain in the work of such scholars as Sir Edwyn Hoskyns, Gabriel Hebert, H. H. Rowley, Alan Richardson, and A. M. Hunter; and
then in the United States in the writings of such as G. Ernest Wright,
Floyd V. Filson, James D. Smart, Krister Stendahl, Paul Minear, Millar
Burrows, and Bernhard W. Anderson.[24] Its academic aim was to understand the Scriptures in terms of their contents; its churchly aim was to
restore the sense that the Bible is revelation, a sense that two generations of criticism seemed to have effectively destroyed.[25] Its central idea

24. Sample writings: Sir Edwyn C. Hoskyns and Francis Noel Davey, *The Riddle of the
New Testament* (London: Faber and Faber, 1947); Gabriel Hebert, *The Throne of David*
(London: Faber and Faber, 1941); H. H. Rowley, *The Relevance of the Bible* (New York:
Macmillan, 1943); idem, *The Rediscovery of the Old Testament* (Philadelphia: Westminster
Press, 1946); idem, *The Unity of the Bible* (Philadelphia: Westminster Press, 1955); Alan
Richardson, *The Miracle-Stories of the Gospels* (London: SCM Press, 1941); A. M. Hunter,
*The Message of the New Testament* (Philadelphia: Westminster Press, 1944. Previously pub-
lished as *The Unity of the New Testament* [London: SCM Press, 1943]); G. Ernest Wright
and Reginald H. Fuller, *The Book of the Acts of God* (New York: Doubleday, 1957); Floyd
V. Filson, *The New Testament Against Its Environment* (London: SCM Press, 1950); James
D. Smart, *The Interpretation of Scripture* (Philadelphia: Westminster Press, 1961); Krister
Stendahl, "Biblical Theology, Contemporary," in *The Interpreter's Dictionary of the Bible*
(Nashville: Abingdon, 1962) 1:418–32; Paul Minear, *Images of the Church in the New Tes-
tament* (Philadelphia: Westminster Press, 1960); Millar Burrows, *An Outline of Biblical The-
ology* (Philadelphia: Westminster Press, 1946); Bernhard W. Anderson, *The Unfolding
Drama of the Bible* (New York: Association Press, 1957).

25. Compare the (probably apocryphal) remark ascribed to Julius Wellhausen about the
teaching of W. Robertson Smith and his supporters (Smith lost his chair at the Free
Church College, Aberdeen, for teaching higher criticism in a way that was held to under-
mine faith in biblical inspiration, though Smith denied that it did): "I knew the Old
Testament was a fraud, but I never thought anyone would make God party to it, as these
Scotsmen are doing."

was that, without jettisoning the "assured results" of higher criticism regarding the composition of biblical books and the true shape of Israel's history, the church should read the canonical Scriptures "from within," that is, as expressions of a faith and a hope in the living God that we in this latter day must re-appropriate. All Scripture, however uneven and unreliable in other respects, is a product of community faith in the almighty Creator-Redeemer, who finally and climactically made Himself known in Jesus Christ. And no Scripture is properly understood save by coming to terms with that faith. It is profitless to know Bible history if one does not go on to grasp the truth about God that Bible history reveals. Joining hands at this point with the theology of the "neo-orthodox" pundit, Emil Brunner, which was also riding high in the fifties, "biblical theology" proclaimed itself the key to a renewing of personal faith and churchly consciousness, and so of corporate Christian life.

This approach led at once to a new seriousness in listening to the theology of the Bible's own theologians and in taking to heart what they most emphasized, namely, the soteriology and eschatology flowing from their belief that their gracious Creator had acted mightily for them in world history in the past and would in due course do so again. That was gain. But the movement had an Achilles' heel. It was trying to ride two horses, that is, to embrace the full biblical supernaturalism of theistic faith without letting go of the rationalistic and naturalistic antitheism of the Enlightenment, which had controlled the development of the "critical" movement from the first. Incoherence and confusion were the inevitable result.

Under interrogation, "biblical theology" proved unable to clear its mind as to whether it saw itself as studying God's self-revelation, which would of course be absolute and abiding truth, or simply the beliefs about God of certain Jewish and Christian writers. Beliefs about God, after all, however exalted and impressive in human terms, do not necessarily express absolute and abiding truth at all. It became apparent also that to gloss over this ambivalence the movement had developed still another one—a form of double talk about God in history that carefully avoided implying anything about God's relation to the life we now live, since "God in history" meant no more than "Bible writers' idea of God in history" (an "idea" that might or might not be true).[26]

*Homiletically*, therefore, the sound and fury of all the talk about the mighty acts of God proved in the end to signify nothing. Also, in the

26. Klaus Bockmuehl, in *The Unreal God of Modern Theology* (Colorado Springs: Helmers and Howard, 1988), castigates the theological version of this double-talk as it deserves; see esp. chap. 4, "The Collapse of the Doctrine of God."

interests of highlighting the distinctiveness of biblical material, exaggerated and simplistic claims were made about the theological unity of the two testaments, separately and together, about the characteristic uniqueness of Hebraic thought forms, and about the way lexical study illuminates the meaning of key Bible words. When in due course it became clear that these claims were overblown, the movement's credibility was felt to be exploded.[27]

At this time, "biblical theology" is in eclipse.[28] "Critical" scholarship is currently preoccupied with the plurality and diversity of the Bible. Liberal churches generally have ceased to believe that any form of Bible-based renewal can help them. And evangelicals study the contents of Scripture on the basis that the text is God-breathed for our learning and that since its contents spring from one divine mind, its unity is a given starting point rather than a possibility to be established. Falling between all three stools and with no one currently calling for its services, "biblical theology" has no obvious future. Its lexical legacy remains a valuable academic aid,[29] but its program for restoring the authority of a well-interpreted Bible to the church must be held to have failed. The movement itself is dying, if not dead.

## INTERPRETATION ACCORDING TO KARL BARTH

To say that Barth (1886–1968) aimed to give the Bible back to the church would be true, but it would not be the whole truth. Barth was a brilliant and powerful systematic theologian whose goal, like that of the Reformers four centuries before him, was to give Christianity itself back to a church that had largely lost it. For more than a century theologians with the mind-set of the Enlightenment in the various Protestant churches had been relativizing Christian faith and morals to the ongoing

27. James Barr, who specializes in demolition work, took the lead here; see *The Semantics of Biblical Language* (London: Oxford University Press, 1961); idem, "Revelation through History in the Old Testament and in Modern Theology," *Interpretation* 17 (1963): 193–205; idem, *Old and New in Interpretation* (London: SCM Press; New York: Harper and Row, 1966).

28. See Childs, *Biblical Theology in Crisis*, 51–87.

29. Gerhard Kittel's massive enterprise, *Theological Dictionary of the New Testament*. 9 vols., 1938–73, trans. Geoffrey W. Bromiley (Grand Rapids: Eerdmans, 1964–74), was sparked by the new interest in Scripture that neo-orthodoxy was generating and out of which "biblical theology" was to emerge. Other ventures, modeled on Kittel, include Colin Brown, ed., *New International Dictionary of New Testament Theology*, 3 vols. (Grand Rapids: Eerdmans, 1975–78); J. J. Von Allmen, *Vocabulary of the Bible* (London: Lutterworth, 1958); and the theological entries in many modern Bible dictionaries.

flow of European secular culture. Barth sought to reverse this by setting forth the self-authenticating witness of a self-authenticating Bible to the self-authenticating risen Christ. This Christ, Barth argued, is present with us through the Spirit as one who by His death and resurrection has already reconciled our sinful race to our Maker.

In his unfinished *Church Dogmatics*, written on the grandest scale (six million words!), Barth's constant theme was the sovereign freedom and amazing grace of God in Jesus Christ. It is Christ who is the incarnate Word of divine self-revelation, whom all Scripture attests as the source, focus, and goal of everything that is. Barth's plan was to offer a version of mainstream Christianity—trinitarian, incarnational, redemptive— that would checkmate the Enlightenment's confidence in reason by being drawn wholly from Scripture and being methodologically impervious to any form of rationalistic criticism. He dismissed as invalid, irrelevant, and irreverent all natural theology and apologetics, both Roman Catholic and Protestant, all claims that historical criticism deepens insight into the real meaning of the Bible, and all ideas of concordats with non-Christian religions.

Barth set himself to draw our entire knowledge of God from narratives in Scripture that show Him in action, particularly from the gospel story of the incarnate Word and primarily within that story from Good Friday, Easter, and Pentecost—the three supreme moments in the Word's incarnate existence. To all of this, on Barth's view, the New Testament witnesses historically in retrospect, and the Old Testament typologically in anticipation.

So far, so good, one might think. But in Barth's working out of his agenda, in which everything depended on how convincingly he handled the Bible, two major problems emerged.

First, Barth would not affirm the God-givenness of the biblical text as a divine-human product—God's instructional witness to Himself in the form of celebratory and didactic human witness to Him. Barth saw, no doubt, that such an affirmation would require him to maintain the inerrancy of Scripture, and he shied away from that.[30] Instead, he construed the inspiration of the text in terms of its instrumentality in God's hands as His means of channeling to us His specific word of the moment, thus causing the written text to *become* the Word of God to us. That God uses Scripture in this way is an important truth in bibliology, and Barth does well to highlight it. But when he categorizes the text as fallible,

---

30. See Roger Nicole's assessment in Gordon Lewis and Bruce Demarest, eds., *Challenges to Inerrancy* (Chicago: Moody Press, 1984), 122–36.

inadequate human witness that God honors by speaking through it, Barth drastically loosens the link between what the human writer was expressing and what God means us to learn at this moment from the passage in its canonical context.

Barth's approach opens the door to fanciful typology while closing it to any treatment of recorded divine commands as universal directives to be applied by systematic moral reasoning. Barth's theological exegesis of the most general of biblical imperatives yields only indicatives, not imperatives, because his method requires him to treat the texts as human testimony to what God once said rather than as God's direct indication to all readers concerning His moral will. Barth's ethics prove to be a kind of situationism, or contextualism,[31] whereby moral priorities are discerned through knowledge of the specific acts in which God's purposes were revealed. Surely something has been lost here.

Second, the attempt to support Barthian distinctives by exegesis repeatedly fails. Barth's negating of general revelation as a basis for natural theology; his insistence on the priority of Christ to Adam and of gospel to law (with the supralapsarianism that this involves); and his universalistic claim that all mankind, having been reprobated in Christ's death, was then elected in Christ's resurrection (a claim that makes the non-salvation of anyone at all an apparent impossibility, as Barth acknowledged)—none of these can be made good by any ordinary form of exegesis. Specific texts stand against them, and Barth's speculative typology proves nothing.[32]

Barth's work over half a century has certainly renewed in some quarters a sense that we must go to the Bible for God's message. But it can hardly be said to have given the Bible back to the preacher and the church as a revitalizing force. The novelty of Barth's exegesis, which makes ingenuity seem more important than fidelity to the text in its context; the almost hypnotic elegance of Barth's formulations, which leaves one feeling that any theology would do, provided it was beautiful; and Barth's paradoxical use of our down-to-earth Bible to construct an abstract Christocentrism, which, as R. H. Roberts puts it, "hovers above us like a cathedral resting upon a cloud, structurally detached

31. See J. I. Packer in Bruce Kaye and Gordon Wenham, eds., *Law, Morality, and the Bible* (Downers Grove, Ill.: InterVarsity Press, 1978), 154f. "Theological contextualism" is the description of Barth's ethics by G. Outka, *Agape: An Ethical Analysis* (New Haven: Yale University Press, 1972), 229ff.

32. For detailed biblical assessment of Barth's distinctive positions, see G. C. Berkouwer, *The Triumph of Grace in the Theology of Karl Barth* (Grand Rapids: Eerdmans, 1956) and Colin Brown, *Karl Barth and the Christian Message* (London: Tyndale, 1967).

from space-time reality"[33]—all these have spawned in today's church an uncontrolled and currently uncontrollable theological pluralism based on selective and fanciful use of biblical material by each thinker. This pluralism, more than anything else, is Barth's actual legacy to us. His theology will undoubtedly be the subject of much academic study for many years yet. But his adventurous expositions of Scripture, throughout *Church Dogmatics* and elsewhere, will ultimately, I think, be rated as experiments that failed in the end to cast much light on the message of the text.

## INTERPRETATION ACCORDING TO RUDOLF BULTMANN

Bultmann of Marburg, Barth's contemporary, who died in 1976 at the age of 92, was another theologian who sought to give the Bible back to the preacher. But whereas Barth's way of doing this was by Christocentric exposition, Bultmann's was by radical demythologization. In addition to being a skilled New Testament exegete and critic, Bultmann was also a Heideggerian existentialist who insisted, on the basis of the Kantian axiom, that God cannot be an object of knowledge as "worldly" realities are. He hit the headlines by dismissing all New Testament affirmations about the words and deeds of God as *myth*, that is, a prescientific way of conceiving reality that is not open to twentieth-century Westerners.

Bultmann assumed that we must, and do, treat science as our sole source of knowledge about the external world. So all those formalized theological beliefs, which earlier generations thought that God Himself had taught us, must be given up, and we must be clear that nothing really depends on knowing the facts about Jesus. Yet, if we ask the New Testament texts to speak to us about our own *existence* (defining that word dynamically and activistically, as is the existentialist way), they will do for us what we and all humankind most need; that is, they will draw, nudge, drive, or lure us into a new view of ourselves, so that we become persons who are no longer in the power either of the remembered past, through guilt, or of the unknown future, through fear. This new "self-understanding," which thus brings freedom, is what the entire New Testament is about—and all that it is about.

The way into the new mentality is by *decision*, that is, by committing ourselves to embrace it and live it out. The making of the decision is

33. R. H. Roberts, in S. W. Sykes, ed., *Karl Barth* (Oxford: Clarendon, 1979), 145.

conceived in Pelagian terms: what we may and should do, that we can do. And the benefit of the decision is conceived in existentialist terms. Thus you achieve your own authentic existence, which the New Testament calls eternal life. This, said Bultmann, speaking in terms of the New Testament myth, is our Easter, our co-resurrection with Christ (although, of course, there was for him no space-time bodily resurrection of Jesus). The only act of God anywhere, ever, that Bultmann allows is the impact of Christian preaching, which, by highlighting our inward predicament and calling on us to decide on our way out of it, triggers the self-understanding that transforms. Thus the preacher's task is to call for demythologization, in which he explains that his new self-understanding (nothing more, nothing less, nothing different) is the whole of New Testament Christianity.

The remarkable influence that Bultmann's hermeneutical reductionism[34] has had over the past half-century was due, no doubt, more to the academic brilliance of his various expositions and the filling of teaching posts in German universities with his technically well-qualified disciples than to any intrinsic wisdom or profundity in what he had to say. The gospel according to Bultmann is like the Cheshire cat's smile that hung in the air after the cat had vanished in Lewis Carroll's *Alice in Wonderland*. It is a phenomenon of reassurance, but there is really nothing there.

It seems clear that Bultmann's idiosyncratic star, which in 1955 seemed to have risen above Barth's, was by 1985 decisively on the wane; and it seems clear too that, whatever else Bultmann has done, he has not given the Bible back to the preacher and the church in a way that can lead to new spiritual life.

## CONCLUSIONS

My narrative has, I believe, hit the high spots of debate about the Bible in the West over thirty years, and I will now conclude.[35] Survey-

---

34. "The effect of [Bultmann's] work is to *reduce* the context of Christian theology to a single idea: that of the act or decision in which man draws his self-understanding and thus his self into conformity with his authentic being as potentiality to be." Robert C. Roberts, *Rudolf Bultmann's Theology: A Critical Interpretation* (Grand Rapids: Eerdmans, 1976), 323.

35. Space forbade any discussion of contemporary Roman Catholic treatment of the Bible; but see my comments in Boice, *The Foundation of Biblical Authority*, 74ff.; also John Warwick Montgomery, "The Approach of New Shape Roman Catholicism to Scriptural Inerrancy: A Case Study for Evangelicals," in *Ecumenicity, Evangelicals, and Rome* (Grand Rapids: Zondervan, 1969).

ing the story from the standpoint of the dual interest (academic and pastoral) I confessed at the outset, what are the appropriate comments to make on it? I offer the following.

First, a Bible that can be read and trusted by all Christians as straightforward instruction from God Himself about His relation to His world and everything in it is a precious gift, one that the church and, indeed, the human race needs. Satanic strategy will certainly seek to obfuscate that instruction by one means or another through generating either some mistrust of the text or some mishandling of it in exposition. Our story bears witness to both types of obfuscation.

Second, we should be thankful to God both for the gift of Scripture itself and for all efforts to uphold its status as an authority and a means of grace to God's people by vindicating its inerrancy and infallibility on the one hand and by expounding the salvation it sets forth in Christ on the other hand. We should see these two endeavors as going together—needing each other for fruitfulness to the church and suffering together if either is undermined or neglected.

Third, we must allow our hermeneutic to be determined *a posteriori*, from within the canonical Scriptures themselves. This means that grammatical-historical interpretation from a redemptive-historical perspective must ever be our method; and if texts are not identified from within the canon as, for instance, myth or type, we should resist the temptation to treat them as such. Our task as interpreters is to read out of Scripture what is demonstrably there, not to read into it what is possibly not there.

Fourth, we must not view the methodological diversity of interpretative styles and conclusions in the modern church as anything but a tragedy. The theological pluralism of our day argues weakness of the flesh rather than vitality of the heart. It is cause for thanksgiving that evangelical theology all over the world, working as it does with an agreed method, remains fairly homogeneous and, if anything, slowly becomes more so. This is how under God it should be, as the Spirit works through the Word, and it is a process that we should try to further. But critical and corrective dialogue with nonevangelical theologies, constructed by use of a partly false method (as they all are), will have to go on. No serious, permanent rapprochement can be considered, even where by a happy accident views on particular subjects coincide, as long as methods diverge.

Evangelical method with the Bible is part of evangelical loyalty to the Bible, just as evangelical loyalty to the Bible is part of evangelical loyalty to Christ. And until agreement reaches to method, the battle for the

Bible in the pluralistic maelstrom of the Christian world today will have to go on. May God strengthen His servants to continue fighting that good fight.

## APPENDIX: A SHORT STATEMENT

1. God, who is Himself Truth and speaks truth only, has inspired Holy Scripture in order thereby to reveal Himself to lost mankind through Jesus Christ as Creator and Lord, Redeemer and Judge. Holy Scripture is God's witness to Himself.

2. Holy Scripture, being God's own Word, written by men prepared and superintended by His Spirit, is of infallible divine authority in all matters upon which it touches: it is to be believed, as God's instruction, in all that it affirms; obeyed, as God's command, in all that it requires; embraced, as God's pledge, in all that it promises.

3. The Holy Spirit, its divine Author, both authenticates it to us by His inward witness and opens our minds to understand its meaning.

4. Being wholly and verbally God-given, Scripture is without error or fault in all its teaching, no less in what it states about God's acts in creation, about the events of world history, and about its own literary origins under God, than in its witness to God's saving grace in individual lives.

5. The authority of Scripture is inescapably impaired if this total divine inerrancy is in any way limited or disregarded, or made relative to a view of truth contrary to the Bible's own; and such lapses bring serious loss to both the individual and the Church.

International Council on
Biblical Inerrancy, 1978

We must regain the sense of Christian "ethnicity," of being the people of God in the world. That consciousness is a strong antidote to pietistical withdrawal from the problems of life and society. Yet as the fellowship of the new humanity in the midst of the world, we must order our lives by the programs and priorities of Christ's kingdom.

"Church, World, Kingdom" (1978)

# 3

# *Christ and Culture*

## *William Edgar*

Christians are becoming increasingly aware of the need to understand culture in order to live out the imperatives of God's kingdom in modern times. In seminaries the discipline of practical theology is expanding at a considerable rate. Along with the traditional subjects of homiletics, liturgics, and counseling, new emphasis is being given to communication, the media, special problems of modernity, and so on. Of course, Christians in every age have recognized the need to deal with the spirit of the age. Whether it be the immediate culture in which they live, that of their neighbor, or even the cultures of far away peoples, it has never been possible to live out one's kingdom responsibilities without measuring them in terms of the world. It is possible, however, that practical theology is being particularly challenged in our day to shape its curriculum in terms of the demands of the surrounding cultural problems.

Alexandre Vinet, a professor of theology at Lausanne in the previous century, characterized practical theology as "la théorie du ministère évangélique." Certainly, a theoretical basis is necessary. But today we are realizing more and more the need to be thoroughly acquainted with the practical. Where should we go? What needs to be developed today, inside and outside seminaries, to bring the claims of the gospel to bear on the lives of men and women in the modern world? Certainly a deep understanding of culture is central to this concern.

Culture . . . what is it? In popular parlance it has a thousand meanings. Artists speak of "visual culture." A Russian dissident is said to be "caught between two cultures." Modernity is seen to be an ideology that is "conceived in reaction to bourgeois culture." We may speak of going to a concert as "cultural activity." There are more strictly scientific terms such as "biological culture." Cultural anthropology studies human behavior, kinship relations, values, symbolization, and so on. Anthropology itself has been hard put to come up with a universally accepted definition. Part of the reason, of course, is that specific commitments are involved. The more universal the definition, the less one has to bother about other notions, such as ethics, religion, and other elements that claim to come from the outside.

In the fascinating studies by Alfred Louis Kroeber on the subject of culture, we met with all-encompassing definitions in which it is likened to "life or matter." He included speech, knowledge, beliefs, customs, arts and technologies, ideals and rules.[1] Culture is "superorganic," rising above somatic, psychological, or even social needs. To be sure, there was variation, there were higher and lower degrees of cultural complexity, and cultures could even die. But Kroeber's successors found it hard to be so all-embracing, even though they struggled to discover how culture could be narrowed to something more specific, without giving in to ideologies that seemed to explain human behavior in abstract terms.[2]

Clyde Kluckhohn, who devoted much of his professional life to the study of culture, saw it more as a way of doing things than as the sum total of human experience. Still, for him, everything we do is characterized by culture—sneezing, walking, sleeping, and making love. Yet by studying a sequence of human acts one should be able to distinguish between separate factors. Take the case of eating, for example. There is a survival factor (biological), one of sharing (social), and a ritual factor, including the fact that one sits in a certain place, sends someone out for the food, uses utensils, etc. (cultural). Thus, culture does not "exist" for Kluckhohn. It is an abstraction that describes trends toward uniformity in the words, acts, and artifacts of human groups.[3] There is a long tradition of culture studies that emphasizes symbolic forms in human experience. Ernst Cassirer, using Kantian categories, posits that each human society organizes its view of the world into various symbolic forms. Each society develops these representations in an autonomous way; and, he added, German high culture seemed to be superior to others.[4]

1. Alfred L. Kroeber, *Anthropology: Culture Patterns and Processes* (reprint, New York and London: Harcourt Brace Jovanovich, 1963), 60–61.
2. See John J. Honigman, *The Development of Anthropological Ideas* (Homewood, Ill.: Dorsey, 1976), 201ff.
3. Richard Kluckhohn, *Culture and Behavior: The Collected Essays of Clyde Kluckhohn* (New York: Macmillan, 1962), 45.
4. Ernst Cassirer, *An Essay on Man: An Introduction to a Philosophy of Human Culture* (New Haven: Yale University Press, 1944).

More recent discussions of culture are perhaps less tied to specific ideologies, at least on the surface. At the same time, one senses that the absence of the basic framework of Genesis 1:26–30 forces anthropologists into an imperialism of culture despite their best intentions.[5] Of course, secular anthropologists are not the only ones to have presuppositional commitments in approaching the subject of culture. Although less may be at stake because the Word of God has resolved the basic issues, nonetheless, Christians in different periods have revealed their specific concerns and biases even as they have tried to define culture from a biblical standpoint. For that reason, perhaps we should leave specific elements of debate for the historical survey that follows. For practical purposes we will avoid defining culture, then, and plunge right into our overview. What culture is will emerge more clearly from the way in which Christ interacts with it (according to the various views about to be described) than from establishing a hypothetical definition of it at the outset.

## A PERIODIZATION

The goal of this study is to survey the theme of Christ and culture over a period of roughly thirty years. Several kinds of limitations will be keenly felt. First, recent history is the most difficult to undertake, as everyone knows. Because we are still mostly in the valleys, a clear view from the mountain peaks is not likely to emerge very often. Certain names will be left out, other trends will be neglected. Some omissions will be deliberate. On the whole, for example, we will simply leave out the vast literature from the Roman Catholic communion. It represents a set of problems and considerations highly worthwhile but of which time forbids consideration.[6] Not that the Protestant world has been uniform by any means; but the main trends can be identified most of the time, at least in Western Protestantism. And the basic questions seem to be shared by most thinkers within each period.

Rather than a history of Protestant views of Christ and culture, I want to propose a periodization that reflects certain basic concerns.

---

5. See, for example, Roy Wagner, *The Invention of Culture* (Chicago and London: University of Chicago Press, 1981), 1–10, 35–50. Vern Poythress has gone a long way toward solving the problem by using the terms *mode* and *function* rather than *culture*. See his *Philosophy, Science, and the Sovereignty of God* (Phillipsburg, N.J.: Presbyterian and Reformed, 1976), 27ff.

6. Besides the usual problems with art, politics, etc., Roman Catholic culture studies have been preoccupied with the relation of the church to the world religions. See Romano Guardini, *Unterscheidung des Christlichen* (Mayence: Matthia Grünewald, 1938).

What task was uppermost, within each time-frame, according to the people and trends we can observe? Of course the dates are arbitrary. Nothing is so simple in reality. Yet from a comparison of the periods I am suggesting below, certain patterns emerge. First, here is a diagramatic overview that provides the skeletal frame we will attempt to flesh out in the ensuing sections. It happens to follow a scheme of decades, but there are overlappings and anticipations.

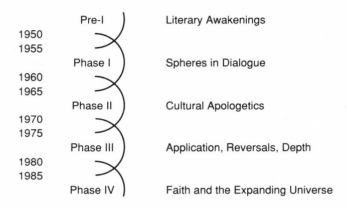

| | |
|---|---|
| Pre-I | Literary Awakenings |
| 1950 | |
| 1955 | |
| Phase I | Spheres in Dialogue |
| 1960 | |
| 1965 | |
| Phase II | Cultural Apologetics |
| 1970 | |
| 1975 | |
| Phase III | Application, Reversals, Depth |
| 1980 | |
| 1985 | |
| Phase IV | Faith and the Expanding Universe |

## BEFORE PHASE I: LITERARY AWAKENINGS

After the First World War, European theology swayed more and more toward Karl Barth's approach. Thomas F. Torrance once described Barth's intention as *diastasis*, "a radical separation between theology and culture, which he felt to be eminently necessary if we were to think clearly again about God, and about man, and of their reconciliation in Jesus Christ."[7] This does not mean that Barth was anticulture; his studies on Mozart should dispel that diagnosis. But Barth was so concerned that Christianity not be reduced to religion, apologetics not trade revelation for reason, that he focused most of the time on the kerygmatic aspect of theology. For very different reasons evangelical Christians during the same time were not so concerned with cultural matters. Among fundamentalists there was often a fear of its harmful potential. The best, like J. Gresham Machen, however, were concerned with culture as a means to defend the faith. Machen replied in the affirmative to the

7. T. F. Torrance, *Introduction to Theology and Church: Shorter Writings, 1920–1928, by Karl Barth* (London: SCM, 1962), 22.

query "What is the relation between Christianity and culture; may Christianity be maintained in a scientific age?" In fact, the problem of modern liberalism is that it is not only un-Christian but unscientific.[8] True science, like true history, is not a detractor but a support for true Christianity. Yet among evangelicals there was not much interest in the value of science and history, let alone other cultural pursuits, in themselves.

A very different relation to culture existed in British Christianity. The Anglican tradition was a seedbed for the most extraordinary revival of Christian literary culture in this century. The outstanding representative is C. S. Lewis, although the Oxford group known as the Inklings included a list of astonishing figures in their own right: J. R. R. Tolkien, Nevill Coghill, H. V. D. Dyson, Dorothy Sayers, and Charles Williams. T. S. Eliot owed a great deal to the Anglican literary tradition, though in a different mode.

Lewis's concern for culture is evident from his output. He wrote three kinds of books. First, apologetics. He explained the credibility of the Christian faith as it meets with problems raised by philosophical objections or those surrounding the matter of evil. By 1956 he had written *The Pilgrim's Regress* (1933), *The Problem of Pain* (1940), *Mere Christianity* (1944), *Miracles* (1947), and *Surprised by Joy* (1955). Lewis was in the Thomistic tradition, although it is difficult to put a label on his approach. Someone once said his method was first to make friends with you, then charm you, then disarm you with his arguments. Second, he wrote a great deal of specialized literary criticism. In works like *The Allegory of Love* (1936), *The Personal Heresy* (1939), *The Abolition of Man* (1943), and *The Arthurian Torso* (1948) he proved himself a redoubtable scholar and a defender of objective values in literary culture. Finally, Lewis is perhaps best known for his actual literary works. In his *Space Trilogy* (1938–45), *The Chronicles of Narnia* (1950–56) and *Till We Have Faces* (1956), he proved that he could not only reflect about culture but also produce it. Lewis emphatically insisted that his novels and fantasy were not allegories. The Christian message comes through, as it does in the works of Tolkien and Williams, indirectly, through literary means. Lewis was always hesitant to put down a set of rules. "Boiling an egg is the same process whether you are a Christian or a pagan," he once said. But at the same time he saw a great contrast between modern principles

8. J. Gresham Machen, *Christianity and Liberalism* (Grand Rapids: Eerdmans, 1923), 5–7.

of criticism and biblical ones. He objected to the modern emphasis on creativity, spontaneity, and freedom. While not a textbook on literary rules, the New Testament gave certain principles that ran quite contrary to these.[9]

## PHASE I: SPHERES IN DIALOGUE

While reflections on the problem of Christianity and other spheres of life were only a peripheral occupation in the previous era, the discussion sharpened and came into central focus during the 1950s. The most important book written about the problem, one which set the tone of the debates for years to come, was H. Richard Niebuhr's *Christ and Culture*.[10] As is well known, Niebuhr gives us five typologies that classify the various ways in which Christians have tried to handle the relationship between Christ and culture. Briefly stated, they are (1) Christ against culture (Tertullian, Tolstoy); (2) the Christ of culture (Gnosticism, Ritschl); (3) Christ above culture (Aquinas); (4) Christ and culture in paradox (Luther, Kierkegaard); and (5) Christ the transformer of culture (Augustine, Calvin, Maurice). The discussion of each position is lucid and on the surface seems convincing. A closer look reveals underlying assumptions, which also belong to that period. Niebuhr is a functionalist when it comes to defining culture. He accepts Bronislaw Malinowski's evolutionist view that culture is an "artificial, secondary environment" imposed on the natural one in response to certain biological needs.[11] Culture becomes a neutral, human response that nevertheless may be challenged by Christ, who "leads men away from the temporality and pluralism of culture."[12] Niebuhr's Christ cannot be grasped by adequate statement. His nature is only accessible to us through the "particular standpoint in church, history, and culture of the

9. C. S. Lewis, "Christianity and Literature," in *Rehabilitations and Other Essays* (London: Oxford University Press, 1939), 183, 186. This conviction is shared by Dorothy Sayers, who once said, "Dogma is the grammar and vocabulary of [the writer's] art. . . . Accordingly, it is the business of the dramatist not to subordinate the drama to theology, but to approach the job of truth-telling from his own end, and trust the theology to emerge undistorted from the dramatic presentation of the story" (*The Man Born to Be King* [Grand Rapids: Eerdmans, 1943], 4–5). Tolkien's views are the same. See Clyde S. Kilby, *Tolkien and the Silmarillion* (Wheaton, Ill.: Harold Shaw, 1976), 56–65.

10. H. Richard Niebuhr, *Christ and Culture* (New York: Harper and Row, 1951).

11. Ibid., 32.

12. Ibid., 39.

one who undertakes to describe him."[13] Thus we find at the end that no one typology has the best answers; we must simply try to find the "reasoning faith" that enables us to make the best of our modern situation in the church and in the world.[14]

Paul Tillich is similarly concerned to define the relationship of religion and culture. Profoundly upset by the state of the church after World War I, he developed what was really a *theology of culture* in response. He felt it was no longer possible to do traditional moral theology. Something more fundamental had to be attacked: the very cultural framework of modern life.[15] Whereas neo-orthodox theology tends to shy away from such involvement with culture, Tillich's liberal theology was the modernist version of natural theology. The influence of Hegel on Tillich is well known. Existentialism, a more recent Hegelianism, helped Tillich define the relationship between theology and culture: "Religion as ultimate concern is the meaning-giving substance of culture, and culture is the totality of forms in which the basic concern of religion expresses itself."[16] Culture is thus formal; it includes styles in art and customs in society. The church's job, according to Tillich, is to reveal the dynamic structures in society, uncover hidden answers to the question of the meaning of life, and bring the healing of hope to that culture. This led to some remarkable analyses of different social forces in his work, but it also led to the same final vagueness we find in Niebuhr. If preaching is going to reach the people of our time, "they must feel that Christianity is not a set of doctrinal or ritual or moral laws, but is rather the good news of the conquest of the law by the appearance of a new healing reality."[17] The problem is that Scripture contains no absolute norms, nor can culture be considered a creation ordinance with the normative structure that would entail. The best we can do is remind people of the centrality of love, although that too demands risk.

Coming from a very different horizon, we are still dealing with the problem of relating two entities in the Dutch Calvinist philosopher Herman Dooyeweerd. Although he defends himself from a Kantian epistemology, his view of culture is quite functionalist in the end. In fact, for Dooyeweerd "the general moral meaning of the law-sphere may be called

13. Ibid., 14.
14. Ibid., 230–56.
15. John Heywood Thomas, "The Problem of Defining a Theology of Culture with Reference to the Theology of Paul Tillich," in *Creation, Christ and Culture: Studies in Honour of T. F. Torrance*, ed. Richard W. A. McKinney (Edinburgh: T. and T. Clark, 1976), 274.
16. Paul Tillich, *Theology of Culture* (New York: Oxford University Press, 1964), 42.
17. Ibid., 50.

a functional modality of the religious fullness of meaning."[18] Within his general theory of modal spheres, culture is aligned with the historical modality. It is not the same as social life. "Culture discloses itself in two directions which in the modal structure of the aspect concerned correspond to the historical subject-object relation. On the one hand culture appears in mastery over persons by giving cultural form to their social existence; on the other hand it appears in a controlling manner of shaping things of nature."[19]

This idea of culture is clearly derived from functionalist anthropology. Yet it is in the process of "disclosing itself" (Dooyeweerd's phrase for the way the creation is subdued and explored by human beings, even after the Fall). We must neither be optimists about culture (because of sin) nor pessimists (because culture belongs to the kingdom of Jesus Christ). Thus we must fulfill the task of the cultural commandment in a "continuous contest with the historical development of the power of sin."[20]

These considerations led Dooyeweerd to some very helpful analyses of modern culture, many of which are indebted to Abraham Kuyper. But they also led him to some erroneous views of the evolution of faith and apostasy. For example, "primitive" culture is a place where man does not realize that he transcends the things of nature, tied as it is to prelogical substrata.[21] Modern studies on so-called primitive cultures have uncovered much evidence to the contrary.

Dooyeweerd's idea of the self-disclosure of culture is related to Kuyper's idea of common grace. People like Herman Hoeksema have actually denied common grace altogether. Klaas Schilder, while not denying it, is very suspicious of the term. For him grace has a very specific content. If culture is done to the glory of God, grace has been there; but he objects to saying that grace is inherent in culture. Neither does the curse lie in culture as such. Culture exists because man exists, and God's commandment to bring the fruits of human labor back to Him is either obeyed or disobeyed, but it is not *common* grace.[22]

---

18. Herman Dooyeweerd, *A New Critique of Theoretical Thought*, vol. 3 (Philadelphia: Presbyterian and Reformed, 1955), 7.

19. Ibid., 198.

20. Ibid., 262.

21. Ibid., 296ff.

22. Klaas Schilder, *Christ and Culture* (Winnipeg: Premier, 1977). He had a strong theology of the covenant of works. His definition of *culture* is similar to Dooyeweerd's, emphasizing mankind's task in "acquisition" and its need to disclose "the potencies lying dormant in creation and successively coming within reach in the course of the history of the world" (p. 40).

Still, there are patterns and norms in history and in culture. When people grab power in a revolutionary way, sooner or later their attempts fail. When civilization rises to great glories, there is Christian inspiration close at hand. The difficulty is in going further into specific events and cultural styles. Can we identify the hand of God in the "facts" of culture? In his enlightening discussion of providence and history, G. C. Berkouwer steers a middle course between two extremes.[23] On the one hand, we must not seek narrowly to identify individual events with a certain interpretation of God's will. On the other, we do not need to be agnostic about His involvements. The key is faith. When we are living close to the Lord, we can judge the relation of historical events to the norms of Scripture, which are established to explain history.[24] This is the only way to avoid relativity.

So, the major preoccupation within this period is relating two realities, two "spheres." The considerations on the whole were abstract (not in a pejorative sense, but simply in that the categorization is fundamental). But toward the end of this phase, we see more and more concern with an application of these findings more specifically to the needs of the present world. This would be developed in the next phase in terms of apologetics.

## PHASE II: CULTURAL APOLOGETICS

While the Anglican literary school continued to have its impact without modification in its basic approach, the Dutch school came into its own with significant qualifying factors. Culture was increasingly focused upon as a tool for understanding the world in which we live in order to set forth the Christian message in a relevant way. Coming out of the Dooyeweerdian framework, art historian H. R. Rookmaaker studied various aspects of modern culture to plead for a balanced biblical answer. His approach to culture, then, is understandably oriented toward epistomology, although his breadth of subject matter is extremely impressive.

His doctoral dissertation was on the Gauguin circle of artists. In them he saw the beginnings of a fundamental shift in art, one that would have deep implications for the course of modern culture.

23. G. C. Berkouwer, *The Providence of God* (Grand Rapids: Eerdmans, 1952), 161–87.
24. Ibid., 24. Edmund P. Clowney, to whom the present essay is lovingly dedicated, shows a remarkable balance in treating the same issues in a neglected article, "Secularism and the Christian Mission," *Westminster Theological Journal* 21, no. 1, (1958): 19–57.

The most important innovation of Gauguin and the group around
him, in trying to overcome the restrictions of the prevailing naturalism, was their understanding of the visual arts as using a picto-
rial language, which I call iconic. . . . This modern movement is
not a style, but more an attitude, a spiritual insight, a feeling for
the predicament of man. Modern art is defined by its content, not
its style.[25]

It is clear that, on the one hand, Rookmaaker's preoccupation is with
the message of art; but, on the other, he points out that modern art is
message-laden, far too much so. In other words, he shares the same concern as the Anglican school for the integrity of the work itself. However,
he has a strong apologetic drive in all of his works. This is partly because of his friendship with Francis Schaeffer, whose pastoral and evangelistic concerns were fully shared by Rookmaaker.

The impact of Rookmaaker's work is hard to measure, but it is certainly very great. The list of his books reveals his concerns only in a
partial way. He wrote *Jazz, Blues and Spirituals* (1960), but he also edited
jazz records and helped young musicians with their problems. He wrote
*Art and the Public Today* (1968), but also functioned in various posts in
public entertainment areas in Holland. His best-known book, *Modern
Art and the Death of a Culture* (1970), along with various smaller books
on art, reveals only one facet of his concern for the art world. He
helped thousands of men and women in many countries to think
through their artistic preoccupations from a biblical point of view. His
lectures and conferences in England were instrumental in the lives of
many young people, several of whom went on to found institutes and
take chairs of art-related disciplines. His premature death in 1977 deeply
troubled the Christian artistic community.

The most famous cultural apologist of the 1960s was Francis A.
Schaeffer. It would have been impossible to predict the enormous impact
of l'Abri and of Schaeffer's position from his background in a separatist
movement within American Presbyterianism. With a zeal to apply the
gospel to every area of life and a prophetic concern born in a personal
spiritual renewal in the 1950s, he developed an apologetic that set forth
the Christian message as it explained and challenged modern culture.

Like Rookmaaker, Schaeffer had a keen interest in art. He spent hours
pouring over art books and visiting museums, but he also understood

25. H. R. Rookmaaker, *Gauguin and Nineteenth Century Art Theory* (Amsterdam: Swets
and Zeitlinger, 1972; originally published as *Synthetist Art Theories*, doctoral diss. [Free
University of Amsterdam, 1959]), iii.

basic trends in philosophy, science, and ethics. His book, *The God Who Is There* (1968), grew out of a lecture series at l'Abri entitled "The Intellectual Climate and the New Theology." It was Schaeffer's conviction that modernist theologies had grown out of the same cultural garden as art, music, philosophy, and modern science. One notable feature of his apologetics was the unusual terminology he used. God is "there." Man is recognized by his "mannishness," his "moral motions," his personal relationships "below the line of anthropology." God is the "infinite-personal God" who exists on the "high order of trinity." Modern man lives after the shift in truth, called the "line of despair," where absolutes are no longer seen as possible. Thus, Schaeffer not only held penetrating insights into culture, but recast certain theological truths in ways that met culture head-on.

Schaeffer's approach to culture was similar to the Dutch school in certain ways. He sought to identify the underlying presuppositions in each expression. This was most often grasped in epistemological terms.

> There is a flow to history and culture. This flow is rooted and has its wellspring in the thoughts of people. . . . This is true of their value systems and it is true of their creativity. . . . The inner thought world determines the outward action.[26]

Culture is oriented through consensus. Our modern culture is "nearly monolithic." Schaeffer's diagnosis of Western culture is quite negative and follows the "rise and decline" of historiography. Yet his preoccupations were more than critical. He also did much to encourage a positive biblical view of culture, especially in the arts. His little booklet, *Art and the Bible* (1973), is full of wisdom for the working poet, musician, sculptor. Perhaps when all is said and done, however, the most important aspect of Schaeffer's ministry in the sixties was to give confidence to thousands of people that Christianity was true and could be applied to every area of life. His most powerful sermon, perhaps, was on Romans 1:16. I can still hear him screaming out, "For I am not ashamed of the gospel!"

Other things were happening in Phase II quite outside the Reformed orbit. In France Jacques Ellul and Jean Brun took on cultural apologetics from their own standpoint. Ellul's critique of technology and other "new demons" was deeply appreciated by struggling Christians. Jean Brun's

---

26. Francis A. Schaeffer, *How Should We Then Live?* (Old Tappan, N.J.: Revell, 1976), 13–14.

thematic approach included unusual studies—one on the human hand
in history, another on nudity, and another on Dionysius today. This kind
of creativity was more than an adventure of ideas. It sought to communicate the Christian message through channels not normally used in order to reach a wider audience and move out of the classic evangelistic
language of the church. Unexpected combinations were found. Robert
Short wrote *The Gospel According to Peanuts* (1964) and used Charles
Schultz's cartoons not only as illustrations but also as presentations of
the Christian message. Churches tried the "jazz mass" and generally
asked a good many questions about the arts in the church, principally
out of a concern to communicate.

The philosophy of science began to provide unexpected encouragement to apologists. I can remember my first year of college, where
Thomas Kuhn's *The Copernican Revolution* (1957) was required reading
in a science class. We found out that the sun-centered astronomy of
Copernicus was more of an invention than a discovery, based as it was
on an aesthetic preference for circles rather than epicycles. This challenged our preconceived idea that science operated through empirical
verification. It was more a question of paradigm shifts, an analysis Kuhn
developed further in his famous work, *The Structure of Scientific Revolu-
tions* (1962). The paradigm concept helped apologists to see the justice
of the Kuyperian insistence on presuppositions (although paradigms and
presuppositions are not strictly the same things). Epistemologists
Michael Polanyi and Karl Popper also helped to bridge the gap between
fact and value, science and human perception. Positivism was losing
ground, and apologetics enjoyed the relativity of scientific affirmation.
Perhaps they did so too much, for few Christians saw the problems of
subjectivism that surrounded many of these approaches. Historians of
science sought in new ways to determine the relationship between Christianity and modern Western science. Authors like Butterfield, Jaki,
Wolthius, and Hooykaas helped us to see the beneficial influence of
Reformational thinking on the rise of modern science in its healthier
aspects.

As we said previously, there was also during the sixties a revival of
interest in the Anglican literary school. Tolkien's trilogy, *The Lord of the
Rings*, became a best seller, and Tolkien, for reasons unbeknownst to
himself, was an overnight cult hero. Students discovered in the writings
of C. S. Lewis a kind of cultural awareness and sophistication rare in
evangelical circles. This opened up an appreciation for other Christian
authors, like Flannery O'Connor and Madeleine L'Engle. Scholars be-

gan to look for themes relating to transcendence in literature.[27] The young aesthetician Calvin Seerveld lectured on "Literature Among the Arts" and "The Office of Literary Criticism" (1964) in which he tried to explain art as more than just the expression of thought. Art is "symbolical objectification" and deals with meaning as art; literature is a special kind of writing, one that calls up "imaginative truth."

We are beginning to move away from Phase II. The "cultural mandate" about which we heard more and more toward the end of the sixties was more than an apologetical tool, even though it could never be less.

## PHASE III: APPLICATION, REVERSALS, DEPTH

In this new phase we see a greater concern for application. We are seeing a movement building on "we can do it" shifting toward a new preoccupation with "how to do it." There is thus an intensive deepening of considerations, but also an extensive one. Not only will thinkers dedicate their research to new ways of connecting Christianity to all of life but new institutions will crop up, new publications as well. Evangelicals make new discoveries, such as the place of culture in missions and the media. Toward the end of this period we will see a hardening along certain lines, which will appear to challenge the more open spirit of the beginning of the era.

Once again Francis Schaeffer and l'Abri were to have great importance. Perhaps more than Schaeffer himself, his students began to carry the baton. They continued to have a strong apologetical emphasis, but took the notion of presuppositions into a wide variety of fields. Os Guinness's *The Dust of Death* was published in 1973. It was received with great enthusiasm in the evangelical world. Nothing quite like it had appeared before. There were chapters on humanism, utopia, the hippies, the new left, technocracy, violence, Eastern religion, drugs, and the occult. And all in one book, well documented and beautifully written. The last section was an invitation to discover the Christian faith as a "third way," a term that has since gained wide acceptance.[28] The idea was to avoid the pitfalls of dilemma. A dilemma entails two options, neither of which is viable; for example, right and left in politics, word

27. For example, John Killinger, who lectured on "The Fragile Presence," eventually published in book form (Nashville: Abingdon, 1973).

28. There is even an evangelical magazine in England called *Third Way*; it deals with all aspects of modern culture and, especially, social questions from a biblical point of view.

and deed in evangelism. After this book was published, Guinness went on to distinguish himself as a sociologist of religion at Oxford, studying Peter Berger's views and their implication for Christian apologetics. He wrote a very practical book about spiritual doubt.[29] Recently he has published a most unusual "spy chronicle," where he uses the format of memos from one spy to another to describe the undermining of the modern church. It gleans a great deal from sociology, but ends with a plea for imaginative presentations of the gospel.[30]

Other thinkers, influenced by l'Abri, developed critiques of various aspects of modern culture. Donald Drew wrote about film,[31] Udo Middleman about a biblical view of work.[32] Still others actually went into the particular disciplines and began to speak more or less as insiders. David Porter developed important views on the media from his work with the BBC. David Lyon has become a major Christian sociologist. His studies on secularization can hold their own in any market of ideas.[33] William Dyrness wrote a very distinguished scholarly work on the painter Rouault. Graham Birtwistle worked on primitivism in modern art. He joined the Art History Department at the Free University of Amsterdam, becoming first a colleague, then the successor, of Hans Rookmaaker. Steve Turner wrote poetry and articles on rock music published in *Rolling Stone*.

What is happening in this phase is not only a broader look at different aspects of cultural life but also a more balanced reaction to trends and views. Judgments in the sixties tended to be black and white. Schaeffer was known to dismiss Beethoven and Sartre in a few sentences. This was probably necessary at the time, just as it was so often the case with the earlier Reformers faced with a decadent Christianity. But in the seventies evangelicals had more confidence and were more aware of the longterm nature of their work. Rookmaaker told his audiences, "Not in my time, nor my children's. Perhaps in the third generation we will see the beginnings of a new Christian culture." David Lyon was not just "against" secularization. In some instances, it was good that the church withdrew from society. David Porter talked of a wise and balanced use of television. Some Christians even dared to discuss the ultimate worldly

29. Os Guinness, *In Two Minds* (Downers Grove, Ill.: InterVarsity Press, 1976).

30. Os Guinness, *The Gravedigger File* (Downers Grove, Ill.: InterVarsity Press, 1983).

31. Donald J. Drew, *Images of Man: A Critique of the Contemporary Cinema* (Downers Grove, Ill.: InterVarsity Press, 1974).

32. Udo Middleman, *Pro Existence* (Downers Grove, Ill.: InterVarsity Press, 1973).

33. David Lyon has recently published what is the fruit of twenty years' work on secularization. See *The Steeple's Shadow* (London: SPCK, 1985).

subject, politics, in a balanced way. Not that there was always agreement, but it seemed possible to speak a bit more calmly, with historical retrospect, on certain issues.

There was a deepening awareness of the importance of the social dimension of human existence—not only among scholars who reminded us that we were more than "ideas with legs" but in a growing concern for economic justice, for social and diaconal ministries, for responsibilities in labor and education. Bob Goudzwaard wrote *Aid for the Overdeveloped West* (1975) and *Capitalism and Progress*.[34] Ron Sider dared to suggest that we were *Rich Christians in an Age of Hunger* (1975). And of course missions began to recognize the gaps in previous strategy due to an overly spiritualized view of man. At the 1974 Lausanne Congress on World Evangelization, evangelicals publicly confessed their shameful indifference to social issues. The impressive thing about Lausanne was the follow-up. There have been a number of gatherings and publications in continuity with Lausanne that have worked on the best way to formulate such issues as the relationship between social action and Christian witness within specific cultural contexts.

A new dialogue between missions and anthropology began to take place during this phase as well. Whereas previously missionaries, and evangelical Christians as a whole, had not wanted much to do with anthropology, this increasing awareness of the social and cultural dimension of men and women pushed them into a field where at least the issues had been discussed for a while. Applied anthropology became a necessary ally, rather than the sworn enemy, of missions.[35]

Perhaps certain missionary failures, and certainly a new awareness of the problems of a postcolonial world, opened many eyes to the need to *contextualize* the gospel. Eugene Nida's *Customs, Culture and Christianity* raised the issue of meeting the spiritual needs of people from remote parts of the world without violating their culture.[36] His idea of "dynamic equivalence," derived from linguistic considerations, began to be applied

34. *Aid for the Overdeveloped West* was published in 1975 by Wedge in Toronto. *Capitalism and Progress*, published by Wedge also, is translated from the Dutch, *Kapitalisme en vooruitgang* (1978). In it rich insights from cultural developments in the past three centuries are applied to economics. See also his *Genoodzaakt goed te wezen* (1981), translated and published in 1984 by InterVarsity Press as *Idols of Our Times*. In addition Goudzwaard published many articles in the seventies in *Philosophia Reformata*, *The Vanguard*, and *The Guide*.

35. It is during this phase that we saw the publication of an important, though short-lived, periodical, *Gospel in Context*. See Harvie M. Conn, *Eternal Word and Changing Worlds* (Grand Rapids: Zondervan, 1984), 138ff.

36. Eugene Nida, *Customs, Culture and Christianity* (London: Tyndale House, 1963).

to evangelism. The idea was that it is possible to reencode the message of the gospel into culturally specific forms without changing the essence of the content. Marvin K. Mayers's *Christianity Confronts Culture* was published in 1974. It set forth a strategy for cross-cultural evangelism that meant to make missionaries more sensitive to cultural and psychological questions resulting from cultural differences. The most thorough study of the cross-cultural problems was Charles H. Kraft's *Christianity in Culture*.[37] Kraft is not only concerned with missions but with doing theology in different cultures. He pleads for a break with the traditional functionalist view of culture, asking for a recognition of the dynamic nature of culture. He is also interested in defining culture in terms much larger than just customs of peoples from different areas; it can be values held by different generations or by different city block dwellers. Following a number of anthropological trends, Kraft accepts the idea that culture is "that in terms of which our life is organized." It consists of rules for behavior, spoken or unspoken. For Kraft God is above culture, but works through it. Recognizing that all aspects of culture are "infected by sin" and also that culture is in constant flux, he affirms the need to transform culture through the influence of the gospel. Yet the gospel never speaks apart from the cultural milieu in which human beings are immersed.[38]

During this phase, many new bodies were created that institutionalized some of these concerns. The London Arts Centre Group, The Society of Christians in the Arts, and the New York Arts Group were founded as places where artists could meet and be mutually encouraged as Christians actually working in music, theater, sculpture, etc. Under the leadership of Nigel Goodwin the London Arts Centre Group grew to a membership of close to one thousand. This is particularly impressive since one of the conditions for membership is to derive at least 70 percent of one's income from the professional arts. Arts and music festivals began to be held. One of the most remarkable is the Greenbelt Festival in England, which gathers for a week every summer to hear Christian musicians playing mostly rock. Tens of thousands gather for each occa-

37. Charles H. Kraft, *Christianity in Culture* (Maryknoll, N.Y.: Orbis, 1979).
38. Ibid., 48, 53, 89–94, 113–14. Harvie Conn has an important commentary on these developments in missiology. He feels that despite their excellent work, Nida and Mayers are still tied to the functionalist model of culture, which limits religion to one aspect of life rather than seeing it as the point of integration. Even Kraft, contrary to his best intentions, tends to divorce culture from its basis in worldview and commitment by speaking of religion as a human need. See Conn, *Eternal Word and Changing Worlds*, 119–21.

sion. The evangelical magazine, *Christianity Today*, began a regular column ("The Refiner's Fire") on the arts at this time. But "culture" included far more than the arts, and other institutes sprang up that sought to apply Christianity to many different areas. The Toronto Institute for Christian Studies, under the leadership of people like Calvin Seerveld and Bernard Zylstra, was primarily an academic research center, while the London Institute for Contemporary Christianity, under John Stott and Martyn Eden, sought to reach pastors and laypersons through public lectures, performances, and a book table in addition to seminars and courses.

Finally, evangelicals discovered the media in an impressive, though not always satisfactory, way. There had always been Christian film companies concerned with evangelism, but most of their work was limited to conveying the gospel message through adventure stories, drama, and occasionally the life of Christ. But then highly trained artists such as Norman Stone in England began to do indirect evangelism, and films that were simply good films in their own right began to be accepted by highly competitive companies like the BBC. Despite some glaring technical problems the film series by Francis Schaeffer in collaboration with his son had a certain impact. They were original and creative, even though not always professionally up to standard. Charismatic Christians as well as "born-again evangelicals" began to exploit television, a hitherto worldly medium. "The 700 Club" and the other programs were often an imitation of late-night talk shows, but with special music and Christian testimonies instead of dirty jokes. Several Christian TV companies broadcast church services, and we see the beginnings of the "electronic church." Paradoxically, liberals had always criticized evangelicals for their cultural shyness, for their backwardness. In the seventies they began to use the media as none else in Christendom could. This resulted in a general awareness, especially in America, of evangelicalism's slogans and bandwagons. It has not necessarily had the moral and social impact for which evangelicals were hoping. Is it because they are not really using the media as anything but a platform for a culture-bound evangelism?

The greater communication provided by the media is one of several contributing factors toward another, apparently contradictory, trend in the seventies: the hardening of lines. Creationists are less and less tolerant of the evolutionist of any shade; rock 'n' roll is either viewed as all good or all bad; the media are either acceptable or worldly; one must either educate children in Christian schools or public schools; apologet-

ics is either presuppositionalist or evidentialist; inerrancy means either
no errors or just general trustworthiness; Christian counseling is either
totally biblical or partly derived from psychology; and so on. Martyn
Lloyd-Jones believed that the importance of preaching was so great that
cultural issues were relatively unimportant. He even refused to allow his
sermons to be recorded. A fierce debate has grown up between the Anabaptist Ron Sider and the postmillenarian David Chilton over economic policy. It is hard to predict where things will go from here. What
scenario will follow? Perhaps these debates will simply force Christians
to sharpen their thinking and be better equipped to handle complex
issues. Perhaps, instead, the church will become even more divided than
it is. All will depend on how willing we are to submit not only to the
specific teachings of Scripture on different points but to the great demands made on us to love God and our neighbor, to promote peace,
truth, and justice in the context of the power of grace.

## PHASE IV: FAITH AND THE EXPANDING UNIVERSE

In some ways the world gets smaller every day. Rapid transportation
and communication seem to indicate this. But, in reality, we are often
bombarded with new facts, new problems, new neighbors, new discoveries, new technical possibilities. Isolationism is less and less possible. One
economy affects the other, one culture confronts the other. I recently
visited a small country in central Africa. On the one television channel, which operated at great cost for about four hours a day, the favorite
program, dubbed into French, was "Dallas"! The rise of Islam in its fundamentalist form has provoked much new interest in religion as a motivating factor in current events. Television coverage of famines and race
riots forces us to reflect on social problems in a new way.

How will this affect "Christ and culture"? That is very difficult to say.
One thing seems clear: Whatever conclusions Christians come to about
certain cultural questions, there will be a new awareness of the multi-
dimensional nature of problems. As we saw, specialists are moving toward a more dynamic view of culture. Tillich's dichotomy of form and
content is no longer admissible. Culture changes, adapts, reacts. It has
very different features from one social group to another. Cultural products and artifacts do not have the same relation to a group of people in
every situation. The telephone is less culture-bound than talking drums.

In light of this Christians will have the formidable task of finding
universals within cultural diversity. There will have to be more and more

studies of pluralism, of world religions, of paradigms and models. Modern physics wrestles with these all the time. Is there a real world out there behind the data? Apologetics is slowly shifting to take into account the problems of relativism, of equivalent models for theistic arguments.[39] Of course, hermeneutic studies are already plunged into the problems of pluralism. But hermeneutics will have to go further, always seeking to preserve the unity of Scripture while respecting the cultural diversity and, for that matter, all the other kinds of diversities in Scripture's language and concepts.

A cautious use of various sciences will continue to be necessary if we are to make headway. Missions, apologetics, and even theology will need to bring various rocks out of the quarries of the human sciences if we are to continue to see God's kingdom come to earth through human instrumentality.

Two areas will become of monumental importance to steer an obedient course as Christians confronting culture.

One is the obvious matter of the politicization of life. In my travels, I meet more and more people who are deeply concerned to define their relationship to the state and to the city of man as it takes on all-encompassing proportions. Many people in the Third World are seriously considering adopting a medieval view of the church's right to control certain aspects of government and legislation. It is not easy to argue the contrary when you see the needs. What are the biblical answers to this cultural problem?

The second area is what we might call *bio-ethics*. With powerful and efficient means at our disposal through technology, we can seriously envision sexual relations without the "risk" of children, choosing the type of children to have should we want them, helping older people die painlessly and when we desire, diagnosing fetal problems within a few weeks of conception, and so on. The answer to these ethical questions is in the biblical concept of life, of the body, of humanity in culture. This too can be faced only if we are clear on the central matter of "Christ and culture."[40]

There are, of course, many other areas in which Christians will have to deepen their understanding. The demands on practical theology will

39. See, for example, William Dyrness, *Christian Apologetics in a World Community* (Downers Grove, Ill.: InterVarsity Press, 1983); also G. H. Anderson and T. F. Stransky, eds., *Christ's Lordship and Religious Pluralism* (Maryknoll, N.Y.: Orbis, 1983); and Stephen Neill, *Christian Faith and Other Faiths* (Downers Grove, Ill.: InterVarsity Press, 1984).

40. At the Centennial Congress of the Free University of Amsterdam in 1980, the three themes were (1) scientific knowledge vs. other types of knowledge, (2) science and ethics, and (3) priorities and control.

continue to present themselves. This discipline will have to continue to grapple with the problems of culture to clarify the way to preach the gospel and live the life of the Spirit with full force and faithfulness. Studies in culture are abundant. One of the challenges ahead is to profit from them while watching carefully for the assumptions involved. We will need to be on the lookout for studies such as *Cultural Analysis: The Work of Peter L. Berger, Mary Douglas, Michel Foucault and Jurgen Habermas.*[41] It is a study of four great modern approaches to man in culture (phenomenology, cultural anthropology, neo-structuralism, and critical theory). Each of these approaches owes a certain debt to immanentist philosophies, to be sure. Yet many of the insights are valuable for the concerns of practical theology. They help us understand a good deal about modern knowledge, language, morality, and sentiment. We cannot ignore them.

If we feel anything of the full force of these issues, we will realize how far Christians need to go, despite some real progress in the previous phases. In fact, we still have not defined *culture*. That item is still on the agenda. We might well ask with the apostle Paul, "Who is sufficient for these things?" (2 Cor. 2:16). Indeed we are driven back to dependence on the Lord, just as Paul was.

And it turns out, as we examine Scripture, as we read it afresh with a view to applying it to the 1980s and beyond, we discover at least one encouraging fact. If we are in an expanding world where culture confronts culture, so was the New Testament church. As we look again at the Bible, we see that the transition from a Jewish culture in Roman territory to a Hellenistic context posed some of the very same problems we face today. Even the Old Testament speaks of such confrontations. Think of Daniel living in exile. It is all there for us to draw from. Let *ethnotheology* begin!

---

41. Robert Wuthnow et al., *Cultural Analysis: The Work of Peter L. Berger, Mary Douglas, Michel Foucault and Jurgen Habermas* (London: Routledge and Kegan Paul, 1984).

*H*ow profoundly the dimensions of leadership are transformed by the Lord! The Lord does raise up leaders; they do organize the ministry of his people, keep before them the goals of Christ's kingdom, and strengthen the bonds of fellowship. Such functions of leadership appear in all human society. But in the freedom of the redeemed community what a completely different meaning they have! Christ's steward seeks his Master's goals in the joyful service of his brothers and sisters. In that fellowship of service every Christian finds fulfillment. Roles and goals both come from his calling and are realized by his grace. The kingdom and the body are the Lord's.

"The Biblical Pattern of Leadership" (1977)

# 4

# The Pastoral Ministry

## Geoffrey Thomas

*I* completed my studies at Westminster Theological Seminary in May 1964. As with every student, many of the privileges those three years had offered were squandered. But not the least benefit received was the assurance that my calling was to be the pastor of a local church. In my coming to that persuasion Edmund Clowney played a key role when, in my final semester, I sought his counsel. My need was to have the opinion of an experienced Christian, whether he considered me to be called and gifted for this office. God used his encouragements to end my uncertainties; the day after graduation I sailed back to Wales on the *United States,* and a month later I had married the girl back home. The following year I commenced my ministry on the western coast of Wales as pastor of a church in a town of ten thousand people, a small academic community complete with a university, some colleges, and a United Presbyterian and Congregationalist seminary. Here I have lived ever since, and, if God wills, amongst these people I would be happy to end my days.

Perhaps a third of the men in our graduating class at Westminster Seminary are in the Christian ministry today. Of course, if one examined the graduates of any seminary then, a minority would be found pastoring local churches twenty years later. Not all who study theology intend to become pastors, and casualties abound in the Christian ministry. No office has come under such scrutiny in recent decades as that of the pastor-preacher of the local church. If one were to probe the ambitions of theological students, how many would indicate that their choice in reading divinity was to enter the pastoral ministry? The only rarer discovery would be the student whose missionary ambitions were to preach the gospel and plant a church in some country other than his or her own homeland. All is not well with theological students if their spiritual ethos can produce this uncertain estimation of the value of the pastoral office and the ambition to do other Christian work.

Yet churches are crying out for pastors to shepherd them, offering security, recognition, a structured life, and rich diversity of responsibility. The Rev. Keith Weston, concluding in the late 1980s his long ministry in the heart of Oxford at St. Ebbes Church, writes of the lasting rewards of the office. "If I were starting all over again, I do not mean to sound proud, but I wouldn't change a lot of things. It was the church that ministered at St. Ebbes, not the Rector. They were the most privileged years of my life, and the blessing was far more to us than through us."[1] But suspicion of the pastoral office is endemic and has been fueled by a bewildering diversity of factors.

Let us examine the reasons for the decline in appreciation of the pastoral office. What attitudes both in the world and in the church have undermined the confidence of theological students in its contemporary significance? What forces have been brought to bear upon the academic discipline of practical theology as it has been taught in the past thirty years?

## THE REASONS FOR THE DECLINE OF THE OFFICE

### THE MODERN CHURCH'S ATTITUDE TO THE MINISTRY

The World Council of Churches is characterized by theological pluralism and dominated by religious and social liberalism. This is manifested in a denigration of the authority of the Bible, and this necessarily gives little prominence to the church constituted by and centered upon the Word and sacrament. The WCC lays its stress upon "community" and "fellowship" and other such matters.[2]

Emil Brunner would appear to have had a profound effect in this area. "He regarded as wholly inadequate the common conception of the church as the congregation where the gospel is preached and sacraments administered. He could see no justification for the prevailing separation

---

1. *Church Leaders in Student Situations Broadsheet*, 25 (November 1985): 4 (U.C.C.F., 38 De Monfort Street, Leicester, LE1 7GP, England.)

2. Colin Williams, *New Directions in Theology Today* (Philadelphia: Westminster Press, 1968) vol. 4, *The Church*, 1–70.

between clergy and laity."[3] Numbers of books have appeared indicating this confusion concerning what the ministry is and what the ministry does.[4] Is it a divinely instituted office, distinct from the universal priesthood of all believers, that exists to preach the Bible and administer the sacraments in the church? Or is it simply one ministry among many ministries in the congregation?

Is everyone a minister?[5] "All Christians are *diakonoi*, ministers called to the ministry," writes Hendrik Kraemer.[6] Even an evangelical author like Paul Benjamin writes:

> Fundamental to our thinking must be the New Testament precept and precedent—every Christian is a minister of Jesus Christ. . . . The idea of every Christian being a minister for Christ is finally dawning upon the American church. During a long night, growth has been thwarted by the "one minister—one congregation" concept of ministry. . . . Once we acknowledge that the congregation is composed of Christ's ministers, then the weekly worship time becomes a meeting of the "ministerial association."

3. J. Robert Nelson, "Emil Brunner," in *A Handbook of Christian Theologians*, ed. Dean Peerman and Martin Marty (New York: New American Library, 1965), 424; see also T. A. Kantonen, *Christian Faith Today: Studies in Contemporary Theology* (Lima, Ohio: C.S.S. Publishing, 1974), 34–38, which takes note of Brunner's emphasis on "fellowship" and "community" and his attacks on the sacraments as means of grace and the pastoral ministry.

4. For example, C. S. Calian, *Today's Pastor in Tomorrow's World* (New York: Hawthorne, 1977); T. M. Gannon, S.J., "Priest/Minister: Profession or Non-Profession?" *Review of Religious Research* 12 (Winter 1971): 66–79; James Glasse, *Profession: Minister* (Nashville: Abingdon, 1969); S. Hiltner, *Ferment in the Ministry* (Nashville: Abingdon, 1969); P. Jarvis, "The Ministry: Occupation, Profession or Status?" *The Expository Times* 86–89 (June 1975): 264–67; W. K. McElvaney, "Ministry, Measurements, and Madness," *Journal of Pastoral Care* 30, no. 1 (March 1976): 55–67.

5. For example, *A Plan of Union for the Church of Christ Uniting* (Princeton: Consultation on Church Union—COCU Executive Committee, 1970), 38–55; Oscar E. Feucht, *Everyone a Minister* (St. Louis: Concordia, 1974); Don Abdon, *Training and Equipping the Saints* (Indianapolis: Parish Leadership Seminars, 1977), 20–25.

6. Hendrik Kraemer, *A Theology of the Laity* (Philadelphia: Westminster Press, 1958), 139; see also Francis O. Ayers, *The Ministry of the Laity: A Biblical Exposition* (Philadelphia: Westminster Press, 1962), 127–64; Howard Grimes, *The Rebirth of the Laity* (Nashville: Abingdon, 1962), 22–41, 66–87. The above men were leaders in the World Council of Churches Faith and Order Movement, which has heavily promoted this "everyone-a-minister" idea. See *The Evanston Report: The Second Assembly of the World Council of Churches, 1954* (New York: Harper and Brothers, 1954), 160–73; *Faith and Order Findings* (Minneapolis: Augsburg, 1963), 55–69; *The Role of the "Diakonia" of the Church in Contemporary Society* (Geneva: World Council of Churches, 1966); Hans-Ruedi Weber, "The Rediscovery of the Laity in the Ecumenical Movement," in *The Laymen in "Christian History,"* ed. S. C. Neill and Hans-Ruedi Weber (Philadelphia: Westminster Press, 1958), 377–94.

Such an experience will provide inspiration, instruction, and fellowship for "ministers." Those who attend are not simply putting in their time. They are finding assistance for their personal ministries.[7]

This emphasis has been compared to a reemergence of Anabaptist anticlericalism.[8] And though literature sympathetic to that movement has increasingly appeared,[9] anticlericalism itself has always represented a powerful force within the professing church.

What changes has this "everyone-a-minister" theology brought into the church? Liturgy and patterns of congregational worship have been modified. The architecture of church buildings has been affected. Among some, it has become one of the theological justifications for the ordination of women. The public administration of the sacraments by the laity has become more common. The very word *laity* has become prohibited in some circles!

Others have expressed concern that the respect for the office of the ministry has been damaged and that it is an endangered profession.[10] James Glasse has written that "much of the literature promoting the ministry of the laity has insisted that the best thing for the church would be the disappearance of the clergy from the ecclesiastical scene."[11]

Surely all Christians need to see and live out their high calling as the children of God. But this has to be done not on the basis of the notion that everyone is a minister but on such convictions as our royal priest-

7. Paul Benjamin, *The Equipping Ministry* (Cincinnati: Standard, 1978), 15–16, 46.
8. On Karlstadt's anticlericalism see G. Rupp, *Patterns of Reformation* (Philadelphia: Fortress, 1969), 84–90. Rupp also writes of the violent anticlericalism of Thomas Muntzer (pp. 164, 167, 174–79, 201, 207, 259). Hans Kung also writes about these men and, in additon, mentions that the Anabaptists and Enthusiasts rejected the "ecclesiastical office as a divine institution. . . ." H. Kung, *Structures of the Church,* trans. Salvator Attansio (New York: Nelson, 1964), 144. Rather than an office of the ministry distinguished from the universal priesthood, the Anabaptists, on the basis of the Great Commission (Matt. 28:18–20), "considered everyone teachers and preachers" (Richard Muller, "Identifying the True Church," *Ministry* 59, no. 9 [September 1986]: 19). For a discussion of the Anabaptist view of the ministry, see Franklin H. Littell, *The Anabaptist View of the Church* (Boston: Starr King Press, 1958), 91–115.
9. Robert Banks, *Paul's Idea of Community: The Early House Churches in Their Historical Setting* (Grand Rapids: Eerdmans, 1980); *The Mennonite Encyclopedia,* 4 vols. (Scottdale, Pa.: Herald, 1955–59); W. R. Estep, *The Anabaptist Story* (Grand Rapids: Eerdmans, 1975); R. Freidmann, *The Theology of Anabaptism* (Scottdale, Pa.: Herald, 1973); W. Klassen, ed., *Anabaptism in Outline* (Scottdale, Pa.: Herald, 1981).
10. Alan Harre, "Can the Laity Be Effective Workers in God's Vineyard?" *Issues in Christian Education* 18, no. 1 (Fall 1983), 22 n 5.
11. Glasse, *Profession: Minister,* 83.

hood and on our concept of calling and vocation,[12] of Christian servant-hood, and of obedience to the cultural mandate. While all Christians hold the general office of the keys and must give a reason for the hope they have to all who ask them, has not God instituted a special office of pastoral ministry for the official and public administration of Word and ordinance in the midst of the whole assembly?[13]

Is it not for this purpose that God calls certain men through the congregation to fill that vocation?[14] A *priest* is not identified with a *minister.* The new birth makes one a priest; one becomes a minister through the gift and calling of God. There is an authority committed to the pastor by God through the congregation (which possesses the priesthood and all church authority) to exercise the rights of the church in its assemblies and on its behalf. The church is a priesthood; it has an ordained ministry.

## UNCERTAINTY ABOUT THE NATURE AND FUNCTIONS OF THE PASTORAL MINISTRY

In a 1988 survey of the largest English theological seminaries, a picture emerged of students in remarkable confusion concerning the nature of their vocation.[15] Most of them believed that "love thy neighbor as thyself" was a political statement. They held forth with passion about apartheid, the poll tax, the British government's underfunding of the National Health Service, and the need for a redistribution of income. Not one raised the issue of the growing godlessness of Britain. The student president of St. John's Anglican Seminary in Nottingham, Andy John, was quoted as saying, "The worst thing in the world for people here is someone who is apathetic about apartheid. Nobody is stirred about Eastern Europe, and even abortion isn't the fashionable passion which apartheid is. The agenda is chosen by the Left."

12. Paul Helm, *Callings* (Edinburgh: Banner of Truth, 1987).

13. Two studies of Eph. 4:1–16 that dispel this "everyone-a-minister" idea are: H. P. Hamann, "Church and Ministry: An Exegesis of Ephesians 4:1–16," *Lutheran Theological Journal* 16, no. 3 (December 1982): 124–27; D. M. Lloyd-Jones, *Christian Unity* (Edinburgh: Banner of Truth, 1980), esp. 196ff.

14. Cp. Joel Nederhood, "The Minister's Call," in *The Preacher and Preaching,* ed. Samuel T. Logan, Jr. (Phillipsburg N.J.: Presbyterian and Reformed, 1986); Edmund P. Clowney, *Called to the Ministry* (Philadelphia: Westminster Theological Seminary, 1963); Robert L. Dabney, "What Is a Call to the Ministry?" in *Discussions: Evangelical and Theological,* vol. 2 (Edinburgh: Banner of Truth, 1967).

15. Graham Turner, "The Gospel According to Marx," *Sunday Telegraph,* 6 November 1988. All quotations from the survey cited in the text are taken from Turner's article.

What was the work they were preparing for? One representative student remarked, "A good many, indeed, come to see their work as taking care of the losers. Looking after those who can't make the most of themselves. That's what Christianity seems to be all about." Another declared, "The church has to be preoccupied with the poor and downtrodden, because nobody else is fighting for them. People who are well off want for nothing." Glen Milne was quoted in the same survey as saying, "There are a lot of middle-class guilt-complexes around, and a lot of paternalistic attitudes. Plenty of clergymen enjoy the feeling that they're the only ones who can fill in forms or deal with the social security, whereas they know that a congregation of professional people would be a lot more challenging." The Bishop of Peterborough, William Westwood, referred to the pastoral calling as "the ninny complex—they love to be in the middle of people who are dependent on them."

This is the Anglican Church with which John Stott is so familiar. He acknowledged, six years before that survey took place, "There is much uncertainty in the modern Church about the nature and functions of the professional Christian ministry."[16] Yet Stott then understood the confusion to be in terms of the diminishing status of the social prestige of clergy in Europe and of the fact that much of the philanthropic work pioneered by the church had been taken over by the state. Stott saw this as causing some who earlier would have offered themselves for ordination to be now involved in the so-called secular city.

Yet within a short time of Stott's assessment, this survey in the largest of the British Anglican seminaries indicated the predominant conviction of the students was that the work of the minister is one of political involvement and community welfare. The themes of the social gospel, lately believed to have become unfashionable, appear to be manifesting an extraordinary durability.

## THE LOSS OF THE AUTHORITY OF THE MINISTERIAL OFFICE

The past half century in the West has seen an enormous increase in crime and a breakdown of the family. The young are being offered a moral morass. The old foci of authority go unheeded because they have lost their self-confidence and the belief in their right to teach objective standards of unselfishness. Individualism and self-assertiveness now rage out of control.

16. John Stott, *I Believe in Preaching* (London: Hodder and Stoughton, 1982), 116.

Churches too have been affected. The falls of televangelists have fueled disrespect for the ministerial vocation, and the significance of the office is widely challenged. Yet there is a natural authority the pastoral office uniquely possesses and of which it can never be divested. That authority contains within it the idea of augmentation, or increase. A person set aside to this vocation is not simply ordained. He is added to, enriched, and so is the relationship between him and those who accept his authority. They have a new source of guidance, advice, instruction, and justice. All of this imposes upon him corresponding obligations and restraints and the need, at times, of counsel from other congregational leaders. It is these relationships, starting with the acknowledgment of parental authority, that teach us how to exercise authority ourselves, how to recognize it in others, and when to challenge its excessive or illegitimate use.

The discreditors of the pastoral office like to depict its authority as, at best, that of a kind of dreary and grim high school principal who confines the flow of existence within the parameters of the status quo. But this cannot be a complete picture of reality. Far from authority being the unswerving enemy of all change, it is scarcely possible to conceive of a fellowship open to the leading of the Holy Spirit that is not at the same time saturated in the understanding of authority. The discussion and testing of various suggestions for change and improvement demand a framework of rule and an authority for carrying out the tests, for judging their results, for agreeing and implementing change. A church lacking such arrangements must have its governing ideas dictated by force and deceit.

We have, of course, all experienced and read of many ministers who have become set in their ways and utterly resistant to reform. But this fossilization is a perversion of proper authority, not its fulfillment. And it is likely in the end to generate a refusal of consent and so to destroy that authority. Long-term pastorates are characterized by a willingness to respond, cautiously and appropriately, to changing circumstances, without succumbing to the paralyzing fear that any change must be fatal.

The restoration and maintenance of the authority of the ministerial office lies in three steps. First, his authority must reside, and must be seen to reside, where it is supposed to reside. "It is not lawful for any man to take upon himself the office of public preaching, or ministering the sacraments, in the congregation, before he be lawfully called and sent to execute the same." So we read in Article 23 of the Thirty-nine Articles of the Anglican church. But once he has been set aside to that office he should be left to get on with his pastoral ministry. Of course, by ordination the church has not made him a minister. It is Christ who provides pastors and teachers. The church has recognized that Christ has sent this man to be His ambassador. That is where his authority lies. As Herman Hoeksema writes:

> A preacher is not a person who merely speaks concerning Christ, but one through whom it pleases Christ Himself to speak, to cause His own voice to be heard by His people. . . . You can have two men that virtually say the same thing, while there is a wide difference between the word of the one and of the other as far as its power and authority and significance is concerned. . . . Our fathers always made a distinction between speaking an edifying word from Scripture and official preaching. The former may be done by any Christian; but the latter one must be sent. And to be sent implies, first of all, that one has received the official commission from Christ to preach, to speak His Word. [17]

That is where the minister's authority resides.

Second, the authority of the pastoral office should be clearly limited to the purposes for which it is appropriate. William Still defines that purpose simply. "The pastor by definition is a shepherd, the undershepherd of the flock of God. His primary task is to feed the flock by leading them to green pastures. He also has to care for them when they are sick or go astray." [18] When the Lord Jesus Christ was summoned, "Teacher, tell my brother to divide the inheritance with me," He replied, "Man, who made me a judge or an arbitrator over you?" (Luke 12:13–14). To be involved in that dispute was a matter outside the purpose of His ministry.

The limits on proper authority are in part a matter of self-limitation, of a true understanding of the minister's own calling, but also of precise and specific authority-defining precepts set out in such parts of the New Testament as the Pastoral Epistles. The essential components of effective authority are that it should be direct, immediate, and tangible. It comes by the Word preached to all the people. And that Word supplies the essential limits to the preacher's authority, so minimizing overflow into a domineering or exploitative relationship. In preaching, the exercise of ministerial authority is clearly defined and subordinate to the particular Scripture. The preacher is constantly acknowledging the existence of

17. Herman Hoeksema, *The Triple Knowledge* (Grand Rapids: Reformed Free, 1970), 2:409ff.

18. William Still, *The Work of the Pastor* (Aberdeen: Didasko, 1976), 3.

that authority overarching his own sphere of activity. It is the dovetailing of the personal sense of call and the objective description of the pastoral office in the Scriptures that makes for stability and continuity and, hence, for ministerial strength and independence.

Thirdly, proper ministerial authority ought to be slow to change its practices. It is not that all such change should be resisted to the last ditch; there are churches and ministers either ossified or giddy—or both (the two qualities are closely linked). But proposed changes ought to be carefully tested, debated, and phased in before being irrevocably adopted. The case against overnight introduction of eldership is not that it is wrong but that its instant adoption suggests a lighthearted abandonment of loyal congregations accustomed to a different tradition of guidance and service. Proper authority must expect now and then to be denounced as "hidebound" or "papal" or a "one-man-show." Such accusations may only be signs that the leaders are doing their job. Most preachers are stuffy about things they know about.

### UNRESOLVED TENSIONS BETWEEN THE MINISTER AND THE CHURCH'S LEADERSHIP[19]

"Is Elder Rule a Threat?" read a headline in *Christianity Today*. It was reporting a Consultation on Congregationalism held at Trinity Evangelical Divinity School in Deerfield, Illinois. Some 160 representatives of twenty conservative denominations and seminaries participated. All of them had been practicing congregational church government, and many of them agreed that in recent years their church leaders were being referred to as "elders." The reporter noted that "Thomas McDill, president of the Evangelical Free Church of America, maintains that the move towards eldership often takes an unfortunate turn. It can lead to the centralization of authority in a group of 'ruling elders' appointed for life, he said, with the pastor relegated to the role of 'teaching elder,' possessing no greater leadership function than is exercised by other members of the elder board."[20]

Professor Donald MacLeod has pointed out that in the New Testament preachers were not characteristically elders. Some were apostles. Stephen and Philip belonged to "the seven." Apollos and Titus had no official designation. Timothy does the work of an evangelist. Preachers

19. Cp. Dr. Keith Davies, "Plurality, Equality and Leadership," *Still Reforming* 5 (May 1985): 17ff.

20. Stanley Grenz, "Is Elder Rule a Threat?" *Christianity Today* 31 (10 July 1987): 48.

are described in a quite independent nomenclature as heralds, stewards, witnesses, and ambassadors. MacLeod believes that the attempt to link preaching indissolubly with the eldership is quite misguided. There is no hint that all preachers must be elders or that all elders must be preachers. In fact, the church never depended entirely on the ministry of "elders." It always enjoyed a distinctive ministry of preaching engaged in by men who were highly mobile, specially gifted and trained, and totally dedicated to proclaiming the gospel.

This must not lead to a depreciation of the eldership. Presbyters were closely associated with preachers from a very early stage in the history of the church. Their responsibility is broadly defined in the Greek words *episcopos* and *poimen;* the former means "overseer," the latter "pastor." The elders' functions, therefore, were to exercise oversight and to engage in pastoral care. According to MacLeod, they fulfilled this by being authority figures, leaders, counselors, guardians of the flock, restorers of the ones going astray, givers of hospitality, and ministers to the sick and dying.[21]

This distinction between the pastoral office and that of the eldership has its own congregational importance. A flock of sheep does not have a multiplicity of shepherds; it has one. So the flock of God, the local church, will relate best to one shepherd rather than to a committee of shepherds. Where plural elders are in existence, the principle of single leadership is necessary. Nowhere in the Scriptures do we find leadership exercised by a committee with one man merely acting as a kind of chairman, although that is the consequence of the concept of parity among plural elders in many cases today.

> Consider the appointment of the apostles by Christ. Clearly with 12 there was a plurality. Yet, within the plurality there was a smaller leadership group (Peter, James and John), and even an individual leader, Peter, the spokesman for the apostolic band. He was their leader when the Lord Jesus was taken from them. The leadership function within the apostolate was quite naturally carried into the foundation days of the early church. In the Acts of the Apostles Peter features prominently as the leader of the church in Jerusalem.[22]

Later, James takes over individual leadership from Peter, and Barnabas has the same role in the new church in Antioch (though others assist him).

21. Donald MacLeod, "Presbyters and Preachers," *Monthly Record* (June 1983): 124.
22. Davies, "Plurality, Equality and Leadership," 18.

Dr. Keith Davies points out that there is no record in the New Testament of the institution of the office of elder, unlike that of apostle and deacon. Eldership was an office taken over, without question, from the organization of the synagogue, which was led by a group of elders, or "rulers of the synagogue." Yet, even with that plurality, there was the ruler of the synagogue, or "chief ruler" (cf. Acts 18:8). Sometimes this would mean laboring in a full-time capacity. It was inevitable that the eldership pattern of the synagogue should be followed in New Testament churches, and it would not need specific comment.

Again, in 1 Timothy 3:1 Paul refers to the office of "bishop" in the singular, whereas a few verses later he refers to "deacons" in the plural (vv. 3:8, 12). His mention of "elders" in Titus 1:5 is plural, but the word "bishop" is singular in Titus 1:7. Again, when Peter speaks of himself as "also an elder" (1 Pet. 5:1), he undoubtedly means that he is an elder like those to whom he is writing. But it also suggests that he is something else as well as being an elder. Today a man may hold the office of pastoral minister and yet be "also an elder."

Davies concludes that

> the people find it impossible to relate to a committee and have naturally and inevitably found it right to relate to one man whom they regard as their shepherd. This singleness of leadership within plurality is, I believe, the institution of Christ. Equality does not work, and I do not believe the Lord would have instituted something totally impracticable. . . . In committee rule the grave danger is that of the rule of veto exercised by the man who wishes to be different and awkward. No one man should ever be allowed to be a dictator, whoever he is. No pastor or elder should ever have that much authority. What I am contending for is the leadership role of the pastor, I am not contending for greater power of authority.[23]

## THE VITALITY OF THE PARACHURCH

There are other reasons for the decline of the pastoral office. One is the vitality of the parachurch and the extraordinary contribution it has made to the coming of the kingdom of God. Many students owe their spiritual birth and nurture to Christian campus organizations. Young people appear to look warily at the man in the pulpit year after year. Just what are they thinking as he preaches to them? It is often at a summer

23. Ibid.

camp that they profess conversion to Jesus Christ. Where would the local church be without the supporting network of camps, conferences, and publishing houses?

There are Christian radio and television stations, Christian retirement homes, Christian education, and organizations that support Christians in farming, Christians in science, Christians in librarianship, Christians in politics, and Christians in all the armed services. All ages have their Christian back-up groups and, a virtual industry supplies materials simply to Christian women. There are prison ministries, music ministries, and hospital ministries. Every kind of disability—the deaf, blind, handicapped, and mentally retarded—all have their specialist organizations and magazines. Then there is the parachurch world of evangelism: home missions and the foreign mission field with hundreds of missionary societies and thousands of staff responsible to them, all independent of the local church.

Youth is the time for idealism and putting forth one's creative energies. Little wonder that the parachurch is enormously attractive—working with one's own peers, freed from the control of church boards, flexible and limited to that sphere with which one is most at ease. Parachurch is self-perpetuating with a dynamism virtually impossible to find within most churches. The innovator and scholar, evangelist, administrator, and specialist will all find themselves at home there. The pastor of the local assembly will experience himself being exhorted and seduced and courted by the parachurchmen. At the drop of a hat they will tell him how to evangelize, counsel, increase his congregation's giving, learn the secret of the successful Christian life, and fill his building. It is his privilege, they see it, to learn from them. They are the specialists. How sedentary his calling can seem in comparison to theirs!

Some of the thinking behind the parachurch is a weariness with the inflexible structures of local churches in contrast to their own stress that union with Christ is the one necessity for salvation, irrespective of denominational affiliation. "Living Christianity," not so much traditions and visible structures, has been their main concern. However, the life of the New Testament church was not a haphazard association of individual believers who met together just as and when they pleased and engaged in work they thought they were good at. Church membership was not a variable, voluntary option. It was the voice of living Christianity that said, "Obey them that have the rule over you, and submit yourselves: for they watch for your souls, as they that must give account" (Heb. 13:17). Paul joyed to behold the "order" of the church at Colosse

(Col. 2:5). In the modern parachurch of independency and individualism there is sometimes an unconscious prejudice against the very spirit that Scripture enjoins. Parachurch must come to grips with what the Holy Spirit has said of the unique role of the instituted church.

## SPECIALIZATION WITHIN THE CHURCH

Similar to parachurch tendencies is the specialization of ministries within the leadership of the local church. Counseling, visiting, music, and discipleship, along with youth, evangelism, administration, and even choreography and drama may all be the province of some of the officers of the congregation. What, within the church, is the minister's calling? He can suffer from a vocational identity crisis!

Is the minister still considered to be the pastor-preacher in the congregation? Is he, preeminently by his preaching, to teach and counsel all the people of God by means of the whole Word of God? Is he necessarily to accompany that with personal pastoring, thus publicly and privately awakening men and women's fears and calming them? There is at the present time a widespread depreciation of preaching, though hitherto it has been regarded as the foremost public work for which the pastoral ministry existed.

> This is not an age of preaching. In many churches midweek preaching died out years ago. Days of revival when preaching was a daily occurrence are almost unthinkable. In many churches preaching is tolerated—people may be willing to hear one sermon per Sunday—but there is a fairly common doubt as to its real importance. Many seem to think that, perhaps, it is out of date for a man to "declaim" from the pulpit to "passive pew-sitters"; discussion or dialogues would be better; perhaps group-Bible-studies are more useful; and that in all probability today visual representations of the gospel in mime or drama are more effective. Certainly a little preaching for most professing Christians seems to be quite enough. It is, then, scarcely surprising that the view which regards the ministerial office as outmoded should be gaining ground at a time when the chief work of that office is so devalued.[24]

In magnifying the preacher's vocation one is aware of the evident dangers. For example, there can be a virtual intoxication with the act of preaching itself. Dr. D. M. Lloyd-Jones describes it thus:

24. Iain Murray, "The Christian Ministry and the Challenge to Its Continuance," *Banner of Truth* (June 1983): 7–8.

> It has often happened that young men with certain gifts who listen
> to a great preacher are captivated by him and what he is doing.
> They are captivated by his personality or by his eloquence. They
> are moved by him, and unconsciously they begin to feel a desire to
> be like him and to do what he is doing. Now that may be right, or
> it may be quite wrong. They may only be fascinated by the glam-
> our of preaching, and attracted by the idea of addressing audiences
> and influencing them. All kinds of wrong and false motives may
> insinuate themselves. [25]

There may also be an absolutizing of the didactic aspect of proclamation. Presbyterian churches properly insist on high academic standards
and years of study for their ministerial students. Graduate school and
further research is an attractive option that many take. At the comple-
tion of all this a man can feel most at ease in his study, staring at a word
processor, and surrounded by shelves of books. His ultimate ambition is
to get back into the familiar academic environment and teach in a seminary. Until that time comes he may conceive of his priority as his hours
in the study, preparing his sermons, descending to the pulpit on the
Lord's Day, and then retreating again to that book-lined room for the
following week. "My gift is teaching the Bible," he may think. True, but
not in isolation from the vocation of pastoring the hurting congregation
of Jesus Christ so as to present his flock to God holy and blameless in
the Great Day.

To a large extent the ministry consists of people management by
means of all the principles laid out in Scripture. It is no place for a man
who wants to spend his days in the ivory tower of a study. It is a potential disaster area for those who are painfully shy, carelessly extrovert,
tactless, or insensitive. Much more is needed from a man who takes to
himself this vocation than orthodoxy or exegetically accurate messages
showered with biblical theological insights. The minister has to motivate, discipline, and inspire a congregation so that every talent in the
church is used and individuals of diverse gifts and temperaments are
molded into a harmonious whole. To achieve that end preaching must
be pastorally relevant from a shepherd who leads his sheep and who
follows up the public Word "from house to house."

## THE INFLUENCE OF THE CHARISMATIC MOVEMENT

The traditional Pentecostal denominations have always recognized the
pastoral office and have established their own seminaries for training

25. D. M. Lloyd-Jones, *Preaching and Preachers* (London: Hodder and Stoughton,
1971), 105.

preachers, but this has been challenged by voices within neo-Pentecostalism. John Stott observes, "Largely as a result of the charismatic movement, the New Testament doctrine of the Body of Christ has been recovered with its corollary that every member has a gift and therefore a ministry. This being so, some are asking whether a professional ministry is necessary any longer. Have not the clergy been rendered redundant? These are some of the trends which have contributed to the contemporary loss of clerical morale."[26]

Iain Murray agrees with this conclusion. "Appeal is made to the Word of God and on the basis of such texts as, 'Your sons and your daughters shall prophesy', 'I would that ye all spake with tongues', 'Let two or three prophets speak', the case is claimed as proven. 'Is it not obvious', charismatics ask, 'that the traditional ministry is a man-made system? Ministers have put themselves in a position where the Holy Spirit never put them."[27] As Juan Carlos Ortiz has commented, the pastor is the cork in the church. Nobody can go out because the pastor is perfecting the saints for the work of the ministry. Rather he is preventing the saints from becoming ministers.

There is no question that ministers should be concerned for the growth and use of the varied spiritual gifts represented in the church. If they are not exercised about this, then they are not ministers at all in any biblical sense. There is much more to be done in every church than can be done by ministers. Indeed many functions are better done by other gifted Christians. The existence of such other "ministries" is not in dispute. What is the issue? It is "whether public worship, as traditionally conducted by ministers, is the cause of spiritual passivity and deadness. That is what is being claimed. There will be no growth, it is urged, unless the structure is radically changed. It is 'the minister' who has bred 'passive pew-sitters' who 'put in their time.' "[28]

What is the response to be made to this evaluation of the ministerial office? It is not to defend ministers as a group of men. The present agitation is itself attributable in part to those things in the pastoral ministry during the past century which deserved to be censured and ought to change.

> In the Old Testament, when the priests failed to do their work faithfully, their office itself fell into contempt. Something very similar has happened during the present century. But as in the Old

26. Stott, *I Believe in Preaching,* 116.
27. Murray, "Christian Ministry," 6.
28. Ibid., 9.

Testament, so now, the evil lay in the misuse and abuse of the office not in the office itself. God's remedy was not to remove the office but to change the men who occupied it: "I will give you pastors according to mine heart, which shall feed you with knowledge and understanding" (Jer. 3:15).[29]

One great need is for a recovery of the considerations that undergird the pastoral office. Are they established on biblical criteria? A mere defense of the traditional ministerial office will not help us.

> The truth is that those convictions have been so little known over a prolonged period that the present confusion is hardly surprising. . . . The danger in this debate is more from ignorance than from any deliberate, conscious opposition to Scripture. When the early (Plymouth) Brethren reacted against the clerical-types of Jane Austen's era their zeal was greater than their knowledge. So it is now with the spate of authors [who want to change the historic view of the Christian ministry].[30]

## THE PASTORAL MINISTRY TODAY

During the past thirty years, the ministerial office has been subject to intense scrutiny—much debate amid not a little criticism. It is conceivable that the Reformed view of the pastoral ministry has been wrong for four hundred years; but it is equally possible that the holders of those evangelical convictions have been as concerned with faithfulness to Scripture as have any contemporary critics of those convictions. They believed that there is an action of Christ in sending men into the ministry of preaching. It is He who calls men, and the church confirms this call (or declines to acknowledge it where the necessary evidence is lacking).

Iain Murray comments:

> Preachers are not made by training nor by some gift which distinguishes them from other presbyters. They are divinely called to their work and office: that office is clearly set forth in the New Testament and if it is argued that men may also belong to the same office who do not preach, or who are not able to preach,

29. Ibid.
30. Ibid.

then the vital meaning of the preaching office is undermined. In short, the real effect of the claim that ruling elders and preachers are the same in Scripture is to undermine the Christian ministry as that work has been historically understood.[31]

What are the marks of a man called to the pastoral ministry?

First, he has a sense of inadequacy and awe when faced with the commission and call to preach. This was true of Moses (Exod. 3:11), Isaiah (Isa. 6:8), and Jeremiah (Jer. 1:6). All men truly called to be pastors live in perpetual tension between shrinking from the office and yet desiring with all their hearts to be God's servants in this way. The preacher is in a position where he actually has to represent God before men. "If anyone speaks," declares Peter, "he should do it as one speaking the very words of God" (1 Pet. 4:11). Elsewhere Paul puts it like this: "We are therefore Christ's ambassadors, as though God were making his appeal through us. We implore you on Christ's behalf" (2 Cor. 5:20). Little wonder that seeing the awesomeness of this calling, and the issues at stake, Paul came to Corinth "in weakness and fear, and with much trembling" (1 Cor. 2:3). The great Methodist preacher William Bramwell once confided, "I die a death every time I preach; I wonder I have lived as long as I have."[32]

Young men especially feel this sense of inadequacy. They have had to battle with reluctance from parts of the congregation when they reveal this concern to become preachers. It is not simply that seminary training is under fire, but that their very youthfulness (mid-twenties) is seen as a disadvantage. They are even being told that they should get a job, see if one day they will be appointed as elders, and then graduate from that to becoming full-time preachers. So Christ would be robbed of their service in their early years. This stems from the confusing identification of the office of rule with that of proclamation. Young manhood with its energy, idealism, and consecration is a good time to preach the gospel of Christ, as Scripture and church history bear witness. Peter was probably in his twenties on the day of Pentecost. The apostle's words to Timothy, "Don't let anyone look down on you because you are young" (1 Tim. 4:12), are just as necessary today. The cause for concern is not the young preacher's sense of inadequacy compounded by this new suspicion; rather, it is its absence in the older preacher.

31. Iain Murray, "Ruling Elders: A Sketch of a Controversy," *Banner of Truth* (April 1983): 8.

32. Quoted by Paul Cook, "Preaching—a Divine Calling," *Banner of Truth* (August-September 1988): 39.

Second, a pastor has a special sense of constraint to do this work. A man becomes a preacher not because of himself, but despite himself. Paul said, "I am compelled to preach" (1 Cor. 9:16). He said again, "I am simply discharging the trust committed to me" (1 Cor. 9:17). And again he said, "Woe to me if I do not preach the gospel!" (1 Cor. 9:16). Paul was reflecting what Peter and John said to their detractors: "We cannot help speaking about what we have seen and heard" (Acts 4:20). That heavy responsibility is uniquely borne by the preacher. It is misleading in holding a service of the ordination of elders to charge them with the words, "Woe to me if I do not preach the gospel." Their charisma is not simply different in degree (that they have less of the preaching gift than has the preacher) but in kind.

Third, he is consumed by his ministry. This was why the apostles did not want to become involved in the problems of administration. They wanted to give themselves "continually to prayer, and to the ministry of the word" (Acts 6:4). MacLeod has pointed out that

> the precise business with which the apostles did not wish to be entangled was ecclesiastical. Not even the work of the diaconate should be allowed to distract a preacher of the Gospel. How much more does this apply to secular pursuits! It is impossible to engage in an effective preaching ministry if we have to snatch our moments of preparation from the demands of business, trade, politics or the caring professions. Men must give themselves wholly to these matters, devoting themselves singlemindedly to reading, teaching and preaching (1 Tim. 4:13 f)—and to prayer (Acts 6:4). They must fan into flame the gift God has given them (2 Tim 1:6), making it their foremost determination to be workmen who do not need to be ashamed, correctly handling the word of truth (2 Tim. 2:15). How else can they be prepared to preach the word in season and out of season, correcting, rebuking and encouraging (2 Tim. 4:2)?[33]

Paul Cook writes of ministers: "Their calling was so total, that they became their message. John the Baptist was his message in every fibre of his being. The way he dressed, what he ate, where he lived: it was all part of his message of repentance. . . . The man and his message had to be one."[34] The example of Paul underlies this again. He is the New Testament model for the pastoral ministry. That is one reason his labors

33. MacLeod, "Presbyters and Preachers," 123–24.
34. Cook, "Preaching—a Divine Calling," 40.

in the Book of Acts and the epistles are so exhaustively preserved. "But he is an apostle!" comes the familiar cry. True, that grace had been given unto him, and so he could write the oracles of God and manifest the signs of an apostle. Any attempt to model a Christian vocation on that would be disastrous. First of all Paul was a Christian, as he says to the Thessalonian church: "We did this . . . to make ourselves a model for you to follow" (2 Thess. 3:9).

But then Paul was a preacher. Note his priorities as he speaks of the gospel "whereunto I am appointed a preacher, and an apostle, and a teacher of the Gentiles" (2 Tim. 1:11). His first calling was to preach the gospel to all people, and in this respect grace has made him a model for anyone who has received a calling to the pastoral ministry. With a single-minded energy of soul Paul gives himself to that ministry as his service to the head of the church. His whole life of consecration is saying to every preacher, "Follow this example!"

Fourth, the pastor sees preaching Jesus Christ to the whole world as the glory of the church. More than its ministry of mercy and more than its godly government, the fact that it freely offers the Savior to all people is its greatest honor. "How, then, can they call on the one they have not believed in? And how can they believe in the one of whom they have not heard? And how can they hear without someone preaching to them? And how can they preach unless they are sent? As it is written, 'How beautiful are the feet of those who bring good news!' " (Rom. 10:14–15). In his lectures to his students and in his addresses to pastors, Spurgeon continually reverted to this same theme:

> We have only one remedy for them [current evils]; preach Jesus Christ, and let us do it more and more. By the roadside, in the little room, in the theatre, anywhere, everywhere, let us preach Christ. Write books if you like, and do anything else within your power; but whatever else you cannot do, *preach Christ.* [35]

Fifth, the pastor acknowledges that effective preaching requires proper training. There is not the same priority given to this in the New Testament as the need for wholehearted dedication. Yet the emphasis is plain enough.

> Paul directs Timothy to impart his message to believing and reliable men who will be able to teach others (2 Tim. 1:2). The Twelve were trained by three years' companionship with the Lord.

35. Charles H. Spurgeon, *An All-Round Ministry* (London: Banner of Truth Trust, 1960), 127.

Paul was taken to "Arabia". Silas, Mark, Timothy and Titus had Paul himself for their mentor. Preachers are not born. Nor are they the products of mere professional training. They must have the gifts of knowledge, utterance, wisdom and courage necessary to effective proclamation. But even those with charismata need to be trained, learning the message and emulating the methods of their seniors. The precise form which such training will take in particular traditions is a matter of Christian prudence.[36]

## CONCLUSION

The whole concept of the pastoral ministry has come under the closest scrutiny and criticism during the past thirty years. What is called for now is as sustained a chorus of prayer for this ministry. Preachers are not to do everything, but they have a work to do that only they are called to do and that far exceeds their gifts and abilities. The first need is to address the Lord of the harvest, "that he will send forth laborers into his harvest" (Matt. 9:38). How wonderfully that prayer has been answered in the history of the church.

---

36. MacLeod, "Presbyters and Preachers," 124.

Seminary is for men who are seriously considering the ministry; it is a place where a man may test his gifts and calling in the service of the Word. It is often difficult for a man to be assured of his calling before the seminary experience. Has he the gifts of insight into Scripture? Can he expound the word fruitfully? The seminary classroom and study help to supply answers to such questions. The academic disciplines of theological study are no more remote from pastoral experience than the drills of the training camp from big league competition. For the man in doubt as to whether he has the teaching gift, the seminary situation may bring grateful understanding as he grows in the Word of God.

*Called to the Ministry* (1964)

# 5

# Theological Education
# Since World War II:
# The American Experience

## Samuel F. Rowen

The period following World War II, though recognizing some of the inherent problems in theological education, was basically optimistic. The war was over, and a sense of hope for the future was on the upswing. Large numbers of former servicemen had returned with plans for entering the ministry and, in particular, missionary work. Theological education was ready for a time of renewal. The optimism was sounded in the 1950 address of John A. Mackay at the biennial meeting of the American Association of Theological Schools (AATS).[1]

In his address Mackay outlined the themes that became the recurring concerns of the next thirty-five years in theological education. These years will not always reflect the positive and optimistic tone he set; they will be variously described as times of chaos, irrelevance, and failure at curriculum reform. While these descriptions of the condition of theological education refer to North America, they will to a greater or lesser extent reflect the concerns in theological education in other parts of the world.[2]

---

1. John A. Mackay, "The Finality of Theological Education," *The Seventeenth Biennial Meeting of the American Association of Theological Schools*, Bulletin 19 (June 1950), 71ff.

2. See Leslie Newbigin, "Theological Education in a World Perspective," *Ministerial Formation*, no. 4 (1978): 3-10. Reprinted in Harvie M. Conn and Samuel F. Rowen, eds., *Missions and Theological Education in World Perspective* (Farmington, Ill.: Associates of Urbanus, 1984), 3-18.

Mackay identified four factors that set the stage for an expected re-newal in theological education.[3]

The first factor was the disturbed conscience of many thoughtful peo-ple. They were disturbed when they considered the progressive descent in academic recognition that theology had suffered in modern cultural history. There was a time when all education was theological, but this was no longer true. It was now time for its reemergence to a place of prominence.

Second, there was the awareness of, and deep concern about, the ma-jor crisis through which civilization was passing. Optimism and a sense of hope for the future was tempered by this reality. Two world wars had left the Western world reeling without a sense of direction. Contributing to this in higher education was what had been called the "treason of the intellectuals." They failed to speak out when they should have, and when they did, it was irrelevant. Now theological education could par-ticipate in helping the church to speak a sure word.

The third circumstance leading to the restoration of theological inter-est was the awakened sense of the church. This new sense of the church was closely related to the discovery of the Bible and the revived interest in church vocations. The only thing comparable to the expansion of communism was the missionary expansion of the church.

The fourth circumstance was the emergence of a dynamic theology. The theology was marked by a strongly biblical emphasis. It represented a renaissance of the consciousness of the church to its responsibility in the world of thought and the prophetic answer to the nihilism in West-ern thought.

The optimistic picture presented by Mackay was not shared by every-one. On the one hand, the awakened sense of the church and the strong biblical emphasis have characterized the development of the largest theological seminaries in North America presently representative of the conservative evangelical segment of the church. On the other hand, after the students returning from military service in World War II had graduated, the more liberal and mainline denominational seminaries be-gan to focus their attention on the state of theological education.

## THE PURPOSE OF THEOLOGICAL EDUCATION

By 1954 the concern about theological education was voiced by H. Richard Niebuhr. In his survey of theological schools presented to the nineteenth biennial meeting of the AATS, he stated:

3. Mackay, "Finality of Theological Education," 71–72.

Great confusion prevails in some quarters about theological education. What, it is asked, is the meaning of this ministry? For what
purpose are we educating? The situation in some circles of theological educators seems to be similar to the one found among certain foreign missionaries and sponsors of foreign missions. They
know that what they are doing is important, but an understanding
of the strategy of their work, a relatively precise and definite understanding of its meaning is lacking.[4]

The survey led to the publication of two significant books edited by
Niebuhr and his colleagues. In *The Purpose of the Church and Its Ministry: Reflections on the Aims of Theological Education* Niebuhr discussed the
idea of a theological school and continued to sound a negative note. He
wrote:

> Perhaps it is a mistake to say that the first impression given by the
> theological schools is one of multiplicity and indefiniteness. Their
> first impression many observers receive is one of inertia and
> conservatism.[5]

The second volume, *The Advancement of Theological Education*, attempted to give some direction to the future course of theological education. The study was influential in advancing continuing theological
education, including the development of the Doctor of Ministry programs that are prevalent today. It also pointed up one of the continuing
tensions—the tension of whether the theological school serves the
church or the academic guilds. Niebuhr said that there is the double
responsibility on the theological teacher for both scholarship and
churchmanship.[6] The theological school must live with its feet in two
worlds. The pull between these two worlds will shape the programmatic
response and the schizophrenic tensions of this period. The introductory
essay to a special issue of *Theological Education* devoted to the history of
theological education in the United States describes theological education as a hybrid institution. "Very few colleges or universities try to
maintain this kind of dual citizenship."[7]

4. H. Richard Niebuhr, "The Survey of Theological Education," *The Nineteenth Biennial
Meeting of the American Association of Theological Schools*, Bulletin 21 (1954): 120.
    5. H. Richard Niebuhr et al., *The Purpose of the Church and Its Ministry: Reflections on
the Aims of Theological Education* (New York: Harper and Brothers, 1956), 95.
    6. H. Richard Niebuhr et al., *The Advancement of Theological Education* (New York:
Harper and Brothers, 1957), 56.
    7. Donald W. Shriver, Jr., "The Accountability of Theological Education to the Mis-
sion of the Church," *Theological Education* 17, no. 1 (Autumn 1980): 59.

The discussion of the purpose and relevance of theological education continues. The consensus is that ambiguity or loss of direction results inevitably in the decline of vitality in theological education. Mackay in sounding his notes of optimism maintains that the "purpose of theological education is not only in the knowledge of God, but also in the service of God. Its supreme objective must be to prepare servants of God."[8] This emphasis—that training and preparation of ministers takes precedence over the study of theology[9]—distinctly sets theological education in North America apart from theological education in Europe. From a European perspective too little respect is given in North American seminaries to theology as an autonomous science.

Moss maintained that the future of theological education would increasingly take place in the context of the university.[10] In spite of this emphasis on context, the dominant concern since World War II is that the purpose of theological education is the preparation for various kinds of Christian ministry in church and society. "Thus the consensus is opting for the professional school as against the graduate school model for the seminary."[11] In 1978 *Theological Education* dealt with the theme "The Purpose of a Theological School: Twelve Years Later." This follow-up study reached a consensus. Both Roman Catholic and Protestant seminaries found the *raison d'etre* to be the church. Grindel sees the purpose of diocesan seminaries as challenging "the student to become a mature Christian man of prayer who listens and responds to God's Word in his own life."[12]

The post-World War II period is marked by an ebb and flow between hope and discouragement. Many attempts will be made to systematically study the theological education enterprise. People in the church have not always viewed these attempts with appreciation (skepticism is a more accurate description). The dilemma is most poignantly expressed in the following poem written by the president of a theological seminary:

8. Mackay, "Finality of Theological Education," 79.

9. Steven G. Mackie, "American Seminaries in World Perspective: A Draft Balance Sheet," *Theological Education* 5, no. 1 (Autumn 1968): 46.

10. Robert V. Moss, "Contexts for Theological Education in the Next Decade," *Theological Education* 5, no. 1 (Autumn 1968): 4–6.

11. Owen C. Thomas, "Some Issues in Theological Education," *Theological Education* 5, no. 4 (Summer 1969): 346.

12. John A. Grindel, "Purpose in Roman Catholic Seminaries: In a Diocesan Seminary," *Theological Education* 14, no. 2 (Summer 1978): 75. See Laurence N. Jones, "A Reflection on Theological Education for the Whole Church," ibid.: 93.

Say, how does the minister function out there?
Is he climbing a wall? Is he tearing his hair?
What problems look large? What forces look sinister
To the poor harried soul who is known as a minister?
Will someone please tell him just what he should do
When he finds that his halo is coming askew?
The young people think that his sermons are dead
The older ones say he's too easily led.
The ladies' aid questions the depth of his piety
And he's not quite in step with the John Birch Society.
His wife wants the freedom to be a whole person
And one gossip swears that she heard him a-cursing.
Say, what is the trouble with old what's-his-name?
If he's such a numbskull just who is to blame?
The answer to who manufactured this fool?
It's that gang at Reformed Theological School.[13]

## ACADEMIC EXCELLENCE IN THEOLOGICAL EDUCATION

The difficulties being experienced in theological education today are in part the result of the necessity for the theological educational institution to live in two worlds—the world of higher education and the world of the church. Colin Williams, dean of the Yale University Divinity School, quotes an article in the *Yale Magazine* by Henri Nouwen about the apparent conflict between the upward pull of the university (toward ascendent power and prestige) and the downward pull of the Christian faith (toward a compassion for human need).

Karl Barth describes the ethics of the New Testament as a downward pull, the pull from the heights to the depths, from riches to poverty, from victory to defeat, from triumph to suffering, from life to death. . . . How can Yale University, which seems to encourage everything except a downward pull, look at itself as an institution which sends its people out into the world to serve? Doesn't Yale University instill within its students the desire to move upward

13. Quoted in Samuel F. Rowen, *Curriculum Foundations, Experiences and Outcomes: A Participatory Case Study in Theological Education* (Ph.D. diss., Michigan State University, 1981), 117.

from weakness to power, from poverty to wealth, from ignorance to knowledge, from servant to master.[14]

"European style," in which integration into the life of the university has been the rule, has been the dominant model for theological education. McCord says, "One cannot think of Luther apart from the University of Wittenberg . . . or of the University of Geneva apart from John Calvin."[15] In the United States as well, Yale Divinity School, Harvard Divinity School, and Princeton Theological Seminary by the very name they bear illustrate the dominance of the European style of relationship between the university and theological school.

And yet the theological school has a way of life apart from the university, as evidenced in the existence of the Association of Theological Schools (ATS), an accrediting agency specifically for theological schools. Some seminaries maintain accreditation both with ATS and the regional accrediting association for universities and secondary schools.

A common thread runs through all of the relationships between theological schools and the accrediting associations, namely, the acceptance of the university model as the appropriate model for theological education. Theological education and higher education at the university level are cut from the same cloth. The institutions belonging to both associations generally do so for the practical reason of facilitating their students' acceptance into graduate-level programs in the university. The professional accrediting associations have some specific concerns for the inclusion of practicum or clinical experience in the curriculum. There is little difference, however, in the educational model. For this reason professional schools (medicine, law, psychology, theology, etc.) function with relative ease within the university. Though recognizing the tension between the upward way of the university and the downward way of the Christian faith, Nouwen sees the relationship between the theological school and the university as useful. He maintains that the relationship provides a challenge to the dominant secular self-image of the university.

A strong pull to maintain the academic search for truth is characteristic of the university. However, Williams asks whether the tension between the upward way of the Greek mind reaching for human autonomy

14. Colin Williams, "Purpose in a University Divinity School," *Theological Education* 14, no. 2 (Spring 1978): 67.
15. James I. McCord, "The Understanding of Purpose in a Seminary Closely Related to the Church," *Theological Education* 14, no. 2 (Spring 1978): 66.

and the downward way of biblical faith, with its insistency on the primacy of divine wisdom, is adequately represented by the curriculum of the theological school.[16] The upward way underlies the charges from the church that the seminary graduates have been affected by professionalism and elitism. The tension between the upward and the downward is seen in the way the "minister as leader" and the "minister as servant" models conflict in the curriculum of the theological seminary. Faculty members experience this tension to the degree they become responsive to the demands to serve the church while, at the same time, seeking acceptance in the guilds of their disciplines—an acceptance measured by the leadership standards of their counterparts in other colleges of the university.

## CURRICULUM REFORM

The period since World War II is dotted with numerous attempts at curriculum reform. Generally these attempts were to include more "practical" subjects in the curriculum. Rather than curriculum *reform*, the results were largely in terms of curriculum *revision*. Wagoner says that no fundamental change occurred. The changes are characterized as chiefly ones of tinkering, of rearranging the same old furniture.

> If we turn to architecture for an analogy we may say that theological education in the United States has never had a Gropius, or a Wright, or a Harrison, or a Saarinen. That is, we have never had a new statement, a genuinely creative response by men who are ruthlessly determined to push beyond the inheritance of the past.[17]

Coupled with an emphasis of adding more practical subjects to the curriculum was the push to "get outside the monastery." Questions were raised about the context of theological education. Is the classroom the place for the individual to learn how to minister to people? Will the student be able to discern the will of God by listening to lectures? Converging patterns of ministry in Asia, Africa, and Europe raised questions of how the changing contexts of ministry should affect the context of theological studies. Mackie identified five elements in this pattern:

16. Williams, "University Divinity School," 65.
17. Walter D. Wagoner, "A Model for Theological Education," *Theological Education* 1, no. 2 (Winter 1965): 90.

1. The minister of tomorrow will be working in an increasingly educated society.

2. The churches will be increasingly involved in ecumenical dialogue.

3. Ministers must be theologians able to bring theological insights to bear on particular situations.

4. Theology must always be taught in "communicable" form.

5. Ministers will work in different areas and sectors of society— therefore, study of sociology and history will be required.[18]

With the emphasis on increasing involvement in the world, substantial changes continued to be made in the curriculum. Some major seminaries eventually had the majority of their students planning on other than pastoral ministries. In spite of this development in the curriculum, the underlying rationale that the seminary is a servant of the church did not disappear. The proliferation of practical courses left much to be desired. The courses lacked theological depth and were without a corpus of significant literature.

In the 1970s three developments were to affect the thinking about curriculum reform in theological education. Each of these had its roots outside the North American scene. They emerged at the frontiers of the mission of the church as it attempted to communicate the gospel across cultural boundaries at the point of contact with dominantly non-Christian societies or with Christian societies in the economically lesser-developed countries.

The first development resulted from the launching of the Theological Education Fund in Ghana in 1957. The concerns were fully articulated in the influential book, *Ministry in Context: The Third Mandate Programme of the Theological Education Fund* (1972). Shoki Coe summarizes them:

> The excellence to be sought should be defined in terms of theological training which leads to a real encounter between the student and the Gospel in terms of his own forms of thought and culture, and to a living dialogue between the church and its environment. The aim should be to use resources so as to help teachers and students to a deeper understanding of the Gospel in terms of his own forms of thought and culture, and to be a living dialogue between the church and its environment. . . . so that the church may

18. Steven G. Mackie, "Patterns of Ministry and the Purpose of a Theological School," *Theological Education* 2, no. 2 (Winter 1966): 82f.

come to a deeper understanding of itself as a missionary community sent into the world and to a more effectual encounter within the life of the society.[19]

The second development is the questioning of the meaning of excellence in theological education. Because theological education was closely wedded to the university model, excellence was generally described in academic categories. However, voices from the churches increasingly resounded that the seminary graduate was ineffective in ministering in the churches. The emphasis on practical courses that took students into experiences outside the classroom were also being criticized. Much of the practical experience was in the context of abnormal human need—psychiatric hospitals, prisons, shelters, etc. While the experience broadened the effectiveness of the seminarian, it provided little opportunity to develop the skills demanded by the average family at the congregational level.

Emerito P. Nacpil, dean of the federated faculty of the South East Asia Graduate School of Theology, expressed the concerns of Asian theological schools as being "in search of a new kind of excellence in theological education." He says:

I detect a shift of emphasis in the pursuit of excellence—from the narrower understanding of it as academic excellence to one that is broader and more adequate to the needs of theological education in the region today.[20]

One of the responses to this concern by ATS has been directed to the question of spiritual formation. The seminary as a community is described as a context for participation in the spiritual formation of the seminarian. However, the changes leading to the "aging of the seminary student" have created some difficulties. Older student populations include many with families. The student must support his family not as part of the theological community but as an employed member of society who is also taking "academic" courses in preparation for the pastoral ministries of the church. The problem is extremely acute if the seminary is to become a community with a responsibility for the spiritual formation of the student.

19. Shoki Coe, "In Search of Renewal in Theological Education," *Theological Education* 9, no. 4 (Summer 1973): 236.
20. Emerito P. Nacpil, "The Question of Excellence in Theological Education," *The South East Asia Journal of Theology* 16, no. 1 (1975): 56.

In the 1970s seminary enrollment increased 68 percent. Conservative evangelical seminaries enrolled about 57 percent of all seminary students in the United States. Excluding the top eleven evangelical seminaries (each with over five hundred students), there was actually a decrease in the size of Protestant seminaries from an average of 263 to 246 students. Including the eleven seminaries, there was an increase in the average from 263 to 343 students.[21] The sense of certainty about the meaning of the gospel in the conservative evangelical seminaries was extremely attractive to potential students. However, the growth was largely among older students and part-time students. Both of these factors made it difficult for the seminary to address creatively the perceived responsibility for the spiritual formation of the student.

The third development of this period was the emergence of the theological education by extension movement. Begun in 1963 at the Presbyterian seminary in Guatemala, it soon spread around the world. Ted Ward maintains that this development was more than a fad, but was actually a reflection of changes occurring in other developments in professional education around the world.[22]

All three developments are interrelated. They all are concerns about how context affects the understanding and practice of theological education. Whereas in the past the debate about the reform of theological education centered on making courses more practical, the discussion of contextualization opened the possibility that reform might be more than simply rearranging the old furniture.

Farley maintains that the reform of theological education is essentially a theological task.[23] While not disputing this, Hough states that a theological solution to the question of the unity of theological education "might emerge partially as a result of attempts to deal with political realities" preceding the theological solutions in time.[24] The political realities are evidenced in the demands of the faculty, students, alumni, and church—each pressuring that its distinctive values be honored.

21. John C. Fletcher, "Theological Seminaries in the Future," *Theological Education* 21, no. 1 (Autumn 1984): 74.
22. Ted Ward, "Theological Education by Extension: Much More than a Fad," *Theological Education* 10, no. 4 (Summer 1974): 248–49.
23. Edward Farley, "Reform of Theological Education as a Theological Task," *Theological Education* 17, no. 2 (Spring 1981): 93–117.
24. Joseph D. Hough, Jr., "Reform of Theological Education as a Political Task," *Theological Education* 17, no. 2 (Spring 1981): 53.

The Presbyterian Church in America in its Sixth General Assembly listed its requirement for the preparation of candidates for the gospel ministry.[25] The discussion at the general assembly level resulted from a dissatisfaction with the readiness of the seminary graduates for functional ministry. There was no fundamental questioning of the curricular pattern in this decision. It was essentially a mandate to the seminaries to include English Bible in the curriculum. The statement proposed a threefold pattern of Scripture, doctrine (including church history), and practical theology.

Although the dichotomy between theory and practice is being questioned as more interaction occurs between Western and non-Western educational philosophies, the present approach of theological education is to accept the fourfold pattern and increase the emphasis on bridging the gap between theory and practice.

The limitations of the theory-practice dichotomy are seen in the ways in which the "bridge" metaphor has been employed. Farley identifies the characteristics of this development:[26] (1) The development of strategies to build the bridge is done by either nominating a particular field (i.e., practical theology) to build the bridge or developing a series of bridgings from each pedagogical enterprise. The end result of these strategies has contributed to a further fragmentation in the theological curriculum. The unity of *theologia* has not been achieved by bridge-building strategies because of the acceptance of the essential validity of the theory-practice dichotomy. (2) The acceptance of the theory-practice dichotomy resulted in a series of bridgings rather than a shaping or formation of the minister of the gospel. A renewed interest in some of the traditional concerns for spiritual formation has emerged.[27] The imagery of a bridge connotes a specific point of arrival. The imagery of formation connotes a process or a pilgrimage that is lifelong. (3) The emphasis on the bridge

25. *Minutes of the Sixth General Assembly of the Presbyterian Church in America, June 19–23, 1978, Grand Rapids, Michigan.* (Decatur, Ga.: Committee for Christian Education and Publications, 1978), 214–17.

26. Farley, "Theological Task," 103–6.

27. "There is a growing insistence throughout theological education that institutions must honestly face the question of spiritual formation. During the mid-sixties theological education addressed itself to concerns involved with a quality of education that would be more experientially based and related to centers of contemporary culture. . . . it became increasingly apparent that the question of the spiritual formation of the individual was becoming primary" ("Report of Task Force on Spiritual Development: Vignette," *Theological Education* 8, no. 3 [Spring 1972]: 153–97). See also Tilden H. Edwards, Jr., "Spiritual Formation in Theological Schools: Ferment and Challenge. A Report of the ATS-Shalem Institute on Spirituality," *Theological Education* 17, no. 1 (Autumn 1980): 7–52.

metaphor has resulted in a preoccupation with technique. Farley concludes by saying:

> Perhaps this bridge metaphor has become the pervasive metaphor in its gradual, unselfconscious process, a metaphor floating into the theological schools by way of the American pragmatic temper and reflecting the valid attempt to correct the academicism of the dispersed encyclopedia. Whatever is the case it is surely a serious distortion of theological study.[28]

## FUTURE DIRECTION IN THEOLOGICAL EDUCATION

The picture of theological education since World War II is one of shifting positions. There is, on the one hand, evidence that much activity was irrelevant. On the other hand, there are signs of a new vitality. The new vitality during this period has largely been in the increasing growth patterns in seminary enrollment along with the increasing number of women seminarians.[29] Nevertheless, the underlying curriculum concerns are evident in seminaries across differing theological persuasions.

Three words characterize the discussions of curricular improvement in theological education in the future—*environment, contextualization,* and *globalization. Environment* deals with the environmental context in which the theological educational process takes place. *Contextualization* deals not only with the context in which the educational experience occurs (environment) and how it affects learning, but also the questions of the meaning of the gospel as it encounters a specific context. This emphasis led many to maintain that the only valid conclusions are those relevant to a specific context and made by people within that context—a view known as "contextualism."[30]

The discussions of contextualization that have made text subservient to context have led to the present discussions on globalization. In order

28. Farley, "Theological Task," 105.

29. In 1850 Antoinette Brown did not receive her degree at Oberlin Theological School. One professor wrote in the *Oberlin Quarterly*, "Women were emotional, physically delicate, illogical, weak-voiced, vain, dependent, and most important, divinely ordained to be mothers and homemakers." By the 1980s the place of women in theological education has been largely reversed in both conservative evangelical and mainline seminaries. See "Special Issue on Women in Theological Education: Past, Present, and Future," *Theological Education* 8, no. 4 (Summer 1972).

30. Max L. Stackhouse, *Apologia: Contextualization, Globalization, and Mission in Theological Education* (Grand Rapids: William B. Eerdmans, 1988), 26–27.

to avoid the conclusions of a contextualism it is necessary to affirm that truth and justice transcend all contexts and are valid for all contexts. Globalization is not simply the idea that theological education will take place in a global community, but that what is true is binding on all contexts. Max Stackhouse in dialogue with theological educators from various parts of the world states:

> Theological Education—if it is to render anything that is worthy of contextualization, globalization, and mission—demands that we reconsider the possibility that at least some texts, however, much they are influenced by their context, have context-transcending elements of potentially universal importance, and that this is why we can take them as source and norm, defend their validity in public discourse, and utilize them to critically assess current contexts.[31]

What is needed in theological education is a "scientific revolution" similar to the one that is found in Thomas Kuhn: a new paradigm for understanding God.[32] The one thing that Thomas Kuhn has done is to demonstrate that all thought is based on presuppositions, that is, conscious choices on the way one views the world. This suggests that a serious reappraisal of the works of Cornelius Van Til is appropriate and timely for the discussions on globalization and the nature of theological education.

There are signs of hope that the future may provide some models of theological education that will give form to some of the issues raised by the discussions on contextualization in the 1970s and globalization in the 1980s. Whenever new models of education are introduced, they have a tendency to "blow the fuses" in the system. There have been several attempts to move theological education outside the "walls of the monastery" during this period.

An example of such an attempt is the Florida Theological Center founded by Westminster Theological Seminary. This model allowed a student to take the first two years of seminary training at the main campus. The third year was taken in a two-year period in an internship context under the supervision of the seminary and the church. The student would spend half of his time on the staff of a church, and both the pastor and the resident faculty were responsible for theological reflection

31. Ibid., 27.
32. Ibid., xiii.

on the actual problems encountered in ministry. In this model there was a close articulation of theological studies along with actual practice in ministry. The cries of irrelevance of theological education were largely absent among the students.[33] However, the management of the program created several difficulties; eventually the center closed, not because of the quality of the education but for management and financial reasons. The model was largely limited to the context of the suburban church and failed to deal with the context of the city in a creative and effective way.

A more recent attempt to create an integrated model of theological studies and practice of ministry is the formation of the Conservative Baptist Seminary of the East (CBSE). This institution is structured to respond to several issues in theological education: (1) the need to have church-based theological education; (2) the need to have theological education serve the needs of the church in a variety of contexts—urban, rural, and suburban; (3) the need for the skills and knowledge base of theological education to be relevant, appropriate for ministry, and capable of articulation with the curriculum of other theological institutions.

CBSE plans three centers of theological education. One center is specifically designed within the context of suburban Philadelphia, the second within New York City, and the third in New England for training people for church work in rural contexts. The curriculum is designed to permit students to be under a supervising pastor and for the faculty to teach in more than one center. CBSE is seeking certification with those agencies which certify formal educational institutions. If CBSE can creatively deal with the tension between the academy and the church, then it will provide a significantly new model for theological education.

The discussions on excellence in theological education will continue to be part of the theological educational scene. A loosely affiliated association of theological enterprises outside the normal stream has been formed. It includes representatives of theological education programs from local church-based groups, denominational alternative educational programs, and some representatives from formal theological educational institutions. The North American Council for the Assessment of Ministerial Preparation (NACAMP) is attempting to develop criteria for the assessment of ministerial preparation.

33. One student evaluated his experience in the following manner: "They do not need to be concerned about the academic standards. I have never worked so hard in my life. When I was at the seminary I always wondered whether or not I could actually function in the pastoral ministry. Now I know I can."

The association will function like an accrediting agency, but with a fundamental difference in orientation. Traditional patterns of accreditation focus on accrediting the *institution*. NACAMP is looking to formulate criteria for the accrediting of *people*. They are looking for ways of commending an individual as being able to function as a minister, rather than assessing the person in terms of number of courses taken. The forerunner of this approach is in the Council for the Assessment of Experiential Learning (CAEL), which began when universities needed criteria to grant advanced standing to students on the basis of experience. Excellence in functional, rather than academic, terms is the goal.

The accrediting associations are struggling for new paradigms for the meaning of excellence. The current approach has been described as "being no more relevant to the 80's than a Model T Ford is for the Indianapolis 500 race."[34] The criteria used for institutions are the number of Ph.D.'s on the faculty, number of books in the library, financial stability, and organizational structure. This approach has not been effective in improving the quality of theological education. It is an instance of the educational maxim, "We generally measure those things which are easiest to measure and often the most trivial."

Theological education will be marked with continued developments in the area of the city as a context. The city is not only a place where there are large numbers of people; as a context with theological significance, it will challenge theological institutions to respond to such needs. Programs like the one begun by SCUPE (Seminary Consortium for Urban Pastoral Education) in Chicago will continue to proliferate. There are programs in Philadelphia, Boston, Detroit, and many other large cities in North America. Some are simply extensions of the campus-based curriculum. Others, like the Center for Urban Theological Studies in Philadelphia (related to Westminster Theological Seminary), are multifaceted and view the city as a place of theological reflection. The curriculum emerges in the process of dialogue between text and context.

The university model of theological education provides the greatest incentive for maintaining the status quo in theological education. Fundamental changes will occur only as there is the openness to experiment on the way in which context rearranges theological curricula. It will most likely be the lessons learned from theological schools in non-

34. Jesse H. Ziegler, "Editorial Introduction," *Theological Education* 14, no. 1 (Autumn 1977): 6.

Western society that hold the most promise. The university model in the West has remained static in structure even in the midst of significant philosophical shifts. In places like Hong Kong, which faces the political realities of how the institution will survive after 1997 when the territory returns to the control of the People's Republic of China, questions are being asked in new and fresh ways about the place of theological education in society. All theological schools must continually remind themselves that they are social institutions. But as Christian social institutions seminaries are to adjust to the social reality as well as change the social reality in which they are to fulfill their calling.

# Part Two
# Disciplines and Directions

When you realize that, with the world the field, this task is as extensive as it is intensive, you may well cry, "Who is sufficient for these things?" Westminster's department of practical theology does not profess to supply an answer in advance to all the problems that will confront you as an evangelistic pastor. But it does undertake to lay upon your conscience the full weight of the responsibility that is yours, and to put before you the principles of Biblical evangelism and Christian education, placing in your hands the most important practical skills which this phase of your calling demands.

"Training for the Ministry at
Westminster Theological Seminary" (1948)

# 6

# Practical Theology: The State of the Art

## George C. Fuller

$T$o speak of practical theology forces the mind to form all kinds of images. The focus moves among all the things that a minister does: preach, pray, mediate, moderate, console, challenge, relate, repair. But this list is incomplete, as is any other compilation. For example, the ministry of lay men and women is omitted. No survey can include all the applications of the gospel and theology.

To ask about the current state of this discipline is to inquire into counseling, missions, preaching, social applications, education, fellowship, worship—the entire spectrum of church life. Is there no limit to the subjects that might quite properly be included under practical theology? Is it the application to life of all the counsel of God? James N. Poling and Donald E. Miller suggest more precise and varied definitions, but for our purposes inquiry will move through the total witness of the church in the world.

Where now to begin? Some assumptions must be made. The first is that the church's training of its ministers reflects what is already happening in the churches or what is about to happen. If that assumption is correct, then today's seminaries either reflect pressure from their constituent churches to provide a specific kind of training, or they carry an impact that will change the nature of the church. In either case, the nature of seminary training should reflect what happens in the church. An important question, but not for our purposes, is, Does the church influence the seminaries or vice versa? We simply affirm that what happens in the seminaries has a parallel in the churches, either just before or soon after the phenomenon appears in the seminaries.

We look then to ministerial training to understand what is happening in practical theology. We assume that what we find is reflected in the church. If a view of the present can be obtained, then perhaps some hope of extrapolating into the probable and ideal future might be gained. That kind of projection, however, requires orientation in the past to understand better the present. A glance through past decades will help us to know where we now stand.

## BRIEF HISTORICAL REVIEW

Beginning a historical survey in eighteenth-century America in itself makes two statements, one about time and another about geography. Recognizing that God's work did not begin in 1700 and limit itself to these acres, we yet note that eighteenth-century ministerial training here was largely done through "reading divinity," a semiformal process by which a minister or professor of divinity served as personal tutor for one or several aspiring clerics.

While the focus of concern was often upon the relation between the knowledge and the experience of religion, no doubt widely varying degrees of attention were given to development of the gifts / skills / abilities requisite for ministry. The tutors oversaw the use of practical work in the churches, as candidates for ministry preached in churches too poor to afford a fully qualified minister and served in other capacities. Virtually all of the ordination examinations was devoted to academic understanding, although a trial sermon was preached. W. Clark Gilpin notes that attention was given to preaching, prayer, some elements of worship; but the clear emphasis in this diverse system was on doctrinal knowledge and personal piety, neither of which is, or was, without practical application.[1]

With the turn of the century came the founding of Andover (1808) and Princeton theological seminaries (1812). The next decades saw the founding of other similar schools. Individualized relationships between pastors or professors and candidates now became institutionalized, as increasing numbers of students gathered in one place to study under the few professors in each new center. A formal curriculum began to appear.

1. W. Clark Gilpin, "The Seminary Ideal in American Protestant Ministerial Education," *Theological Education* 20, no. 2 (Spring 1984): 85–106.

Andover included a department of sacred rhetoric, but Robert Wood Lynn warns his readers not to assume this to be a direct forerunner of later practical study: "The Andover offerings . . . were more akin to an eighteenth century college course in rhetoric than to the preoccupations of late nineteenth century practical theology."[2]

As more American professors studied in Europe, however, they became convinced of the benefit of a curriculum divided into four distinct disciplines: exegesis, doctrinal theology, ecclesiastical history, and practical theology. The call went forth for a more systematized seminary curriculum, and the response to challenge was heated then, as now: " . . . two Andover professors assaulted the witless spawning of 'feeble, mendicant institutions' and stated that 'every seminary that is not plainly needed is plainly a nuisance.' "[3] The expression *practical theology* gradually came into use to describe one of the four foci for formal theological investigation and study, but obviously not without birth pangs. Growth pain has been experienced through the subsequent years.

As the century drew to its close, William Rainey Harper, founder of, and scholar at, the University of Chicago, noted what he saw as academic and professional retrogression in the seminaries. "So far as I know," he said, "the only professional curriculum which is essentially the same as it was fifty years ago is that of the theological seminary."[4] He indicated that preaching no longer was the single high calling of the pastor. Lynn summarizes the changing situation: "A working knowledge of Greek and Hebrew, the ability to excel in closely reasoned theological debate in addresses and sermons were considered less significant than the capacity to organize a Sunday School, to work with the women's auxiliaries, to inspire missionary interest and giving, and to building denominational loyalty."[5]

Harper called for a drastically revised curriculum that devoted its first year to the study of English Bible and theology and then placed major focus on clinics and other study devoted to areas of ministry specialization. "By the time of graduation the religious professional would be the equal of the newly anointed engineer, lawyer, and doctor."[6]

2. Robert Wood Lynn, "Notes Toward a History: Theological Encyclopedia and the Evolution of Protestant Seminary Curriculum, 1808–1868," *Theological Education* 17, no. 2 (Spring 1981): 118.

3. Ibid., 125.
4. Ibid., 128.
5. Ibid., 129.
6. Ibid., 130.

## THE TWENTIETH CENTURY

Many features now easily recognized in the field of practical theology are observed in incipient and developing forms through the decades of this century. While the other three departments of theological inquiry have "rich internal histories," comments Robert T. Handy, "practical theology has probably grown the most as it has added such various sub-departments as religious education, supervised field education, clinical training, and sociological and psychological studies."[7] Changes of this type recognize and encourage specialization in ministry. As such, they display the horizontal expansion of practical theology in the former Bachelor of Divinity and now Master of Divinity programs.

Other developments have enlarging impact on the practical theology horizon: new continuing education programs for clergy and the development of lay theological education. These changes indicate a vertical extension in practical theology, as the field reaches levels where it had not before penetrated. Included in this delineation must be the relatively new Doctor of Ministry degree with its important implications and consequences.

The recent decades have seen rapid expansion and innovation. But the need seems insatiable. Or is it that the supply is simply insufficient? Lynn refers to 1966 and 1967 studies, one sponsored by the American Association of Theological Schools (Charles Fielding, *Education for Ministry*) and two others that were denominationally oriented: "The principle theme of these investigators can be summed up in the 1967 verdict of *Time* magazine: 'Seminary teaching often lacks contact with life.' Fielding, for instance, found that the theological schools were too academic in orientation and too distant from the concerns of the churches to be effective professional schools."[8]

As the decade of the 1980s began, all of practical theology's expansion and effort were regarded as insufficient, perhaps in light of the vast array of individual and corporate problems in the world. Leon Pacala, executive director of the Association of Theological Schools, set forth his "Reflection on the State of Theological Education in the 1980s," in which he first commented on trends developing in the previous decade. He saw those years as a time of "increased professionalization of theological curriculums. It was a time during which the practice

---

7. Robert T. Handy, "Trends in Canadian and American Theological Education, 1880–1980: Some Comparisons," *Theological Education* 18, no. 2 (Spring 1982): 182.

8. Lynn, "Notes Toward a History," 137.

of ministry was conceived as the major problematic of theological education and professional competence as its major objective. Both were the results of the widespread acceptance of the professional model of ministry as the dominant model for theological education."9

Practical theology then seems to have moved from a position of uncertain importance in early theological training to a pivotal position. In the tutor-candidate relationship the focus was on Scripture / doctrine on the one hand and experience / personal piety on the other. Trial sermons and personal observation of the mentor at work were surely part of the interaction. But what is today the practice of practical training was allocated a very informal role in a system that itself was not structured.

Through the phases of theological education's development, practical theology first had found its place as one of the four carefully delineated fields designated for inquiry and study. But it is not unreasonable to assert that it now takes a place of prominence, even dominance, among the other seminary disciplines. In fact, as the role of the training institution becomes that of preparing the professional / practitioner / pragmatist, it can be argued that practical theology is what all of seminary education is about and that to speak of one is to affirm the other. There may exist now a practical equivalence between what begrudgingly had become one of four facets of seminary training and that entire discipline of the training of ministers (and others) for service.

But if there is any truth to this affirmation of the staggering growth in practical theology's role and influence, a sense of frustration is also apparent. Whatever has happened in the practical preparation of ministers, it has been inadequate. It is not enough; we are simply not meeting the needs. The target is changing so rapidly that innovations in preparation seem outmoded, inappropriate, even before they have been put into position.

This effort to understand the broad situation will now be localized as we look at three seminaries that find themselves part of this history and part of the present. It will be obvious why these three schools—Princeton, Reformed, and Westminster Theological Seminaries—are of special interest in this study. They are all part of the same heritage, each arising from Calvinistic and Reformed roots. The only issue before us is the development of practical theological training. And in this regard we will understand Princeton to be either a predictor of, or a reactor to, what is happening in the church at large. It is to be seen as a pacesetter or an early responder to trends that are widespread now in the church. Princeton also has played a pivotal role in the development of theological education in the United States.

Reformed Seminary's history now spans more than two decades, and it has grown significantly in size. Located in Jackson, Mississippi, it serves many Presbyterians and others of conservative commitment. It is of special interest because of the radical curricular changes made in 1986 and 1987. These need to be observed against the background of practical theology's history and its present status in the general seminary curriculum. A full study of Reformed's new direction must also be made in the light of tensions regarding the role of a seminary and its proper goals. Is a seminary to train people who are prepared for a life of learning, or is its goal an already finished product? No simple answer is proper. It is not an either / or kind of question, but the curricular tension between the question's poles is apparent.

Westminster supplies the third case study. Its interest to the contributors to this volume does not need to be explained. But it can serve as a helpful example of an institution that has sought to maintain loyalty to the traditional balance of courses and weight in the curriculum and at the same time to offer training that is relevant to an increasingly complex and more rapidly changing world.

This review will look specifically at requirements for the three-year program designed for the training of ministers. At the several seminaries, this program was concluded with the awarding of a certificate, the Bachelor of Theology (Bachelor of Divinity or Master of Divinity) degree. The expansion of courses offered in practical theology, particularly at Princeton and Westminster, was accompanied by the offering of new programs in which many of these courses were relevant. Reformed Seminary also began to offer specialized programs other than preparation for the pastorate. The review of the next pages, however, will focus only on the traditional three-year program of preparation for church (and parallel) ministry.

A review of developments at Princeton Seminary opens our eyes to what is happening at a "mainline" institution. To a significant degree what has been happening at Princeton will have its parallels at many other institutions that share Princeton's commitments. Princeton offers then a concrete case study that gives form to an abstract generalized history of practical theology. And, to a significant degree, to know where Princeton Seminary is today is to have good insight into the state of the generalized situation for practical theology.

## CASE STUDY ONE: PRINCETON THEOLOGICAL SEMINARY

The Princeton 1880 catalog describes requirements in major divisions of the curriculum: (1) Old Testament; (2) New Testament; (3) theology; (4) biblical and ecclesiastical history; (5) ecclesiastical, homiletic, and pastoral theology. Apart from the division of exegesis into its two components, the structure follows the fourfold differentiation that had begun to appear almost a century earlier.

Of special interest is the surprising breadth of requirements in the last department, that which came to be known as practical theology. Too extensive to duplicate in full, excerpts from the department's requirements show its extensive concerns: "Sacred Rhetoric, analysis of texts, and writing of skeletons. . . . Church government, nature of the Church, Church polity, membership, the baptized, communicants, officers, commission, succession, and parity of Ministers; ruling Elders, Deacons, Church courts. . . . A call to the Ministry; the aptitudes and attainments required; the duties, relations, and responsibilities of the pastoral care . . . worship, including the sacraments and public prayer, preaching and praise . . . systematic beneficence. . . . Discipline. . . ." This concluding sentence is added to the full statement, "These and other topics connected are treated historically, as well as discussed in the light of Scripture, and according to the standards of the Presbyterian Church." Even though a suspicion arises that some of the content of these courses was more academic than specifically practical, the spectrum of concerns addressed was extensive. Perhaps some of the emphases of recent decades have not been all that innovative. It could be that our predecessors in the discipline had a more balanced approach than we want to imagine.

Princeton soon began to delineate requirements in terms of specific course requirements. The 1910 catalog offers this comment: "The Seminary Course of Study . . . occupies some one thousand four hundred and forty hours of instruction, and the accomplishment of the whole of this Course is required for graduation." The prospective student is told that he will be expected to attend 16 hours for three years of approximately thirty weeks each. The total semester hour requirement in practical theology was about 15 hours, approximately 16 percent of a required curriculum of 96 semester hours.

Several phenomena are of special interest, especially in the light of later developments at the seminaries under scrutiny. Entering students were expected to know Greek and to take a full year of study in Hebrew.

Courses in the content of the English Bible were required but were included among the offerings in the "Department of Practical Theology and Homiletics." This inclusion should not be regarded as strange; it simply recognized the place of English Bible study in the curriculum as being of practical orientation, quite distinct from the required exegetical study. The inclusion of a course in doctrine of the church ("Ecclesiastical Theology") in the practical department indicated a desire to study practical issues on the basis of firm theological grounding.

Through the next decade (until 1920) little change was made in the nature or extent of the requirements of practical theology. But the course offerings in the department were beginning to expand, as specialization began to exert pressure for expression in the general curriculum of the institution. The total requirement for the Bachelor of Divinity student continued in the 14- to 16-hour range. However, by 1920 each student was entitled to elect 5 hours of course work. The issue of elective options will become increasingly important and may be seen as a response to the need for personal development and specialization in ministry.

## PRINCETON SEMINARY: DEVELOPMENTS AFTER 1930

The struggle at Princeton that led to the founding of Westminster Seminary in 1929 focused on tension between members of the Department of Practical Theology and J. Gresham Machen and some members of the other departments. That tension is not, however, reflected in Princeton's curriculum structure in 1930. Minor changes in requirements are observed, and these appear as precursors of later developments. One hour of "religious education" was by now required, and the student was permitted to elect 10 hours of his program. Course offerings were expanding rapidly.

The three-year curriculum of 1940 shows only 17 required hours in practical theology, a modest gain over previous years. The student was free to elect 23 hours work. The catalog by now listed ten courses in what had become known by the title "Christian education." The department continued the tradition of strong offerings in speech.

By 1950 the seminary had moved to the quarter system, and the requirement in hours for the Bachelor of Divinity degree was correspondingly increased to 135. As 29 hours were now required in practical theology, that stipulation moved to over 21 percent of the full requirement for graduation. Students were now entitled to elect 42 hours of their programs (31 percent). With Greek and Hebrew still required, and with 29 hours required in practical theology and 42 hours of elective credit available, it is apparent that some course material in the other departments was "feeling the squeeze." Those whose oxen are not being gored may forget that to add a valuable course in the practical theology program must mean to eliminate some other requirement from the curriculum. To offer 3 hours of elective credit means to remove 3 hours of required credit from somewhere in the catalog.

PRINCETON SEMINARY: RECENT DECADES

The 1950s seem to have been a period of rethinking. By 1960 the elective opportunities were reduced to 25 hours, while the requirements in practical theology remained steady. Specialized programs in education, in clinical pastoral studies, and in other areas had been developing at the institution. Senior courses not in the Department of Practical Theology included "The Christian Mission in Today's World," "Christianity, Society, and the Individual," "The Doctrine of the Church and the Christian Life," "Christian Ethics," and "Christian Social Ethics." If it might have been proper to suggest that "ecclesiastical theology," offered through the years in the practical department, was perhaps in reality a study in systematics, it might now be reasonable to see what had been regarded as within the spectrum of investigation for practical theology as becoming the content of courses in other departments. Was practical theology beginning to be the dominant focus on campus? Or was it even becoming identical with the total thrust of the institution?

The curriculum at Princeton had been going through decades of growth and change, moving toward general flexibility in student choice and in the practical area moving toward wide diversity of content. By the end of the 1960s the seminary had found a new innovative way in which to deal with the statement that had been appearing in its catalog through the recent years: "The program of study set forth for the Bachelor of Divinity degree is designed to prepare students for the parish ministry, for graduate study in theology and related disciplines, for various types of chaplaincy, for mission work at home and abroad, and for other forms of church vocation." The student would now (1970) be required to complete thirty units of study (twenty-four courses and six practicums), but he or she would have considerable freedom of selection for these units. Such selection, however, was guided by restraints. Three units, for example, had to be in the field of history, three in theology. Greek and Hebrew were no longer required, and alternative tracks were available for those who elected either, both, or neither of the biblical languages in their courses of study.

In 1970 each student was required to complete nine units (three courses and six practicums) in practical theology. This requirement represented 30 percent of the total required curriculum. Three of the units were in homiletics / speech; one in polity; one in work with small groups, teaching, Christian education, or administration; four were to be elected from other offerings in the department. Freedom and flexibility, within broad outlines, were the dominant themes, as the Bachelor of Divinity program was seeking to prepare students for a wide variety of diverse service in an increasingly complex world.

By this time, courses listed under the Department of Practical Theology covered twenty-four pages of the catalog. In light of the history of practical theology's curriculum development, the variety of course subject matter is staggering. Full sections of the practical curriculum are devoted to church administration, church music, Christian education, preaching, and worship. A series of courses was taught jointly by members of the biblical team and homiletics professors. In these courses a focus was on exegetical preaching.

From 1970 through 1980 only minor changes were made in the general degree requirements in practical theology. Of the thirty total units still required for graduation, nine continued to be required in this department.

Five years later (1985) the seminary had returned to a system of credit hours, rather than its previous policy of marking progress in terms of courses and practicums. Although "a program of senior studies in some area of the curriculum" had been added, the requirements in practical theology continued at approximately the same levels as those instituted in 1970. The degree, of course, had by now been changed from Bachelor of Divinity to Master of Divinity. Under that new heading the recent catalog affirmed what had been apparent for many years: "The curriculum is planned to provide the maximum of flexibility and independence consonant with a broad theological foundation."

## CASE STUDY TWO: REFORMED THEOLOGICAL SEMINARY

Reformed Seminary is of interest for a number of reasons. It was begun only recently (1966), but has grown remarkably to an enrollment of approximately three hundred students. As a seminary committed to the

Reformed tradition, it belongs on the same family tree as Princeton, and, for that matter, Westminster. Reformed and Westminster both desire to perpetuate those theological and biblical commitments which characterized Princeton during the first one hundred years of its history and which they believe Princeton now to have significantly diluted or abandoned.

Reformed is of special significance for this study, however, because of the radical transformation that it has instituted in its curriculum, especially as that change reflects on the current state of the study of practical theology. It is difficult to imagine any institution moving more thoroughly or more quickly in its preparation program for ministers.

By 1970, just several years after its founding, Reformed had settled upon a basic curriculum that closely resembled the requirements at Princeton in 1930 or, for that matter, in 1920 or 1910. This correspondence was not without significance, as Reformed was among those institutions which wanted to perpetuate many of the theological and other commitments of "old Princeton." In 1970 Reformed was operating on the quarter system; 135 credit hours were required for graduation. Of these, 118 were specifically stipulated, including work in homiletics / speech (14 hours), pastoral care / counseling (6 hours), worship (3 hours), evangelism (3 hours), missions / world outlook (2 hours), education (3 hours). The catalog listed corresponding courses in preaching / speech (20), pastoral care (6), worship (1), evangelism (4), education (1), and spiritual formation (2). Elementary Greek was required, but credit was not given for its study. Apparently the student was free to elect about 17 hours of his study. Required practical theology courses accounted for 31 hours, or 23 percent of the total curriculum.

Change was radical and not gradual. After consultation with a number of pastors and others in various kinds of service, the seminary in 1986 instituted its new curriculum. Having moved to the semester system, Reformed now required 105 semester hours. The only flexibility among these hours is a "three semester hour elective in theology." Two important features were introduced. The seminary now requires 40 hours in practical theology, including the entire third-year program. In the last year, the degree candidate studies communication (12 semester hours), leadership and management (6 hours), outreach (5 hours), worship (2 hours), Christian education (2 hours), polity (2 hours), pastoral ministry (2 hours), and pastoral counseling (3 hours). In the first year two hours of introductory study are required, and in each of the first two years a two-hour course in spiritual formation is required.

In the first year the student must complete 10 semester hours of study in the Old Testament. Obviously these are in English Bible, and the catalog indicates that the focus is on "the relevance of these books for the church and world today" and on "expository study." The same emphasis seems apparent in the 10 hours of New Testament study required in that same first year. In the tradition of Princeton (and of Reformed and Westminster Seminaries) these courses would properly be listed in the Department of Practical Theology.

The current Reformed catalog lists, indeed needs to list, only very few elective courses. It is fully yielded to the professional / pragmatist / practitioner model for training and assumes that those training for the pastorate must all follow, at least through their three years of seminary, a tightly prescribed path. This movement from one end of a continuum to the other has not been made without recognition of the underlying assumptions. Vice-president for Academic Affairs Richard G. Watson quotes Benjamin Rush's dictum, ". . . to spend four or five years learning two dead languages, is to turn our backs upon a gold mine, in order to amuse ourselves catching butterflies." Then he writes, "To require pastors to spend three years studying theories of textual criticism and technicalities of linguistic construction to the neglect of the Bible in English, the essential doctrines, and practical theology, is to turn our backs on fields white unto the harvest, in order to amuse ourselves catching butterflies."[10] Dr. Watson is thereby quite prepared to defend a curriculum that is almost 40 percent in the field of practical theology; if English Bible survey courses are included in the practical department, that percentage rises to almost 60 percent.

## CASE STUDY THREE: WESTMINSTER THEOLOGICAL SEMINARY

Westminster was founded in 1929 to continue the tradition and commitments of Princeton Theological Seminary. Generally the issues were in the areas of the recognition of biblical authority and fidelity to the historic Reformed faith. But postures in those matters may express themselves in curricular structure. Westminster believes that a thorough biblical and theological and apologetic undergirding is necessary for ap-

10. Richard G. Watson, "Secularists Did Not Steal the Colleges," *Presbyterian Journal* (28 June 1986): 10.

plication of practical principles throughout one's ministry. The need for academic tools is seen as foundational. Without question, this need can be overstated to the point that no practical building at all grows on a foundation overbuilt and of no practical use. Westminster's curriculum at its founding must be seen, however, as part of its intended reason for being.

In 1930 each student was expected to complete 97 semester hours of study, in addition to a full year of noncredit Greek. Fourteen hours were devoted to practical theology: homiletics / speech (10 hours), missions (2 hours), and pastoral theology (2 hours). Of the 97 required hours, 15 were elective. The 14 hours in practical theology represented about 14 percent of the full curriculum. The catalog lists only six courses in practical theology, all required.

In light of gradual change at Princeton and radical change at Reformed, consistency (or stubbornness, depending on one's perspective) identifies Westminster's history in its curriculum development. By 1940 only 16 hours in practical theology were required (of the full curriculum of 96 hours). The modest increase in required hours seems to have been at the expense of elective flexibility, as those hours fell to 11. Practical theology now commanded 17 percent of the required curriculum.

For Westminster the next decade saw only minor extension. By 1950 practical requirements for the Bachelor of Divinity degree had reached 18 hours—homiletics / speech (10); missions (2); public worship (2); church government (2); poimenics (1); and Christian education (1). Elective hours fell to 6, and it seems apparent that other departments were not willing to suffer dilution or were not asked to do so. The situation was virtually unchanged in 1960, except that "Doctrine of the Church" had replaced "Church Government" in the department's requirements. This is of some significance, since the new course was more clearly (in its title at least) a study in theology, although with obvious practical overtones. Westminster by this point might be regarded as experiencing the invasion of its practical department by other disciplines, rather than the contrary experience of many other seminaries.

By 1970 Westminster had moved temporarily to the quarter system and was requiring 25 hours of study in practical areas. But the portion of work in this department was part of a total required curriculum of 137 quarter hours and therefore less than 20 percent. The courses required remained similar to those of previous decades. The courses listed in the catalog included a required introductory course, others in homiletics /

speech (ten courses), pastoral theology / counseling (three), doctrine of the church (one), Christian education (three), missions (one), evangelism (five), and literature (four).

During the 1970s the seminary (a) returned to the semester system and (b) initiated a program for prospective pastors that included a two-year Master of Arts in Religion degree, followed by a one-year program leading to the degree of Master of Divinity. With both of these significant changes, however, the practical department's total requirements of such candidates was still only 18 hours out of a three-year required curriculum of 92 hours (19.5 percent). By this time, however, students were expected to pass entering examinations in Greek and Hebrew or to take a full year of course work in the deficient language(s). The full required load for most students had therefore now reached 112 semester hours, of which 18 (16 percent) were required in practical theology.

By 1985 Westminster had returned to the three-year Master of Divinity curriculum, eliminating the two-year Master of Arts in Religion degree as an intermediate stage. The required program encompassed 92 semester hours in addition to one year of basic study in both Greek and Hebrew. The 18 hours required in practical theology were not far removed from the 14 hours required in 1930 or the 16 hours required in 1940. Against this background of requirement restrictions, the department nevertheless expanded its course offerings exponentially. For 1985 the catalog showed courses in homiletics (six courses), counseling (twelve), doctrine of the church (two), education (two), evangelism (four), current issues (e.g., women, race, poverty) (five), and missions (twenty-three). If Reformed Seminary is remarkable for its radical and swift change, Westminster is nonetheless notable for its consistency. Striving for the new is no more to be cherished than is refusal to change. Neither extreme is necessarily to be desired, and each may be at some times and under certain conditions appropriate.

While Westminster's curricular structure, aiming at the preparation of people for pastoral ministry, has remained constant, the seminary has moved in two directions typical of seminary activity today. First of all, new degree programs have been developed to meet perceived needs in the church and in the world. For Westminster the most notable new practical areas developed are in counseling and missions, specifically urban mission. Secondly, Westminster has formalized and extended its work in field education. Each of the institutions mentioned above has regularly had such a required program in operation under some kind of supervision by the local pastor (or his parallel in specialized ministry) and / or by personnel in the seminary. No seminary assumes that the totality of practical training can be obtained through formal course study. During the past two years Westminster's progress in this regard has been great and importantly augments the classroom experience, which has not been enlarged.


## THE IMPETUS FOR DRAMATIC CHANGE

The decades of this century, especially those since 1930, have brought forth radical change in the practical theology programs at most seminaries. Specific examples of departure from earlier modes have been seen in the broad history and in the specific examples that have been noted. The next paragraphs briefly identify five factors that affect practical theology today. Of course, not every seminary is influenced by each of these factors to the same degree, but their cumulative impact is ignored only at great peril.


### EMERGENCE OF THE NEW PROFESSIONALISM

Of primary significance is a new and general commitment to the professional model as the proper form for the training of ministers. It was never properly argued that the training of ministers was simply an academic exercise. But, to an increasing extent, the drive toward professional expertise, toward the goal of a consummate practitioner, has brought the work of practical theology to a point of supremacy in the curriculum, perhaps even to a point where all seminary education must be thought to be "practical." Watson argues pointedly that "all courses must stand the test of usefulness in the ministry."[11]

If the professional model can stand alone, then why must college education precede admission to seminary? Why not admit well-motivated applicants who have demonstrated communication skills and shown some degree of attainment in business or in their professional lives, with particular emphasis on their interpersonal experience? Training in liberal arts, traditionally sought among seminary applicants, would be of little importance in a curriculum whose first goal is to train a professional.

11. Ibid., 11.

## THE CHANGING ROLE OF THE SEMINARY

A second modern phenomenon influencing the discipline of practical theology is the obliteration of former distinctions between the church and the seminary. I generalize from my own observation and assume that many facets in the preparation of pastors formerly committed largely to the church have not been faithfully exercised: evaluation of spiritual gifts, testing of ministerial skills, spiritual formation, determination of readiness for ministry, general pastoral oversight of candidates.

These activities are recognized as important, and it has fallen to the seminaries to see to their application. The Association of Theological Schools (ATS) therefore calls for more extensive, better supervised, and fully evaluated field work experiences. Seminaries seeking to serve more usefully are called to develop additional programs, sometimes at great effort and expense, perhaps even at some cost to other parts of the seminary program. Identification, even quantification, of ministry gifts/ skills/abilities has become an important, growing factor in practical theology today.

## IMPORTANCE OF THE LAITY

A third impact factor is the role of the laity. Confusion seems to exist with regard to the relative roles of the ordained clergy and Christian lay people.

On the one hand, we live in the midst of a movement toward equality between ordained ministers and lay membership in churches. In the Presbyterian Church in America, for example, careful effort is exercised to identify lay elders as "ruling elders" and the ordained clergy as "teaching elders," seeking thereby to emphasize that each has an office on parity with the other. Writing from a Roman Catholic perspective, Thomas Franklin O'Meara affirms: "Both historical theology and the expansion of the ministry have challenged the claim that the distinction between clergy and laity is basic, perennial and of Jesus' institution. In its historico-social forms it exists as a product of culture; it is a pointer to the importance of ministry."[12] Jasper L. McPhail pleads, "Why cannot the Christian perceive himself as ministering in his daily life and work?"[13]

---

12. Thomas Franklin O'Meara, *Theology of Ministry* (New York: Paulist, 1983), 161–62.
13. Jasper L. McPhail, "The Church in Society," *The Theological Educator,* no. 29 (Fall 1984): 5.

Good fruit is coming forth. Seminaries are initiating creative, specific training for lay leaders. One-day, weekend, and week-long seminars are beginning to appear. The use of audio and video tapes is multiplying; the possibilities for computer-based education seem open ended. New emphasis is being placed on diaconal ministry, and the only hope for doing all that serving at tables involves today is to train lay leaders who will be able to mobilize others. Increasingly ministers are being trained to motivate and train other leaders.

On the other hand, the vast array of needs in the world and in the church calls for increasing specialization. The solution often applied is extensive and varied professional training for the candidate in important areas of ministerial expertise—management and motivation skills, organizational insight, interpersonal abilities. We recognize the important role of lay people in the church. But have we perhaps lost the unique position of the preaching pastor, as we seek to make him a jack-of-all-trades? One of the minister's first tasks always is to give away every job possible, to the end that he might devote full energy to his first calling. So that there be no misunderstanding at this point, let it be recalled that the apostles themselves continued to minister to the needy and those without the gospel, even after the deacons were appointed to relieve them of first responsibility for work other than prayer and the ministry of the Word. An era that quite properly emphasizes the high calling of the laity prepares its ministers for work that might better be assigned to lay leaders.

## AN AGENDA FROM WITHOUT

A fourth factor is the influence of the world's agenda on the agenda of practical theology. Current concerns with regard to the role of women, racial inequities, and severe material deprivation have originated largely in the world. Whatever truth there is in that statement stands as an indictment of the church. But the fact remains that issues of social importance have been thrust upon the seminary world, especially into the practical theology departments. Jerry Falwell's *Fundamentalist Journal* speaks to the issue of South Africa and other social matters as these subjects become material for reflection among many Christians of widely differing perspectives.

The practical theology department is asked to wrestle with the question of the church's role in society. How does the church as institution address the other institutions of society and when, if at all? Richard J. Mouw recognizes the prohibition in the Westminster Confession against such communication except when "required by the civil magistrate." But he states, "There is a profound sense in which churches in democratic societies are under a continuing mandate to speak to nonecclesiastical issues."[14]

All kinds of questions are raised by new interest in the role of women in society and in the church. Practical theology departments respond with courses that address these subjects from various perspectives. Seminaries that train women for the ministry find a growing percentage of their students are female, and this places new demands on the curriculum and the faculty. Many seminaries must wrestle with the question of how to minister to women and how they can best minister in the family, in the church, in society. The study of black theology and the training of black pastors open new questions.

Westminster's commitment is to traditional orientation in message and ministry. But today 30 percent of its students were born in countries other than the United States. Seventy-five are of Korean origin. An effort has been initiated to serve the needs of city church leaders, most of whom are black. The part of Philadelphia adjacent to the campus is a composite, a collage of many ethnic bits and pieces. How shall the gospel be preached in contexts other than those in which God made it clear to us? The agenda of the world has invaded the campus; there is no place to hide.

In his keynote address to the Thirty-fifth Biennial Meeting of the Association of Theological Schools (1986), Francis Cardinal Arinze focused on "Globalization of Theological Education." Major concerns for him were inculturation, dialogue with followers of other religions, ecumenism, and evangelization and human promotion. In a reply to Arinze's comments, Professor Don S. Browning concluded his search for a definition of *globalization* with the suggestion that all uses of the term "in theological education have one element in common: the context for theological education can no longer be simply the local congregation, the local community, a particular region, state, or nation. The context of theological education must be the entire world, the entire global village that influences our lives in multitudes of direct and indirect

---

14. Richard J. Mouw, "Spiritual Identity and Churchly Praxis," *Theological Education* 23 (Supplement 1987): 98.

ways and which we influence and shape in ways we do not fully un-derstand."[15]

What is happening in the world is affecting the work of practical the-ology. New importance is being attributed to the various contexts in which the gospel is to be proclaimed. Reasonable concerns for equity among people are being addressed from biblical and theological perspec-tives, as the seminary is challenged to seek out proper foundations for social posture. Those who cannot agree with the presuppositions or con-clusions of liberation theology must nonetheless address the issues of poverty, hunger, inequality.

## THE CHALLENGE OF DIVERSE NEEDS

From a pastor's study, from a denominational office, from the front seat of a car, on a subway platform—everywhere the needs of the world look so complex, so varied, so multiform. And the demands of the church itself appear to call for such diverse gifts. The seminary responds with all kinds of specialized programs, especially in practical theology. Specialization becomes the hallmark of the ministry: youth work, adult ministry, ministry of evangelism, or visitation, or administration, and on and on. In some institutions training is offered to each ministerial candidate in many fields; in other schools it is assumed that specialists will be trained for each need. Carl S. Dudley sets forth a church case study and describes responses from various different perspectives: psycho-logical, ethnographic, sociological, theological—perhaps unwittingly suggesting the need for specialization in dealing with ecclesiastical prob-lems in today's world.[16]

Probably no field has grown so much in recent decades as that of counseling. E. Brooks Holifield has documented an extended period of change and growth in *A History of Pastoral Care in America*.[17] The rela-tionship between secular theory and biblical principles creates a contin-uum of perspectives among the seminaries.

The Doctor of Ministry degree is a recent arrival in the practical the-ology family. For 1986, seminaries reporting (89) to the ATS indicated

15. Don S. Browning, "Globalization and the Task of Theological Education in North America," *Theological Education* 23, no. 1 (Autumn 1986): 44.

16. Carl S. Dudley, ed., *Building Effective Ministry* (San Francisco: Harper and Row, 1983).

17. E. Brooks Holifield, *A History of Pastoral Care in America* (Nashville: Abingdon, 1983).

that 6,430 candidates were enrolled in D.Min. programs. This degree is an evidence of desire to provide continuing education for ministry in a complex world.

## THE CONTINUING TENSIONS

Thorwald Lorenzen, professor at a Baptist seminary in Switzerland, poses a critical question: "Should a theological school turn out a 'finished product', or should theological education in a seminary provide the basics in information, attitude and methodology for a continuing lifelong theological pilgrimage?" Obviously not all will agree with his conclusion: "If the former is the case, given the brief span of time allowed for a basic theological education (three to five years), there will be a tendency to do away with time and energy consuming language study, and one will move toward survey and 'how to do it' courses. The result is a ministry without theological depth and little creative inspiration in preaching and praxis."[18] What stage of development should a seminary diploma specify: trained professional or well-grounded apprentice?

A second question not yet answered inquires into the relation between so-called practical courses and academic courses, so designated. Is it possible to imagine any seminary course totally devoid of academic insight or foundation or, on the other hand, any course of absolutely no practical application? Any curricular decision is simply a question of priority. How is the seminary to balance academic foundation with practical application? What interaction is necessary? How is it to be achieved? In "The Education of Practical Theologians" Joseph C. Hough, Jr., calls for "reflective practitioners."[19] How is the balance inherent in each of those words to be obtained, maintained?

A third question asks Christians to reflect on the nature of the church's ministry. What is the church's calling? What can the church do that no other institution can do? To what degree can it, and should it, join with others in service to the world? Finally, how do our responses to these questions impact the training that seminaries offer, especially in the field of practical application of the gospel?

18. Thorwald Lorenzen, "Theological Education between Church and World," *Ministerial Formation*, no. 32 (December 1985): 15.

19. Joseph C. Hough, Jr., "The Education of Practical Theologians," *Theological Education* 20, no. 2 (Spring 1984): 55–84.

$B$ecause the church is the assembly of heaven gathered already on earth, worship is the first responsibility of the church. Paul describes the church as those "who call upon the name of the Lord Jesus Christ in every place" (1 Cor. 1:2). . . . God who called Israel to assemble at Sinai and to gather for the feasts of worship at Jerusalem now calls us to his festival assembly in heaven. We sing our songs of pilgrimage as we enter the courts of Zion. In worship we can hear with the ear of faith the answering "Amen" of the choirs of angels. Jesus Himself is the heavenly choirmaster as, in the midst of the brethren, he sings the Father's praise (Heb. 2:12).

*Living in Christ's Church* (1986)

# 7

# Evangelical Worship in Our Day

## Robert G. Rayburn

Professor Bard Thompson of Drew University wrote in 1961, "We live in an era of liturgical revival."[1] Technically he may have been correct. There has been in the last few decades a great surge of interest in the study of the sources and content of the liturgies of most of the Christian churches in the world, especially the Roman Catholic, Eastern Orthodox, Anglican, Lutheran, and even some of the Reformed churches. However, a renewed interest in historic origins of liturgies and even making changes in the liturgies of some churches do not at all indicate that a genuine revival in worship has come in our day. In some theologically liberal churches liturgical revival has focused upon the introduction of dance and drama into the services, often as a substitute for the sermon. Liturgical revival does not necessarily include a revival of true corporate worship.

Worship may be considered from two different viewpoints. There is a sense in which it is synonymous with the whole of our lives, but it also must be considered as a specific activity of our lives. It is this latter aspect of Christian worship with which we are concerned in this essay. We further limit our concern to corporate, or common, worship in the evangelical churches of America during the last few decades and in the present day. It would be quite impossible to discuss in any adequate way the dangerous heresy of modernity, which substitutes good deeds, kindness, and social concern for worship. Many who give much time to social injustice and deeds of compassion have no place for God in their

1. Bard Thompson, ed., *Liturgies of the Western Church* (Philadelphia: Fortress, 1980), ix.

131

lives. Their religion is secular humanism. The Bible, however, makes it very clear that corporate worship is an essential part of the life of the child of God (Heb. 10:25; Pss. 34:3; 95:2, 6).

It is renewal in the corporate worship of God's people with which we are concerned. Participating in a liturgy, even a good liturgy, may not mean that one is worshiping. It is actually possible to sit through a worship service, to read all of the common prayers, the litanies, and the versicles, and to chant the ancient hymns of the church with complete satisfaction of one's aesthetic tastes as well as historic sensitivities without actual participation in common worship "in spirit and in truth." Members of a congregation may have experienced only a sense of personal satisfaction instead of having participated in the offering up to God as a corporate body a pure act of worship.

The quality of one's worship is determined by his or her personal understanding of God. The conception people have of the deity they worship will certainly shape their worship practices. If they think of God as good-natured, indulgent, and permissive, they will feel that His greatest pleasure is found in their pleasure, and their chief concern will be what they personally appreciate and enjoy in a service. If they look upon God as an angry, aggrieved potentate who must be placated, they will feel the need to worship him by offering painful sacrifices that will move Him to be merciful. If, however, they understand Him as the Bible presents Him—infinitely holy, perfect in wisdom, absolute in His justice, and glorious in His gracious salvation provided through the eternal atonement of His Son on the cross—their great desire will be to glorify and exalt Him for the wonders of His being and His works. In response to His love they will render in their worship glad obedience to His holy revealed will. When they gather in their places of worship, their controlling purpose will be to proffer to Him that glory, praise, honor, and reverent submission to which He is due. It certainly would seem reasonable to expect that all evangelical Christians would have such a purpose, but an examination of their worship practices in the last thirty years must call into question their commitment to true spiritual worship or their understanding of how this act is performed.

Owing to the wide diversity in the theological presuppositions that lie behind the worship practices in the Protestant church in general and especially in the evangelical churches, it is impossible within the limitations of this essay to give a clear and comprehensive survey, to say nothing of an appraisal, of all the evangelical churches of our day. One of the problems is that many of those churches which would identify themselves as evangelical would not be recognized as such by churches with more rigid standards of doctrinal subscription. Another is the wide diversity of worship practices.

It must also be noted that the characteristic evangelical presence today is found more typically in such parachurch organizations as the Navigators, InterVarsity Christian Fellowship, Young Life, Youth for Christ, Campus Crusade for Christ, and others than it is in any of the individual denominations generally classified as evangelical. Corporate worship has never been a particular concern in any of these organizations, although in each of them Christians would be urged to "attend church." Moreover, the evangelical and interdenominational theological seminaries such as Fuller, Dallas, Gordon-Conwell, and Talbot have placed very little emphasis upon corporate worship, and they have given practically no instruction as to the minister's responsibilities in teaching the congregation how to worship and in the conducting of common worship. Certainly this makes it easy to understand why multiplied thousands of those who attend churches regularly confess that they have never had any instruction in corporate worship.[2] They may have been carefully indoctrinated in the theological distinctives of their own churches, but they have been given no background for understanding the proper movement of a corporate worship service.

In Roman Catholicism there is a basic uniformity of liturgical practice characteristic of the vast majority of Roman Catholic churches. This is not the case with Protestants. While the structure of the worship of the Reformation provided some continuity with medieval and primitive elements, it also represented a genuine revolution in Christian worship. It introduced a new and fundamental emphasis upon the Word of God as well as the need for every believer to participate regularly and frequently in genuine corporate worship in line with the scriptural injunctions. A basic requirement of corporate worship is real intelligibility on the part of the worshiper based upon simplicity in all elements of the liturgy. It seems necessary at this point to examine a few of the basic concerns that have dominated Protestant worship throughout its history and then see how these concerns have been present in recent decades and in our day. It takes only a limited acquaintance with the history of worship in the church to recognize the fact that the contemporary distortion of evangelical Protestant worship has been centuries in the making.

2. Through questionnaires and samplings in scores of classes and seminars throughout the country, I have personally confirmed this fact.

## WORSHIP AND THE WORD

The first great emphasis of Protestant worship, as indicated above, has been the supremacy of the Word of God. By this I do not mean primarily God's self-disclosure in Christ Jesus as liberal theologians would interpret it.[3] Rather I speak of the revelation of Himself in the infallible Scriptures of the Old and New Testaments, which alone give us the revelation of God in His Son, the Living Word. It is clear that, because the inscripturated revelation of God to His people demands a primary place in their worship, the reading of the Scripture in the vernacular and the preaching of the Word of God as a single unit became prominent in all Protestant worship. Martin Luther is said to have put it this way: "Where God's Word is not preached, it is better that one neither sing nor read, nor even come together."

Although the terms *liturgical renewal* and *liturgical reform* are very common in the theological literature of the second half of the twentieth century, there is no indication that this renewal or reform has brought about significant results in the preaching heard in the evangelical pulpits of our day. There is a recognizable shortage of great preaching.[4] This is not to say that there are no great evangelical preachers, but their number is very small. The emphasis in the seminaries has not been on preaching as art or upon the minister's function as an artist under the guidance of the Holy Spirit. When Princeton Seminary moved from its position of historic orthodoxy, it also ceased to produce the steady stream of outstanding evangelical preachers that had characterized it since its founding. Genuine liturgical renewal, which will be a part of a genuine renewal of worship, will involve a return to the emphasis upon the artistic, clear, and powerful expository preaching of the Word of God. The majority of the most prominent evangelical preachers of our day are so heavily involved with the complex administrative problems of their large churches or with radio and television programs, which make incessant demands upon their time and energy, that they could not, even if they would, give themselves to the preparation of great sermons.

After the Reformation it was not long before the new emphasis upon the preeminence of the Word took precedence over the other elements of corporate worship, especially in Reformed churches. Liturgies were discarded and sermons grew longer and longer. By the time of the Puritans in England and Scotland, there was very little concern for anything

3. For this viewpoint, see Cyril C. Richardson, "Word and Sacrament in Protestant Worship," in *Liturgical Renewal in the Christian Churches*, ed. Michael J. Taylor (Baltimore: Helicon, 1967), 33ff.

4. Reuel L. Howe, *Partners in Preaching* (New York: Seabury, 1967), 39.

in the service except the sermon and the long prayers of the pastors. The congregation participated actively only in the singing of one or two metrical versions of the Psalms, often with mediocre tunes and without any instrumental accompaniment. This Puritan emphasis, with the congregation largely composed of spectators or listeners rather than active participants, was transferred to our country and dominated the worship services of the churches of New England and the Middle Atlantic states.

Because of its association with the Royalist cause, the Episcopal Church in the American colonies was practically destroyed when the British lost the Revolutionary War. The Methodists asked Wesley for help, and he prepared for them a liturgy that was an abridgement of the Anglican Book of Common Prayer, but its use was short-lived in American Methodism. The American Lutheran Church had fixed forms, but it has never been able to secure uniformity in the use of a liturgy. And while Lutherans have remained more or less liturgical, they have not escaped the free spirit that has dominated the worship of American Protestant churches. In 1788 the First General Assembly of the Presbyterian Church in the United States adopted the Directory of Worship of the Westminster Assembly but used it simply as a guide to worship. Most Presbyterians have had no knowledge of the content of this directory. From earliest days the worship of the American Presbyterians was nonliturgical and informal. None of the other leading bodies, such as the Congregationalists and Baptists, used any fixed formularies in their worship.

As great segments of the population moved westward, the worship services of the frontier underwent significant changes. In many places there were no church buildings, and the worship services were held in homes or schoolhouses. Thus great informality took over. There were not enough ordained ministers to conduct the services, and the worshipers represented a variety of denominational backgrounds. Liturgical services were for the most part out of the question. In general, then, with the exception of two or three denominations, Protestant worship services in the United States from the first may be accurately designated as nonliturgical and evangelical.

In the year 1855 there began what some church historians have called a liturgical revival stimulated largely by the publication of Charles W. Baird's *Presbyterian Liturgies.*[5] Baird focused attention on the liturgies of Calvin, Knox, and other early Presbyterians and urged the restoration of their use in liturgical worship. A revival of interest in worship spread

5. Charles W. Baird, *The Presbyterian Liturgies* (1855 as *Eutaxia;* reprint, Grand Rapids: Baker, 1957).

from the Presbyterians to many other churches, and worship guide books were printed for many denominations. However, this so-called liturgical revival movement did not seriously change the practice of the evangelical churches of this country; it continued for the most part to be non-liturgical with individual pastors and congregations free to establish their own orders of worship.

The revival movement had a profound effect upon the worship practices of American Christians, but it only served to increase the emphasis upon informality as well as complete liberty from any liturgical forms and to add to the special stress upon the sermon. This emphasis continued right into the twentieth century, and it is well entrenched in contemporary worship services.

Preaching alone, of course, is by no means the only manifestation of the supremacy of the Word of God needed in corporate worship. Christian worship should always include the response of the congregation to what God has revealed of Himself and of His will in the Scriptures. Worship, when rightly understood, is a dialogue, a two-way conversation between God and His people. This dialogue requires careful attention to the liturgy, or what evangelicals prefer to call the order of worship, so that it will be clear to gathered worshipers that they are hearing the Word of God throughout the service and are responding to God in their acts of worship. Through the centuries the divine-human dialogue has been seriously distorted. In the Middle Ages the people did not hear the Word of God at all. When it was read to them, it was read in a language they did not understand, and it was very rarely preached to them in the vernacular. They were for the most part mere spectators to what was transpiring on the altar. There was utterly no sense of corporate worship, much less corporate response to the Word of God.

This neglect of the Word of God before the Reformation led to an extreme reaction following the establishment of Protestant worship. In some traditions, particularly those of the Calvinistic or Reformed convictions, almost all of the emphasis was placed upon the sermon as the means by which God communicated with His people. Very little provision was made for any corporate response of the congregation. The music was confined to the singing of the Psalms, which were themselves the inspired Word of God. There was little or no opportunity for the congregation to offer its corporate praise and thanksgiving or to present its common prayers of confession and intercession to God or to make its offering of the fruit of its labors as a sincere act of worship in response to the goodness of God. There were no opportunities for the congregation to respond to God, not even as had the ancient Christians when they heard the simple word of divine greeting, "The Lord be with you," and replied, "And with thy spirit."

Preaching at its finest is preaching delivered and received in the context of corporate worship. It should always be preceded by the worshiping congregation's responding in wholehearted devotion to God's Word as it calls them to various aspects of their worship—adoration, confession, thanksgiving, intercession, stewardship, and the like. Does this mean that there should be a recognizable structure to the order of worship? Indeed, it does. However, it does not mean that a fixed liturgy from week to week is necessary or desirable. The dialogue structure that appears so frequently in the Scriptures is by no means difficult to establish and maintain without meaningless repetition or stilted formalism.

When one examines the order of worship for the majority of the evangelical churches of the last few decades in our country, however, one finds that the typical order is little more than a number of items arranged according to the inclination of the person responsible for conducting the service with no apparent structure in mind. These items may be shuffled like a pack of cards for the next service or allowed to remain rigidly the same over a long period. There is no evident reason for such repetition, except that perhaps the congregation likes to find itself familiar with the sequence of the parts of its worship service and the pastor himself finds it easier to make no basic changes. He only needs to change the hymn numbers, the Scripture passages, and sermon titles from week to week. His order has not been subject to any special criticism by his congregation. So few who worship in contemporary evangelical congregations have had any instruction in worship that most of them would not be sufficiently intelligent in the subject to offer a suggested change in the structure of the service. Many, however, seem to realize that their worship services are quite meaningless. For this reason many have deserted the evangelical churches in which they were reared and have moved to the more liturgical churches, especially the Episcopalian.[6] Although they have often found the preaching disappointing, these evangelicals have been moved and blessed by a participation in common worship they had never known in their former

6. An example of this is the popular professor at Wheaton College, Robert E. Webber. Another prominent evangelical, Thomas Howard, formerly of Gordon College, after moving to the Episcopal Church later moved on to Roman Catholicism. Both men became discouraged over the worship services in their former evangelical churches. See Thomas Howard, *Evangelical Is Not Enough* (Nashville: Nelson, 1984).

churches. Of course, many others have abandoned their churches entirely because they recognized the apparent lack of significance in what was called worship. It seemed to them to be an exercise in self-gratification on the part of those participating. An equally good, or much better, sermon could be easily heard on the radio or television.

Perhaps this is an appropriate place to make certain observations concerning the music in our churches during the past thirty or forty years. The musical program, especially the part taken by the choirs, has contributed greatly to the distortion of the dialogue in corporate worship. Because choir lofts have almost uniformly been placed in front of the congregation, either directly behind the pastor or to one side of him, the choir appears to be singing to the congregation instead of singing for the congregation in praise directed to God. This judgment is reinforced by those congregations that break into applause at the conclusion of the choir's anthems. Thus the congregation responds to the choir's skill, but not to God's glory. Thanks and appreciation is expressed to the choir for the beauty of its music, but not praise to the one whom, if they understood their ministry, the choir should have been exalting. How rarely do worshipers in our churches today understand that the choir, when it sings an anthem, is offering to God musical praise on behalf of the congregation, beyond the musical capacity of the congregation as a whole. The congregation can and should unite in the singing of hymns. But well-trained and gifted musicians can praise and magnify the Lord with greater skill and beauty than can the congregation. The Levites (together with other highly trained musicians) of David's and Solomon's era did the same, as they brought the musical praise of the eternal God to a height of splendor and perfection probably never again equaled. Contemporary congregations need to learn that the choir sings to God, to glorify Him, and the congregation's participation comes through sincere participation in the praise, even as they participate in the prayers offered by their pastor or others who lead in public prayer.

## WORSHIP AS OFFERING

A second basic principle of worship established in the Reformation, although not recognized by many liturgical theologians, is that corporate worship in all of its parts must be a declaration of the *gloria Dei*. Calvin put this principle succinctly when he said, "We are born first of all for God, and not for ourselves." Thus worship must be theocentric and certainly, for the evangelical, Christocentric. With this necessary emphasis it is not surprising that Protestant worship in the early days of the Reformation began with a clear enunciation of a portion of the Word of God and not with the ringing of a bell as in the Catholic mass. Since all authentic Christian worship depends upon God's revelation in His Word, our worship today should begin with His Word. It springs from divine initiative, not from the will of man. While this is true, it is necessary that worshipers understand that their worship is offering—the offering to God of the honor, praise, adoration, glory, and submission to which He is due. The true worshiper comes to the place of worship with an offering. At the very beginning of the Bible we are confronted with this fact. Cain and Abel, the children of the first parents, both brought offerings to the Lord. Although blood sacrifices ceased as acceptable offerings to God when the once-for-all offering of Himself was made by Christ on the cross of Calvary (Heb. 10:12, 14), the New Testament makes it clear that we are continually to bring offerings to God (Heb. 13:15). For the modern American Christian, however, our offering is merely the amount of money placed in the plate at the proper time in the service.

Stephen Winward, a well-known Baptist pastor in London, wrote in 1964, "In Great Britain today the average worshiper goes to church to receive rather than to give, to 'get a blessing' rather than to 'make an offering.' "[7] Certainly anyone with a wide acquaintance with the worship services in American churches today would affirm Winward's judgment as equally true in our own country. American Christians seem to be almost totally concerned with what they get out of any service, with what they *receive* from God rather than with what they *give* to Him.

It must be stated emphatically that until evangelical Christians in our churches begin to understand the biblical teaching that worship is offering, yes, worship is sacrifice, we shall never be able to say with assurance that we are experiencing a genuine revival of corporate worship. Certainly it is the responsibility of the evangelical pastors of our day to sound the call of the psalmist, "Ascribe to the Lord the glory due to His Name; bring an offering and come into His courts" (Ps. 29:2). I am convinced that the average worshipers in the evangelical churches give little or no thought to what they are going to offer to God when they go to a church service. Nor is it of any concern to them when the service is over whether they have offered an acceptable sacrifice of praise and

7. Stephen F. Winward, *The Reformation of Our Worship* (Richmond: John Knox, 1965), 7.

thanksgiving to the Lord and whether they have purposed anew in the offering of their bodies as living sacrifices (Rom. 12:1–2) to submit to the will of the Lord as it has been revealed through the reading and exposition of the Scriptures. They will, however, be very conscious of whether or not they have "enjoyed" the service, particularly the sermon. A genuine revival of worship in our land will come only when the radical self-centeredness so characteristic of American worshipers, which manifests itself in all spheres of life, gives way to a humble focus upon the supreme glory and majesty of the divine Savior and Lord.

One of the influences that has made it difficult for worshipers to think in terms of worship as offering is the presence of the dominant personality—a condition seemingly characteristic of most of our larger churches and one readily portrayed on the television screens of our country daily. While it is difficult to estimate accurately the influence of the television evangelists upon the worship of the churches of America during the last two or three decades, there can be no doubt that these preachers command huge audiences week after week and their influence is substantial. According to *Time* magazine, sixty-one million Americans tune in to these TV shows each month frequently enough to have "at least minimal exposure."[8] It is especially significant that the overwhelming majority of those whose religious programs are carried on the television tube are certainly evangelical in a broad sense. In fact, most of them would gladly accept the classification of fundamentalist. Thus it cannot be denied that during the last two decades of the twentieth century the influence of the television preachers and their video programs will have been a major factor affecting the religious attitudes and activities of Americans. Since worship is at the very heart of all religious activity, the influence of religious television shows upon worship practices, which is already consequential, is sure to become even more notable.

Let us analyze the impact of television preacher/evangelists on their viewers, the majority of which are church members. Since only six of the most popular TV preachers reach fifty million households per month, it is fair to use these six as representative and to assume their audiences as composed of typical individual listeners and observers. It will be readily recognized that the preachers have learned much from show business and have adapted their programs according to good show business techniques. Clearly, this fact presents one of the problems, for a

8. *Time,* 17 February 1986, 63.

worship service is not a show and should never be looked upon by its participants as entertainment. However, it seems evident that, as a result of these religious television programs, multitudes have expected the worship services of their churches to provide good entertainment, even though it is religious entertainment. One of the most striking evidences of this fact is the comment evangelical ministers hear most often following a service as they stand at the church door to greet the departing members of the congregation: "I really enjoyed the service!" Certainly one major result of religious television programming is a demand for good entertainment as a feature of worship.

The most strikingly theatrical of all the television church services is that of Dr. Robert Schuller of the Crystal Cathedral in Garden Grove, California. This eighteen-million-dollar structure serves as a glittering backdrop for a service that is more a theatrical show than a corporate worship experience. Well-known singers, some of whom are movie or TV personalities, grip their microphones and pour forth emotionally charged songs apparently designed to make the listeners feel happy, in line with the pastor's emphasis on "possibility thinking" and the "be-happy attitudes." The gospel of salvation through the shed blood of Jesus Christ is never preached on his program, although Schuller claims to believe in the historic Reformed faith with its strong doctrinal position. Affiliated with the Reformed Church of America, he insists that when inquirers come to his church they are given a clear gospel witness. This, however, does not in any way nullify the effect of the televised service with its pleasant Hollywood atmosphere.

Of course, there are exceptions to the rule. Dr. D. James Kennedy of the large Coral Ridge Presbyterian Church in Fort Lauderdale, Florida, while not one of the ministers who commands the largest audience on television, certainly has an audience numbering in the millions. His program is simply a broadcast of one of his three morning worship services held in the large and impressive sanctuary, which is usually (at least in winter) overflowing with visitors, built by his congregation. His service is a formal one, although it could not be called liturgical. The huge, well-trained choir sings anthems that are theologically sound and musically appropriate. The only touch of pure entertainment comes when the cameras focus a little too much upon the highly capable organist; the enormous, imported pipe organ gives her immense opportunities for musical showmanship. Kennedy himself preaches the Word of God without compromise and makes simple and clear the gospel message. His worship service is adequate, although the individual worshiper has little actual participation except in the singing of the hymns. A significant problem arises, however, from the fact that the television viewer is only an observer to what is being done in the church; he or she is not able to join even in the singing and could not be considered a participant in the corporate worship. One can derive much benefit from the sermon, but in the rest of the service one listens and watches without participation. Even a fine service as this encourages the spectator syndrome in the lives of American worshipers.

Rev. Jerry Falwell, pastor of the twenty-one-thousand-member Thomas Road Baptist Church of Lynchburg, Virginia, also televises his Sunday worship services. They are not characterized by evident showmanship, although Falwell himself is by personality a supersalesman. He not only has acquired a vast television audience but has also been able to launch an influential political lobby called the Moral Majority. His personality dominates the entire televised service. This confirms in a special way one powerful influence upon the worship in evangelical churches of our day—the dominance of the charismatic leader. Humble pastors in thousands of medium-sized and small churches in towns and rural areas cannot generate anything like the forceful and influential effect upon their people that the masters of television engender.

In addition to the fact that entertainment is a large component of the television "service" of the major religious broadcasters, there is the additional problem that a great deal of time is taken with the raising of the vast amounts of money needed to support the programs. Of course, the television preachers insist to their listeners that their gifts are offerings to the Lord, but no local pastor could get away with putting so much emphasis upon financial support in his services of worship. The gimmicks used—books offered when gifts are sent, medals and jewelry used as "come-ons"—would be deemed inappropriate in a service properly focused upon bringing glory to God. It would stretch the imagination to think that those who mail in the millions of dollars to support these television programs and the dynamic and forceful men who direct them are in any sense participating in corporate worship of God. Even in the local church there is always the danger of the people observing and responding to a powerful personality rather than making a humble offering to the God of all grace.

Here we must consider another aspect of the musical ministry of the church in the last few decades. The economic expansion that followed both world wars provided many opportunities for church music and musicians, especially because of the fine modern church buildings with large organs and big choirs. Unfortunately, most of the evangelical churches used their economic prosperity for purposes other than enhancing their musical worship. The finest music in recent years has been found, with a few significant exceptions, in the liberal churches.

The immigration of many musicians with outstanding talent from Central Europe in the years preceding and following World War II greatly assisted in raising the musical standards of our country. Most of these musicians were not committed to church music, but those few who composed for the church have been musicians of great artistic skill and creative imagination. Few evangelical churches have been the beneficiaries of these talents, however. The emphasis found in most churches upon hearty singing went along with a predilection for what was easy to sing. And when it came to the choral music for their services, a substantial population of evangelical churchgoers created a demand for music that would carry the same sensual appeal as the music of the nightclubs, radio, and television. No thought was given to offering such music to God. While there have been exceptions, as a general rule evangelical churches, instead of offering to God highly artistic and beautiful music, have preferred music that is easy to sing and easy to listen to. Resembling the pop music styles of the day, it gives immediate musical enjoyment and sometimes even amusement to those not musically educated.

Along with this kind of music, so often preferred, a cult of amateurism has grown up within the evangelical church that guarantees mediocrity. People who have no special musical gift and very little skill often "perform" in the services. At its worst this has actually brought in musical vulgarity. Robert Berglund has remarked in this connection, "There is little room for mediocrity in church musicians, pastors, bankers, teachers, or in any other vocation. God deserves the finest that man can produce."[9]

Regrettably, most evangelical churches of our day do not consider the musical ministry of the church as important enough to be a necessary and substantial part of the church's budget. There are very few openings for Christian musicians of spiritual maturity and musical skill in the churches of evangelical persuasion. Until the churches recognize the importance of raising the level of their musical offerings to God and provide for skilled musical leadership at least on a part-time basis, there is little hope for a genuine revival of corporate worship in the days ahead. Congregations will continue to demand entertainment.

Before we leave the discussion of worship as offering, we need to ask ourselves if in emphasizing this principle so strongly we are not in dan-

9. Robert Berglund, *A Philosophy of Church Music* (Chicago: Moody Press, 1985), 10.

ger of downplaying the grace of God. If a worshiper is to be more concerned with giving to God than with "getting a blessing," are we
distorting the gospel and substituting human effort for divine grace? Is
there not a sense in which God's people assemble themselves in their
houses of worship to receive from God His gracious ministry to them?
Indeed there is, beyond a doubt! But what we receive from our ever-
giving, gracious God will never be what He wants it to be until we have
first learned the depths of joy found in the pure worship of God unadul-
terated by thoughts of what we desire for ourselves.

Frederick Schroeder puts this in proper perspective when he says:
"Worship at its highest and best is the act of giving to God the honor
and glory that are his due, without regard to any personal satisfaction or
benefit accruing from the act of adoration. It would be a mistake, however, to assume that people always reach to this high level of self-
immolation in the act of worship. Human need in some form or other
does enter the picture, even if it be no other need than the need to
worship; that is, the need to relate one's self to God."[10]

We learn from the Scriptures that both God and man receive in sacrifice and offering. For us the receiving has already preceded the giving.
In the sacrifice of Christ, His eternal Son, God has given to us a salvation that includes riches beyond measure. In the light of this glorious
redemption we bring our offering of worship, our sacrifice of pure devotion. However, the God who both received and gave everything in the
sacrifice of His Son continues to manifest His never-ending grace to
those who, in recognition of the inestimable value of what they have
received from Him, come regularly and joyfully together to pour out the
homage of their hearts to Him. As Christ gave His life that they might
receive life, so in giving their lives they receive blessings without number—indeed, the abundant life!

## WORSHIP AS COMMUNAL

A third principle of Christian worship to be emphasized is that the
worship of the church is essentially corporate, congregational, communal. The church is the body of Christ, and each local church, if its
members are true Christians, is a local manifestation of that body.
Therefore they must function as a body. While each member respects

10. Frederick W. Schroeder, *Worship in the Reformed Tradition* (Philadelphia: United
Church Press, 1966), 32.

the differing gifts of other members of the body, they all function together as a body, and each member is important to every other member. The apostle Paul prayed for the members of the church at Rome, "May the God who gives endurance and encouragement give you a spirit of unity among yourselves as you follow Christ Jesus, so that with one heart and mouth you may glorify the God and Father of our Lord Jesus Christ" (Rom. 15:5–6, NIV). While Paul doesn't specifically mention their worship services, the unity of heart and mouth for which he prayed (because it would glorify God) would certainly need to be manifest in their worship, the supreme purpose of which would be the glorification of the Triune God.

We have already commented on the fact that one of the obstacles to corporate devotion in the contemporary church, particularly in the past few decades, is the dominance of the charismatic minister over the entire service. While this is most evident in television services and not a serious problem in some of our churches, there are very few churches where lay members of the congregation function as actual participants in anything except the singing of the hymns and taking of the offering. The minister not only preaches the sermon, he reads all the Scripture, he offers all the prayers, he conducts the communion service, and he usually makes the announcements, which are all too often a part of the worship service itself. Any kind of ritual that would bring members of the congregation into active participation (for example, in prayer) is looked upon with profound suspicion and has generally been discarded as inappropriate for use in the evangelical churches of our day. Why should not both men and women from the congregation be used for reading Scriptures or even leading in prayer during worship services? They sing in the choirs of all evangelical churches. It is inconsistent to deny them any other part in the common worship.

It is a decided sign of inadequate appreciation of the value and significance of corporate worship that in most of our evangelical churches no provision is made for vocal participation in common prayer. Congregations are not even encouraged to participate in a unison "Amen" at the close of the prayers of the pastor, although this ancient and thoroughly biblical practice is common in most other countries of the world. The use of a prayer book or of any printed prayers for congregational use is looked upon as decidedly unspiritual. It seems strange indeed that no one ever hears objections raised to the singing of hymns, many of which are addressed directly to God as sung prayers of praise and devotion. To sing them the individual worshiper must use words provided by someone else. Actually, there is no basic difference between singing with the use of words not one's own and praying with words provided in a prayer book or printed in the church bulletin. Both are addressed to God.

Some congregations, particularly those of Reformed persuasion, are providing prayer books for their people to use in their common worship.[11] Others are printing prayers in their church bulletins for use in their services. While extempore, or unpremediated, prayer has always had an important place in Protestant worship, the contemporary denial of any other way of praying deprives the congregation of all the substantial advantages of liturgical prayers, chief of which is the value of vocal congregational participation.

Those who prize their heritage in the Reformed, or Calvinistic, tradition should remember that no Sunday morning worship service could be considered authentically Reformed from the historical perspective if it did not include very early in the order of worship a corporate confession of sin. Calvin, Knox, and all the early Reformers included this confession as a basic component of Christian worship. For multitudes of worshipers in evangelical churches today there is hardly a word of confession offered, even in the pastor's prayers. Is it any wonder that professed believers are unable to focus their attention upon the glorious holiness and the ineffable majesty of God when they have not been reminded that only those with "clean hands and a pure heart" are able to stand in the presence of the infinitely pure and holy God and have not then confessed their sin before Him?

It would be a mistake in connection with our discussion of communal participation in prayer for us to fail to mention the importance of providing proper means for members of worshiping congregations to kneel when they pray. One's physical position does help or hinder when praying. Nowhere in the Bible do we find any mention of anyone sitting while praying. All references to any physical posture—and there are many—indicate either kneeling or standing. Yet the vast majority of American Christians in Protestant churches sit through all of the longer prayers of their worship services. American evangelicals have accepted a false antithesis between the spiritual and the material, the soul and the body. The Bible tells us that we are to love God with our whole being (Mark 12:29–30). If this is true of our lives in general, it certainly should be true of our participation in common worship. It is not evidence of any carnal appetite for men and women to kneel when they

---

11. The Grace and Peace Fellowship of St. Louis, a congregation of the Presbyterian Church in America, and several other churches in this denomination have done so.

pray. On the contrary, it may be evidence of carnal sluggishness when we sit stolidly in our pews instead of kneeling in proper reverence before our Savior God.

In summary, it seems quite clear from our brief study of evangelical worship in our day that a genuine renewal in the churches will be the fruit of a refreshing revival of corporate worship. Such a revival is not to be looked upon as utilitarian. What happens when Christians worship is not to be confused with their purpose in worship. In our day a renewal of corporate worship will be contingent upon the people of God coming to a clearer understanding of the true meaning of worship as well as the way they are individually to participate properly in the act of corporate worship. This will come when pastors take seriously not only the worship that precedes and follows their sermons but also their own preparation and leadership of this worship, as well as their responsibility to continuously instruct their members in the meaning and practice of common worship. They must also be willing to provide for and encourage every means by which common worship can be made more meaningful and more truly biblical.

Christians who desire to worship God in a manner acceptable to Him need to realize that, while He takes the initiative in worship and His Word is of primary importance in all true worship services, they not only must make their response to Him an offering but also must participate freely in a divine-human dialogue, responding joyfully to the divine initiative. May their response be that of the psalmist who addressed the Lord and said: "My heart says of you, 'Seek his face!' Your face, Lord, I will seek" (Ps. 27:8).

No Christian in this life has yet become what he is called to be, and the church too is still under construction. It must be seen in its design, not in its incompleteness. Yet the fullness of Christ indwells the church and to that fullness the church shall come.

"The Ministry of Hope" (1966)

# 8

# *Ecclesiology: Reformed and Reforming*

## *Roger Nicole*

$I$n view of Dr. Clowney's manifest interest in the doctrine of the church, I will concentrate my attention in this area and proceed to present some observations in three directions.

First, this essay will begin with a study of the principle of the reformation of the church as delineated, e.g., by John Calvin, and show how this principle requires of us continued vigilance and ever-renewed preparedness to submit to reformation. The *reformata* implies *reformanda*.

Second, the organization of church government provides an illustration of the way in which subtle changes may occur resulting in a shift from one type of church order to another. This too manifests the truth that we cannot rest content with a status quo, confident that the recovery of a biblical stance achieved at the Reformation is bound to safeguard us from deviations. On the contrary, every church and every individual must be alert to the possibility of gradual shifts that cumulatively may vitiate the best type of organization. Here specifically *reformata* demands *reformanda*.

Third, in an effort to tie in with the period of 1952–84, the special focus of this festschrift, I will offer some comments about certain reforming efforts of the last three decades.

## CALVIN AND THE REFORMATION PRINCIPLE

In 1543, in preparation for the Diet of Spires, which was to be convened at the end of February 1544, Calvin wrote a treatise known as *The Necessity of Reforming the Church*; its original title, in the style that was then prevalent, was *A Honorable Exhortation to the most invincible Emperor Charles V and the most illustrious Princes and other Orders, now holding a Diet of the Empire at Spires that they seriously undertake the task of restoring the church presented in the name of all those who wish Christ to reign.* This work was immediately translated into French (1544) and subsequently into Czech (1546), Dutch (1602), English (1838), and German (1924); it was incorporated into the collections of Calvin's treatises in Latin (1563, 1567, 1597, 1611, 1617, 1667, 1867), French (1566, 1611) and English (1844, 1959). The introduction and the second part of his treatise have been translated afresh and incorporated in J. K. S. Reid's edition of Calvin's *Theological Treatises.* This treatise should not be confused with another of Calvin's works entitled "The True Method of Reforming the Church and Healing Her Divisions" (1549), which appeared in the same year in French and later in Italian (1561) and in English (1851, 1959). To be sure, there is some overlapping between these two treatises, but they remain distinct; the latter one deals with the controversy at a later stage and in specific refutation of a document entitled *Interim*, intended by Charles V to regulate the churches until a general council should have rendered its verdict.

Calvin defines his task as follows:

> To accomplish [my end], I must take up together the three following points. First, I must briefly enumerate the evils which compelled us to seek for remedies. Then I must show that the particular remedies which our Reformers employed were apt and salutary. Last, I must make it plain that we were not at liberty any longer to delay putting forth our hand, inasmuch as the matter demanded immediate amendment.[1]

The "evils" that Calvin identifies are divided into three categories.

One, some evils relate to the mode of worship—specifically, the inordinate attention given to deceased saints in prayers, the worship of images, and the concentration on outward ceremonies—to the detriment of the biblical emphasis on true repentance on the part of sinners.

Two, some evils relate to a misrepresentation of the revealed truth concerning the source of salvation. This includes a proper sense of the utmost gravity of sin, an emphasis on turning to Christ alone as the ground of salvation and resting on Him alone for assurance. By contrast,

---

1. J. K. S. Reid, ed., *Calvin: Theological Treatises*, vol. 22 of *The Library of Christian Classics* (Philadelphia: Westminster Press, 1954), 19.

Calvin avers, the Roman Catholic Church has come to envision original sin as merely physical and leaving some remnant of free will in fallen humanity. The church asserts that human good works are a part of the ground of salvation, and thus it undermines the principle of assurance to the point where no one can be certain of salvation except by some supernatural revelation not vouchsafed to any but the apostles.

Three, the evangelical view of sacraments and of ecclesiastical government has also been grievously disfigured. The idea and function of sacrament has been severely damaged by numbering seven sacraments instead of viewing merely baptism and the Lord's Supper as such. Furthermore, even the nature of these two true sacraments has been subverted by representing them, respectively, as operating regeneration and renewing the sacrifice of Christ instead of seeing them as a dramatic representation by symbols of the truths of salvation. The government of the church has been also damaged by minimizing the teaching office, by failing to insist that those who lead should be moral examples to the flock, and by unbiblical standards of ordination and appointment. This has placed the faithful under a tyrannical bondage from which deliverance must be sought.

The Reformation was simply a movement designed to correct these fearful excesses. No further delay could be allowed; the Reformers could not be accused of having rashly and prematurely set in motion their own program. They must be viewed as having in the nick of time averted a complete disaster toward which the Roman Catholic Church was moving headlong.

It must be noted that this strong Protestant manifesto was not an isolated voice clamoring for reformation. For more than two centuries many sincere believers had been anxiously seeking a reformation "in the head as well as in the members" of the church. For some time, there had been hope that councils could axe out a rottenness only too apparent. But these forces proved helpless to accomplish such a gigantic task. In some cases they manifested themselves as part of the problem rather than a solution to it. Nothing short of the powerful movement of the Reformation of the sixteenth century could wake up the church from its spiritual torpor. Even Roman Catholic scholars are prepared to acknowledge that the Counter-Reformation was, in fact, beneficial for the church and that it could not have taken place as it did had the Roman Catholic Church not been confronted by this monumental revolution—a revolution that made it imperative for the church to muster its utmost energies to survive. This is not to say that this reaction, epitomized by the decisions of the Council of Trent (1545–63), was a source of unmixed blessing. Indeed, in opening a period of four hundred years characterized in a dominant way by an anti-Protestant stance, the Counter-Reformation tended to freeze the church into a rejection of the biblical insights of the Reformers. Yet there were ways in which the Roman Catholic Church made substantial progress. Those men elected popes after 1550 were generally capable and honorable, not morally flawed as several of the scoundrels who occupied the throne from 1350 to 1550. After 1550 only one pope ruled at a time, not two or even three pretenders at once. Several of the most flagrant disorders were corrected, particularly in lands where Catholics and Protestants lived side by side. One, therefore, did not need to side with Luther or Calvin to say that the church needed reformation.

Very manifest in this proposition is the fact that even an institution established by God and in some real sense subject to the guidance of the Holy Spirit is not on that account immune from corruptive influences. In our fallen humanity even those with the best starting point may deviate in their course; therefore, they always need to be prepared to submit to appropriate corrections. Surely the history of Israel gives us ample examples of this truth. For indeed the nation was established by God's special call and instructed by the light of His revelation. Yet the children of Israel were prone to veer astray even during the lifetime of Moses. From the death of Moses to the time of the exile to Babylon, the history of Israel seems to be a long succession of periods of disobedience, even of idolatry, when most of the kings "did evil in the eyes of the Lord" (1 Kings 14:9, 22; 15:3, 26; and passim). After the exile, while idolatry seemed less besetting than before, there was nevertheless a great estrangement from the spirit of God's law. When Jesus came, His most determined enemies were the scribes and the Pharisees—the very ones who should have been best prepared to receive Him because of their great knowledge of the Old Testament. Jesus' verdict was "You nullify the word of God by your tradition" (Mark 7:13; Matt. 15:6). And Stephen, full of the Holy Spirit, could say, "You stiff-necked people. . . . you always resist the Holy Spirit!" (Acts 7:51).

The very fact that a church calls itself "reformed" implies that the church is not immune to deviations. The solution, therefore, lies in a spirit of continued submissiveness to correction. A Protestant tradition is no more inherently "infallible" than one in the Roman Catholic or Eastern church. If the church is indeed "reformed," it follows that it is always subject to reformation. *Reformata* implies of necessity *semper refor-*

*manda.* The norm by which this reformation needs to be regulated remains the infallible Word of God—the Bible in its entirety as the word of God written, therefore inerrant in the autographs.

If any further evidence were needed than the logic of reformation, it would certainly be provided by the history of Reformed churches. Less than three centuries after the death of Calvin, the church of Geneva was so deeply corrupted that a pastor could be suspended from the ministry there for using Calvin's catechism rather than a recent one permeated with Pelagianism![2]

A similar downward course may be observed in many churches issuing from the Reformation. In 1883 Abraham Kuyper found it necessary to publish his *Treatise on the Reformation of the Churches,*[3] precisely because the state Reformed church in the Netherlands had veered so far astray from Reformation principles and doctrine.

In the perspective of the Reformation what is essential is not physical continuity, but spiritual conformity. Genealogy is no guarantee of orthodoxy or orthopraxis. In the matter of ordination the basic unity of spirit and doctrine with the apostles and with the Reformers is more important than an uninterrupted chain of hands on heads from them to us.

## CHURCH GOVERNMENT

The principle that the church is always subject to reformation may be illustrated from the vantage point of the government of the church.

There have been elaborate controversies on this topic, and even in the Westminster Assembly the delegates engaged for many months in what has been known as "the Grand Debate concerning Presbytery and Independency," a debate that absorbed the utmost powers of some of the most distinguished members of the great assembly. A common premise seemed to prevail throughout the debate that there is only one scriptural system of church government and that this system is mandatory for all times and places. The practice of the church in the apostolic times, particularly as reflected in the writings of the New Testament, provides us with the details of this mandate. But we must distinguish carefully

2. For more details see Léon Maury, *Le Réveil Religieux dans l'Eglise Réformée à Genève et en France* (1810–1850), 2 vols. (Paris: Fischbacher, 1892), 1:149–73.

3. *Trectaat van de Reformatie der Kerken, aan de Zonen der Reformatie hier te lande op Luther's vierde eeuwfest aangeboden* (Amsterdam: Hoveker, 1883). A fairly lengthy discussion of this work is found in J. C. Rullmann, *Kuyper-Bibliographie* (Kampen: Kok, 1929), 2:93–106.

between what is portrayed and what is enjoined. It appears possible to hold that several forms of church government are *compatible* with Scripture, although not any one of them can be asserted on that account to be obligatory.

The spectrum may be represented by the following diagram:

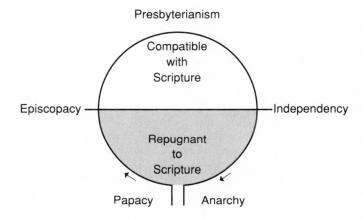

If we move clockwise around this circle starting at 6 o'clock with *papacy*, we face a form of government where authority is supremely vested in one person who is free to make decisions and issue mandates. Such power may be exercised in isolation and, in the most extreme cases, is construed as an infallible pronouncement authenticated by God Himself. Practically in most cases a number of counselors, often with a high degree of competence, assist the central authority with their advice and wisdom. In the Roman Catholic Church, canon law, although subject to modifications from time to time, functions as a protection against arbitrariness. Perhaps the worst type of papal authority may be seen in the sect led by Jim Jones in Guyana.

The distinguishing feature of *episcopacy* lies in the distinction between two classes of priesthood, or ministry. The upper class is designated by the word *bishop* or *supervisor*. This form of government may become abusive when it tends to "prelacy," or the abusive exercise of power by bishops with an infringement of the rights of ordinary clerics or lay people (the lower class). Some of the difficulties experienced in the Church of England under Archbishop Laud may be traced to his prelatical conception of his office. In most cases the bishops have the right to ordain and to appoint clergymen to the service of particular churches. They may have judicial powers for the resolution of difficulties arising in the relationship of a parish to its clergy. In many cases the power of the bishops is carefully defined by canon law. Often assemblies constituted by clergy and laity and meeting at regular intervals maintain a certain level of democracy, which may be so dominant that the form of government approximates Presbyterianism.

*Presbyterianism* may be described as a confederation of churches united under a common profession of faith. It advocates a hierarchy of ecclesiastical assemblies, or courts, in which a careful balance is maintained between clerics and lay people. The nature and range of jurisdiction as well as the form of procedure are carefully established in a book of church order. The principle of accountability for local churches as well as individual ministers is firmly established as well as a mechanism for appeals by those who deem themselves aggrieved. When the church at large is healthy, this system may well provide an ideal equilibrium between the rights of autonomy of the local churches and the need for concerted action ensured by a common bond that includes jurisdiction. Certain matters in which the local church may not without difficulty proceed in isolation (such as the ordination and call of ministers, the establishment of major undertakings in education or mission, the administration of the discipline of ministers and churches) are remanded to an ecclesiastical representative assembly of a higher order. Problems do develop in cases of conflict by excessive wrangling over ecclesiastical procedure and by the oppression of ministers and local congregations loyal to the confession of faith on the part of a majority that may have defected from the original standards. Both of these defects are amply illustrated in the church history of Scotland, not to speak of other nations.

The more the rights of the individual local congregation are emphasized the closer we get to *independency*, the system in which no jurisdiction can exist over any local church; the congregation remains at all times free to take any decision it pleases, subject to its own by-laws. (A violation of the by-laws might be appealed to a secular court.) Matters in which the church cannot well function in isolation, such as the ordination of candidates for the ministry, are accomplished by a recourse to other independent churches with which there is an *association*. This relationship, however, does not, as presbytery, curtail somewhat the autonomy of the local church by conferring on a higher assembly some jurisdiction over it. Limited to a process of advice and fellowship, such a relationship may be terminated at will by an appropriate vote of the congregation. Since ordination is not very meaningful if it does not involve recognition outside of the local church, the need of some concurrence at this level tends at times to infringe on independency. The establishment of funds vested in the association rather than in local congregations also acts as a centripetal force making disassociation more difficult. On the one hand this approach has a certain looseness that makes safeguarding the accountability by individual ministers or congregations difficult. On the other hand, when the larger body is not in good spiritual health, it does ideally preserve the rights of the local church to keep itself free from infection.

Beyond independency there are various forms of church order, or rather disorder, that may generally be described by the term *anarchy*. When this occurs, a strong personality frequently takes over where a constituted order should preferably prevail. This state of affairs then rejoins the principle of papacy, but often without the checks and balances found in the Roman Catholic Church.

It would appear that the upper portion of the circle is compatible with Scripture, while the lower shaded part includes some features that violate the rights of God's people. It is easy from any vantage point to slip into that lower part, and a church that has emerged out of it (*ecclesia reformata*) must be ever on its guard not to return there (*semper reformanda*).

## RECENT REFORMATION STRUGGLES

The mere fact that reformation is perceived as allowable, and indeed as necessary, does not guarantee that every reform undertaken will be to the good. The *semper reformanda* may indeed be involved to justify backward steps or injurious novelties that cannot by any stretch of the imagination be viewed as constructive. A manifest example of a backward step is the move to reunite with Rome on the papacy's terms. A clear example of injurious novelty might be the ordination of practicing homosexuals.

In the Netherlands the (Free) Reformed churches (*Gereformeerde Kerken*) were the product of the confluence of two reformation movements: the *Afscheiding* (1834) and the *Doleantie* (1886). A veritable resurgence of Calvinism occurred under the notable leadership of Abraham Kuyper (1837–1920) and Herman Bavinck (1854–1921). The Free University of Amsterdam, founded to reflect and promote a Reformed world-and-life view (1880), fulfilled this mandate with great brilliance for some seventy years. In the 1950s, however, some new directions began to appear. G. C. Berkouwer (1903–   ), perhaps the leading theologian of that church, after a period in which his advocacy of Reformed orthodoxy was indubitable (articulated by an aggressive stance against neo-orthodoxy and Roman Catholicism), began to soften his attitude. His improvements in courtesy and generosity actually led him to a certain permissiveness. In his own structuring of the Christian faith in the series *Studies in Dogmatics,* a weakening of the confessional Reformed position appears through the rejection of the Dort doctrine of reprobation, advocacy of traducianism, some vacillation on original sin, an affinity with Amyraldianism, and finally a weakening of the doctrine of scriptural infallibility. This trend was aggravated in some of Berkouwer's noted disciples, particularly H. M. Kuitert, who propounds a very diluted doctrine of scriptural authority, and Herman Wiersinga, who rejects penal substitution and favors a moral influence view of the atonement. Between 1954 and 1984 the *Gereformeerde Kerk* has moved so far away from its moorings that it is now hardly distinguishable from the church from which it seceded in the nineteenth century. A strong drive toward participation in the World Council of Churches and a considerable permissiveness toward practicing homosexuals are significant features of the life of the church. As leaders of an earlier generation are passing away, the backward reformation becomes more and more accentuated. A very painful schism in 1944 with the active participation of Klass Schilder (1890–1952) may turn out to have been a blessing in disguise. It permitted a significant group of people and churches to escape the weakening that has affected the body from which they originated.[4]

In the Christian Reformed Church in the United States and Canada the period of 1954–84 was marked by considerable turmoil. As a channel of public expression, those whom James Bratt describes as "the progressive" established *The Reformed Journal,* while the "traditionalists" countered in *Torch and Trumpet* (later named *The Outlook*). It is difficult to apportion right and wrong in this continuing debate, although it is easy to perceive some wrongs on each side. The progressive appear to me

---

4. For greater details about the destiny of Reformed thought in the Netherlands, see W. Robert Godfrey, "Calvin and Calvinism in the Netherlands," in *John Calvin: His Influence in the Western World,* ed. W. Stanford Reid (Grand Rapids: Zondervan, 1982), 95–120, 377. For a very critical evaluation of Berkouwer's journey, see Henry Krabbendam, "B. B. Warfield versus G. C. Berkouwer on Holy Scriptures," in *Inerrancy,* ed. Norman L. Geisler (Grand Rapids: Zondervan, 1979), 413–46, 485–89.

surely wrong in their weakening of the doctrine of an inerrant Scripture, in their advocacy of universal grace and universal atonement, in their objections to the Dort doctrines of reprobation, and in their very negative attitude that seemed to ignore the tremendous strengths of their church. Dr. Harry Boer, sometime chaplain in the Navy, appeared to be in the forefront of all these battles. The traditionalists by contract were concerned to preserve the doctrinal heritage of their church (and who could fault them for that?). But they did damage to their own cause by an excessive tendency to suspect others, by a caustic tone in controversy, and by an unwillingness to give serious consideration to such minor improvements in church order as the acceptance of women for the office of deacon. The progressive wanted to press *semper reformanda* to the point of eroding their doctrinal heritage; the traditionalists were reluctant to accept any change at all.[5]

Until 1967 the United Presbyterian Church in the U.S.A. functioned with the formidable fence of the Westminster Confession of Faith. At the time of ordination every candidate had to answer affirmatively the question "Do you sincerely receive and adopt the Confession of Faith of this church, as containing the system of doctrine taught in the Holy Scriptures?" There was an embarrassing disparity, however, between the doctrinal views of many ministers and the express statements of the confession, resulting in the impression of a lack of integrity in the ministerium. Furthermore, the confession did not touch upon some subjects on which many felt the church should take a resolute stance. Thus a movement was initiated to write a briefer confession of faith much less decisive on many theological points and more clearly related to the issues and concerns of the modern age.

After considerable debate such a confession was adopted in 1967 and made one of several in a *Book of Confessions* by which an ordainee was to declare he or she would be instructed and led. Thus the church bought integrity for its officeholders at the expense of its moorings in the Confession of Faith. Under this approach it would be well-nigh impossible to convict anyone of heresy, and indeed heresy trials have not taken place since 1967. A challenge to the vote to receive into the National Capital

---

5. For more details and documentation one should consult James D. Bratt, *Dutch Calvinism in Modern America* (Grand Rapids: Eerdmans, 1984). A condensed presentation is found in his essay "The Dutch Schools," in *Reformed Theology in America*, ed. David F. Wells (Grand Rapids: Eerdmans, 1985), 135–52. His sympathies fall more fully with the "progressive" than mine would.

Union Presbytery the Reverend Mansfield Kaseman, who refused to affirm that Christ is God, did not succeed (1977–81).

On the other hand, the church did refuse to ordain candidates, otherwise well qualified, who could not in good conscience participate in the ordination of women. And this in spite of the fact that there is little in the *Book of Confessions* on this subject.[6]. Such refusal was viewed by the Permanent Judicial Commission as a rejection of the mandate of the church's constitution and consequently as a disqualifying feature.[7] Thus the "church" lost the services of a number of well-prepared and well-qualified candidates who could not in good conscience interpret the restrictive statements of Scripture as compatible with the ordination of women. At the same time people whose views were directly contrary to Scripture on major doctrines (deity of Christ, virgin birth, physical resurrection, substitutionary atonement, etc.) could be and were ordained as ministers of the gospel. Here surely we have reformation of the worst kind.

Not all efforts at reformation in the recent decades have been negative, however. The Reformed Presbyterian Church of North America, a notably conservative body that functioned with the Westminster standards and a Testimony and Declaration of the Church as subordinate standards, recently revised its Testimony in order to adapt more fully to the needs of the present time (1980). It proceeded to publish the Westminster Confession of Faith in the one column and its Testimony in a parallel column, thus interpreting and amplifying the 1648 statement and at many points adding features not found in the original document, notably the express rejection of faulty views. This revision constitutes a

6. The one statement of the *Book of Confessions* that seems to have relevance is in the Scottish Confession of Faith, which condemns the Roman Catholic Church for allowing "women to baptize, whom the Holy Ghost will not permit to preach in the congregation" (Art. 22) (Philip Schaff, *Creeds of Christendom* [Grand Rapids: Baker, 1966] 3:471; *Book of Confessions*, 3.22). Of course, ordinands are not bound by this, only "instructed"! The Second Helvetic Confession, Article 20, adopts the same position (Schaff, *Creeds of Christendom*, 3:490, *Book of Confessions*, 5.191).

7. This was made apparent in a ruling of the Permanent Judicial Commission in November 1974, overruling the decision of the Pittsburgh Presbytery to ordain to the office of minister of the Lord Mr. Walter W. Kenyon, who averred that on biblical grounds he could not participate in the ordination of a woman, although he would not refuse to work cooperatively with ordained women. This ruling was confirmed at the next session of the general assembly in 1975 and again in 1976 and 1977. Overtures requesting that ministers be asked whether they will "submit to" rather than "endorse" the government and discipline of the church were defeated (Overtures 43 and 53, *Minutes of the General Assembly,* 1977. *Journal*, pp. 747, 752, 91, 92). Thus the Book of Order was placed above the Confession of Faith, which was seen merely as a guide and instructor. Even the Roman Catholic Church does not demand such an allegiance to its canon law.

volume of eighty-six single-space typewritten pages, a most helpful updating of more ancient documents.

In the Lutheran Church (Missouri Synod) the largest seminary, Concordia Theological Seminary of St. Louis, had become suspect of harboring professors and students not wholeheartedly committed to the inerrancy of Scripture. Under the presidency of Jacob Preus the church pursued a vigorous inquiry and dismissed President John Tietjen in 1974. This led to an exodus of a large portion of the faculty together with an important fraction of the student body to form a rival seminary in St. Louis, Seminex (that is, Seminary-in-Exile). In spite of strong pressures from various quarters, the original seminary's chairs were filled with competent teachers wholly committed to the authority of Scripture. Depleted at first, the student body was gradually restored to its previous levels.

In the Southern Baptist Convention, the largest Protestant body in the United States, a certain unease has been for some time prevailing concerning the soundness of the six seminaries officially affiliated with that denomination. The overwhelming majority of the members are very conservative in doctrine, but unless the cadres of the denomination were of that persuasion, it was realized, no clear movement of reformation could be expected. Conservative leaders then proceeded to encourage the election of conservatives who would, in turn, appoint conservatives to all boards of the church. This has occurred so successfully of late that we may well expect a turning point in the denomination and its seminaries.

## CONCLUSION

*Reformata, semper reformanda*—reformed, but always subject to reform. This perspective is truly in the logic of Calvinism with its realistic perception of the depth of sin's impact upon all areas of human life, and its glorious vision of the potential for healing and recovery to be found in the redemptive grace of the Triune God. On one hand because of sin's impact, the consistent Calvinist will never imagine that on this earth one can achieve perfection either in personal or corporate life. We cannot indulge the utopia of a paradise regained under the sun, and therefore even the best individuals and the best institutions are always subject to reform. On the other hand, because of the sovereign grace of God our Savior, the lost sinner becomes the object of a radical renewal by the

Holy Spirit, who revels in the transformation He can work even in a valley of dry bones. The church as the company of the redeemed can be developed and purified so as to be ultimately presented to Christ "a radiant church, without stain or wrinkle or any other blemish, but holy and blameless" (Eph. 5:27). Our sinfulness makes reformation always imperative; God's grace makes it worthwhile.

We are to preach all the riches of Scripture, but unless the center holds all the bits and pieces of our pulpit counseling, of our thundering at social sins, of our positive or negative thinking—all fly off into the Sunday morning air. Paul was resolved to know nothing at Corinth but Jesus Christ and Him crucified. Let others develop the pulpit fads of the passing seasons. Specialize in preaching Jesus!

"Preaching Christ from All the Scriptures" (1986)

# 9

# Preaching for Modern Times

## Derke P. Bergsma

$P$reaching is the proclamation of the Word of God in all its relevance to the contemporary situation in which real people are called to responsibility before that Word. Such a view of preaching implies the necessity of biblical interpretive gifts (skills), as well as insight into the nature of the times during which one's ministry is exercised. While the truth of the Word is unchanging and the eternal Spirit of God the guarantee of that truth, the responsibility of the preacher is not exhausted when he has done careful exposition. At that point a very fine interpretation of a passage may have been produced. But the sermonic task necessarily includes the application of the truth to a given contemporary situation. It follows therefore that an effective preacher of the Word must be a sensitive observer and interpreter of the "times and the seasons," understanding the cultural ideals, the political realities, the influential movements, and the challenging crises of a given era.

This is not to say that the pulpit reflects and reinforces the situational circumstances of a particular time period. Such a travesty occurs whenever a preacher prostitutes his role to allow particular social or political movements to set the agenda for his preaching. Historical events necessarily raise questions, the responses to which must be sought through diligent search of the Scriptures to determine what mature Christian belief and action ought to be. Principles of Christian life and behavior do not emerge from existential experience. They are divinely revealed. But challenges and opportunities do confront believers in life's situations, requiring studious recourse to the Bible for the guidance needed to respond with Christian appropriateness. The worshiper in the pew should expect such guidance from the occupant of the pulpit.

## THE PREACHING SITUATION

The last four decades have presented as great a challenge for effective preaching in North America as any prior period of similar length. The placid, complacent years of the 1950s ended, a decade in which religious interest and church attendance reached unprecedented levels.[1] According to most observers at the time, the '50s were expected to serve as a plateau from which virtually unlimited social and technological advances were certain to be made. But it was not to be, at least not without conflict, struggle, and enormous cost. As if on cue, the 1960s opened with society in turmoil and continued as a decade of social and political conflict. A brief mention of some major events of the time reflects the general sense of disquietude that prevailed, a fear that something was going wrong, badly wrong, within the structures of society.

Traditional American optimism and pride was blunted by the tragicomedy of the Bay of Pigs and the assassinations of John and Robert Kennedy and Martin Luther King, Jr. These events were followed by unrest triggered by unfulfilled expectations among ghetto blacks whose frustration exploded in "burn, baby, burn" riots in the major cities. The Civil-Rights Act of 1964 offered hope to those whom society's majority had relegated to second-class status, but basic attitudes changed little. The changes which the act required in the areas of school desegregation and real estate practices precipitated confrontational crises that disrupted neighborhoods in all major cities.

Dominating national life and policy during the latter half of the '60s was Vietnam. With a troop level steadily increasing to a peak of one-half million men by 1969, the war was the first ever televised for daily replay in one's living room. Battlefield casualties were shipped home for burial, usually in a week or less—the first time the tragedy of war impacted the home folks so tangibly and immediately. Protests against government policy erupted on the streets of cities and were regular occurrences on college campuses, overshadowing everything else that happened at the 1968 Democratic Party Convention in Chicago. Casualties of these events included a president discouraged to the point of refusing to seek reelection and, more seriously, the loss of faith in the rightness of American causes and distrust of American leadership. On July 20, 1969, astronauts landed on the moon, a human achievement of tremendous technological proportions, while relations on planet earth resembled the primitive order of the jungle.

1. DeWitte T. Holland, *The Preaching Tradition* (Nashville: Abingdon, 1980), 86.

The years between 1970 and 1980 were hardly more stable than the decade preceding them. True, the war in Vietnam gradually diminished as far as American involvement was concerned. But trust in the authority of government and its spokesmen declined precipitously. It seemed that "lying in state" was a definition for diplomacy. Richard Nixon's lies, designed to cover up his knowledge of the burglary of Democratic party offices in the Watergate Hotel, eventually forced him to resign the presidency in disgrace. Cynicism toward political leaders at all levels prevailed.

Public morals suffered. Evils long practiced in private were openly championed. Pornography in pulp literature, on movie screens, and via cable television was widely and legally disseminated in the land. Homosexuality was increasingly promoted as a simple matter of sexual preference with no moral implications or consequences. The Supreme Court established the legality of abortion on demand, and thus placed the law on the side of the casual destruction of human life. Churches, Catholic and Protestant alike, began to realize their impotence toward influencing the shape of the ethical standards of society. Shaken out of their naive belief in the essentially Christian character of our democratic society, some churches began to speak a more prophetic word of judgment on a nation drifting away from its earlier orientation to a divine source for its laws. Secularism as a way of interpreting life began to be challenged by the conservative religious bodies of the land.

The 1980s have inherited the influences of prior years with little diminution of their impact. Mood-changing illegal drugs are used by a broader segment of the population as increased supplies and lower prices make them available to more people. Further, minority demands for equality continue, as does the feminist attack on entrenched masculine domination in church and society. And yet, perhaps the decade of the '80s will be most remembered as the era of the terrorist. Though terrorism was once largely restricted to regions where belligerents confronted each other, now Europe and North America are vulnerable to the designs of terror groups.

In the face of the realities briefly sketched above, what was the message heard from the pulpits of the land during these years? Was there a sure word to proclaim? While "change and decay" seemed to be the order of the day everywhere, was there a guiding light to lead us through the maze of events that threatened to undermine our world? What could be trusted not just for survival but to provide an unshakable foundation for contemporary life? What could provide the assurance that life is fundamentally good, fulfilling, and purposeful? Was there a word of hope to which people could be confidently called? Such questions were unavoidable. The variety of presumed answers from pulpits everywhere was diverse and contradictory.


## LIBERAL PROTESTANT PREACHING

Traditional liberal Protestant pulpits continued to emphasize the necessity of the life of love to God and fellowmen for which humanity's own resources were adequate to attain if only its inherent potential were exercised. "When all is said and done," wrote H. Richard Niebuhr, "the increase of this love of God and neighbor remains the purpose and the hope of our preaching of the gospel."[2] But the weakness of the liberal pulpit lay in the naive belief in human goodness, trusting that loving God and neighbor was a simple, attainable, human possibility apart from the transforming grace of God. It failed to take seriously the biblical portrayal of the human condition as lost in its rebellion against God and, therefore, prone by nature to hate God and neighbor. The indispensable need for conversion and a renewed heart was implicitly denied. In the context of a world disturbed by conflict and hostility, liberal churches were especially ineffectual as agents of reconciliation, refusing as they did to acknowledge the source of the alienation that prevailed in human relations. Their pulpits had no sure word of hope to proclaim.

The Barthian corrective for traditional liberalism had little influence for restoring Scripture-based pulpit power. Barth was far more realistic regarding the human condition and far less optimistic about human potential, insisting that divine initiative was indispensable for the renewal of the heart. Preachers under his theological influence brought a message with greater urgency than liberal pulpits had customarily done. Unfortunately, the Barthian movement did not signal a return to the Bible as, to use Calvin's statement, "the very words of God." Rather, for them the Bible "witnessed to" the Word of God or "contained" the Word of God but was never to be identified or equated with the Word of God. Both in reading the Scripture and in hearing it preached, one was admonished not to listen *to* the Word of God but rather to listen *for* the Word of God. The difference between the prepositions is nothing less than the difference between an objective authoritative written revela-

2. H. Richard Niebuhr, *The Purpose of the Church and its Ministry* (New York: Harper and Row, 1956), 39.

tion and the subjective response to a fallible testimony to revelation. As a consequence, Barthian theology provided no more confident basis for preaching than the liberalism to which it claimed to stand in judgment.

## PREACHING AND RADICAL THEOLOGY

Radical Protestant theology, emerging to the forefront of theological dialogue in the '60s, was more consistent than traditional liberalism and, consequently, had a more devastating effect on the preaching task. Radical theologians not only rejected the Bible as authoritative revelation (as traditional liberalism had done) but also discarded the belief in a transcendent, sovereign, creator God. In 1963 Bishop J. A. T. Robinson wrote, "There is a growing gulf between the traditional orthodox supernaturalism in which our faith has been framed and the categories which the 'lay' world finds meaningful today."[3] The most striking example Robinson used to illustrate the "categories" that are "outmoded" was the biblical idea of a transcendent God who exists "up there" or "out there," separate and distinct from the created world as we know it. The bishop argued that the idea of the Christian God was formulated at a time when myth still prevailed, when people still had a childish awe and sense of dependence upon an all-powerful, heavenly daddy God, when the words *supernatural* and *transcendent* meant something. If Christianity persists in stressing this relic of the past, says Robinson, it relegates itself to irrelevancy today. We have come of age and discarded medieval religious myth—much as the idea of Santa Claus, however pleasant and real he may have once seemed in one's childhood, is discarded as myth when a young person grows up and comes of age.[4]

The same position is far more sharply expressed in *Radical Theology and the Death of God*. There William Hamilton and Thomas Altizer argue "that there was once a God to whom adoration, praise and trust were appropriate, possible and even necessary, but—now there is no such god."[5] Hamilton explains, "We are not talking about the absence of the experience of God but the experience of the absence of God."[6] This gives us a hint as to the final authority to which he appeals in

3. J. A. T. Robinson, *Honest to God* (Philadelphia: Westminster Press, 1963), 8.
4. Ibid., 11–14.
5. Thomas J. J. Altizer and William Hamilton, *Radical Theology and the Death of God* (Indianapolis: Bobbs-Merrill, 1966), 28.
6. Ibid.

formulating this theology—human experience. According to Altizer, the "death of God" means the impossibility of attaching any meaning to the classical Christian image of the Creator-creation relationship.[7]

The only possible response to the death of the outmoded transcendent God concept is to radically embrace life in the world as we know it, hopefully waiting for a modern, relevant God concept to emerge out of man's secular, this-worldly experience, freed from any kind of a beyond-the-world-of-human-experience reference point. The British lay-theologian John Wren Lewis finds justification for such an immanentistic search for God in the words of Jesus, "the reign of God is among you." He defines God as "the creative power between persons" and asserts that from this point alone our understanding of religion can begin.[8]

In a similar vein, Paul Van Buren called for discarding traditional language used to describe God since it is meaningless for us today. The gospel must be understood in a thoroughly secular fashion, he claims, to be significant for contemporary society. Biblical categories must be translated into the empirical terms of a scientific, technological society.

Toward the close of the last century Freud analyzed the Christian heavenly Father concept as the projection into the heavens of the world's corporate super-ego. He called the idea a "heavenly nobodaddy," a daddy who is nobody. Radical theology seemed to have made his idea theologically respectable.

Common to all these approaches is the presupposition that mankind and its experience of reality is the fundamental source of truth. Humanity is its own authority. God is dead. Human beings, as independent creators, are autonomous (their own law). Paul Tillich made this position clear in his book *The Courage to Be*. He insisted that the God of theism was dead and deserved to die. He claimed that a God who stands above human activity and who controls the cosmos is ultimately the enemy of human self-fulfillment, because He opposes human freedom.[9]

This phenomenon of mankind's usurpation to itself of the role as final reference point and authority for the establishment of truth is not new. It is as old as the devil's successful temptation of Adam to assert independence and autonomy vis-a-vis God, to know good and evil, everything, on his own—to praise man from whom all blessings flow! In the past it was customary to give lip service to God as ultimate Lord while practically and empirically He was forgotten. But radical theology as-

7. Ibid., 11–14.
8. John Wren Lewis, *God in a Technological Society* (London: SCM Press, 1963), 32–33.
9. Paul Tillich, *The Courage to Be* (New Haven: Yale University Press, 1966), 184–85.

serted that human beings can finally get along without God, because they have come of age, they've grown up. Now they have the strength, resources, and technical competence to shape their own future and the courage to take responsibility for their own world. This is the message recommended to preachers addressing modern man.

The radical theologians were not denying the existence of the "Divine" in reality. They were, however, rebelling against the idea of a personal, transcendent God who is the source of all truth. Preachers within such a theological framework had the responsibility of interpreting and clarifying the "experience of the Divine" in existential life. Worship was understood as the celebration of the emancipation from all restricting superficialities which prevented humans from experiencing "depth relationships." "It is the assertion of the beyond in the midst of life, the holy *in* the common."[10] The preacher's task was to encourage "authentic" living. That is, to live in an honest, open relationship with others, avoiding superficiality and role playing. Whenever people relate in genuine openness, so it was claimed, there the divine emerges in the process, because of the ultimacy of pure personal relationships. [11]

Since the presence of the divine in reality comes to be when persons relate authentically (that is, as honest authors of their actions and words), it was just a short step to the claim that "God is where the action is." Relationships are dynamic, not static. The divine is identified with change and the demonic with static preservation of the status quo defended by those desiring to freeze life at the point of their personal advantage. The pulpit, therefore, was enlisted on the side of protest movements bent upon social transformation. It was the social gospel come of age—not just preaching redemption through the shaping influence of a wholesome social environment but encouraging confrontational actions to inaugurate a new order. It is not surprising that the church's agenda was determined by the secular order since there, it was believed, the divine action was unfolding.

## PREACHING AND SITUATION ETHICS

Closely allied to the theology of Christian atheism and sharing its spirit was the parallel rise of situation ethics. It, too, deprived the pulpit of any authoritative word of direction and hope for the present life or

10. Robinson, *Honest to God*, 86.
11. Ibid., 87.

that to come; for it claimed that no fixed standard for the moral life of mankind could be normative for any specific situation, except the one abiding standard to "do what love requires."[12] This one rule must be obeyed always and everywhere and is, therefore, the one exception to the rule that all rules are relative to the situation.

It may be true that the nature of love as an other-directed concern for the welfare of people in all circumstances assures the best interests of all in every act. But such a position also assumes that we have the capacity to know and the desire to pursue what love requires. It suggests that loving our neighbors as ourselves is a simple human possibility without the need for regeneration and redirection of the naturally self-seeking human heart to one of love toward God and neighbor. Preaching, from this perspective, is reduced to encouraging people to be sensitive to others so that they will always do what love demands. The preacher's task is to provide "an analysis of the depths of all experience, interpreted by love."[13]

## PREACHING AND THE SELF-REALIZATION MOVEMENT

Radical theology has not been very prominent in more recent years, but the spirit of the movement lives on and is reflected in the preaching from many Protestant pulpits. The most prominent example arises from the "self-affirmation" school of religious thought. Under a variety of subjects, such as "self-realization," "self-fulfillment," "self-actualization," or "self-esteem," a common theme lurks; that is, humanity has the capacity, resources, and power to affect positive change in its moral and spiritual life. The emphasis now is on mind power. "Think and grow rich! Think and succeed in any venture! Anything the human mind can believe, the human mind can achieve."[14] What is needed is a "positive mental attitude" or "possibility thinking" or "the power of positive thinking," with no prior need for repentance and a heart renewed by God's grace.

What is implied from such a perspective is that a low ego image is the "sin" from which people need to be "saved." The purpose of worship in general and preaching in particular therefore must be to effect psycho-

---

12. Joseph Fletcher, *Moral Responsibility* (Philadelphia: Westminster Press, 1967), 29–41.
13. Paul Tillich, *Systematic Theology* (Chicago: University of Chicago Press, 1952), 1:15.
14. Napoleon Hill, *Grow Rich with Peace of Mind* (New York: Ballantine, 1967), 158–60.

logical uplift through the exercise of the "will to self-love." Since "the need for dignity, self-worth, self-respect, and self-esteem is the deepest of all human needs,"[15] preaching must be designed to supply what is needed. The preaching method followed betrays its claim for the basis of truth, namely, human experience. For the sermon consists primarily of anecdotes, example stories of people who, caught up in apparently overwhelming circumstances, prevailed against all odds by the exercise of indominable courage and right thinking. Their experience is both example and proof that positive attitudes produce positive results. "It works! Try it! Tap the inexhaustible reservoir of human resources! Take charge of your own life!"[16]

The old social gospel is to be preferred to its contemporary grandchild. Though just as thoroughly creature-centered in its approach, the social gospel at least recommended seeking personal fulfillment in service to others. It at least recognized that broken relationships need to be healed for human welfare to be secured. By contrast, the new liberalism recommends narcissistic preoccupation with one's individual self. It is a radical form of salvation by self-effort. Both the old and new liberalism contrast sharply with the biblical insistence that reconciliation to God through repentance of sin and faith in Christ Jesus as Savior is the only way to restored human dignity. For only in Christ is it possible for anybody to become somebody, redeemed, forgiven, restored. Those who are forgiven can then forgive others. Those who are accepted into the restored family of God for Christ's sake can accept others for Christ's sake. Self-esteem, rightly understood, is the happy state of those who know themselves to be the objects of God's love and grace in Christ Jesus. All other pursuits are psychological exercises in auto-suggestion, which substitutes individualistic, self-centered ego building for humble surrender of the will to the loving mastery of Jesus Christ.[17] He alone

15. Robert Schuller, *Self-Esteem* (Waco, Tex.: Word, 1982), 34.

16. The method and content of the preaching by "self-help" theorists is remarkably similar. Living as I do between San Diego and Garden Grove, California, I frequently have watched on television Pastor Terry Cole Whittaker, of Religious Science United Church, San Diego, and Robert Schuller, of the Reformed Church in America. Even though the traditions they represent are very different, they could trade sermons without changing a single sentence.

17. Robert Schuller identifies the "will to self-love" as the deepest and purest expression of human will. He contrasts the will to self-love with the will to materialism (Marx), the will to pleasure (Freud), the will to power (Adler), and the will to meaning (Frankl). He fails to acknowledge that it is precisely the human will that is flawed. What is needed is the will surrendered to the will of Christ, who possesses us and redirects us to love God preeminently and our neighbor as ourselves. (Cf. Schuller, *Self-Esteem*, 32–33).

can raise us up "to sit with him in heavenly places."[18] This is the ultimate worth, esteem, and dignity, attained not through human effort but by divine grace.

There are two reasons why the gospel of self-affirmation is so deceptive and attracts the interest of such large numbers of people. First, it appeals to the natural tendencies of unregenerate human hearts. It repeats the false gospel to which Adam and Eve surrendered. They too were promised self-esteem, complete human fulfillment through a positive attitude of self-assertion. If they would exercise their inherent capacity to realize their own potential, apart from God, they would be like gods, knowing everything, good and evil. The essential appeal is to self-deification.[19] It absolutizes the individual and either has no need of a God or reduces Him to an impersonal creative force, available on demand, to be tapped when needed. It is the essence of hubris, the haunting pride and arrogance of heart that denies human creatureliness and dependency in relation to a personal God. Such a message has always attracted its multitudes. It proclaims what human ears have always been itching to hear.

The second reason the message of self-affirmation attracts such a large following is that it appeals to a valid principle of human activity. Motivational power is indispensable for the achievement of human potential. Another way of presenting the same idea is to say that without possibility thinking the possible will never be actualized—it will remain possibility and never become reality. But, and this is the rub, what is thought *must be possible.* The resources and opportunities must be (providentially) provided for the mentally visualized results to become visual, objective reality. A person with a severed spinal column cannot possibility-think himself to walk. Someone free falling from an airplane without a parachute cannot possibility-think himself to a soft landing. In other words, motivational principles apply wherever in God's providence the necessary resources and opportunities are present. Certainly, most human beings do not make use of the enormous resources the Lord has provided. But this fact does not justify preaching as gospel that motivational principles apply in all circumstances. It also runs the serious risk

18. Eph. 2:6.
19. Dave Hunt and T. A. McMahon, *The Seduction of Christianity* (Eugene, Ore.: Harvest House, 1985). Chaps. 1 and 2 provide a penetrating analysis of the humanistic basis for the gospel of self-generated success. Cf. Herbert Schlossberg, *Idols for Destruction* (Nashville: Nelson, 1983), 39–43.

of causing the depression and discouragement of a guilt trip for those whose "thinking" failed to produce the "possibilities" expected.[20]

Furthermore, the human mind is capable of thinking and acting on the basis of evil possibilities. When the potential resources and opportunities for doing great evil are present, a perverted mind can fashion plans and objectives that may be actualized in destructive ways. Some of the most prominent examples of evil people in human history were possibility thinkers, destructive of the lives and welfare of uncounted numbers of their fellowmen. The Holocaust was a possibility first conceived in depraved minds. Thought itself requires transformation by the work of grace before God-honoring possibilities become the subject of reflection. The renewal of the mind is absolutely essential before its capacities can be exercised in ways that please God and bless our fellowmen. The renewed mind, says the apostle Paul, thinks of possibilities in harmony with the will of the Lord.[21]

The Bible clearly portrays the unregenerate heart as "deceitful" and "desperately wicked," and however much a preacher may be embarrassed to proclaim it, it is the truth, revealed truth.[22] Spiritually considered, our possibilities are warped, flawed, and incapable of thinking and realizing the good. Radical change of heart is required, which is a divine possibility alone. And the good news is that God has sovereignly taken the initiative to right the wrong of the human condition and restored its dignity. This is good news. An appeal to inherent human capacity and potential in the spiritual realm can only be bad news. To promise power of self-renewal to the natural heart is to practice pulpit deception.

## PREACHING TO NEEDS

The last two decades have seen the rise and often uncritical acceptance of the theory that preaching must be addressed to people's needs.

20. It is irresponsible and unloving to promise people success beyond the personal and circumstantial resources available. A pastor acquaintance of mine returned from a conference on successful church leadership determined to apply "the principles which guarantee success." When the expected results were not realized, he blamed himself and became discouraged to the point of being institutionalized with severe depression.

21. We are not distinguishing between terminology used in the self-realization movement, but there are subtle differences. One could argue, for instance, that the word *positive* in *positive thinking* implies thinking shaped by wholesome Christian attitudes avoiding negative or sinful patterns of thought. The phrase *possibility thinking* is more neutral and lacks any inherent qualifying implication as to what possibilities ought to be the object of thought.

22. Jer. 17:9.

Dr. Lloyd John Ogilvie, pastor of the Let God Love You ministry, urges preachers to listen to people for their needs and then turn to the Bible for answers. And Dr. Robert Schuller's similar statement is well known: "Find a need and fill it." There is certainly a place for recognizing people's needs in the total program of the church. Pre-school nurseries, youth programs, social groups of many kinds, and many other efforts may fill a variety of needs in a community and be legitimate in the life of the local church. But preaching must address what the *Scriptures* identify as needs, which goes deeper than the needs people customarily identify. The average persons tends to understand needs in emotional, social, and financial categories. Should preaching then be geared to provide emotional satisfaction, social acceptance, and encouragement in the pursuit of wealth, since these are the felt needs arising out of hurting experiences of depression, loneliness, and poverty?

Suppose the felt needs of people are the external expression or consequence of a deeper, though unacknowledged, need? Suppose they are symptoms of a basic spiritual disease? Rather than treating the symptoms, preaching must be radical in addressing the root of the human condition. To do anything less would be unloving, dishonest, and without hope. The truth of mankind's spiritual condition is revealed in Scripture, though it may embarrass some to hear it. The natural human condition is spiritually fatal. But there is good news. God in His Word identifies the deepest human need and meets it by His Spirit through the faithful preaching of the gospel. This is the absolute necessity in the ministry of the church before it can genuinely minister to the emotional, social, and volitional needs of people. No amount of human "placebo" preaching, while it may avoid embarrassing people and may attract millions, can fill the real need of the human spirit.[23] It will only blind many to the cure, making them complacent in their lostness, or, worse, reassure the wealthy and successful that their achievements are a guarantee of their wholeness, reinforcing their pride.

## PREACHING AND THE ELECTRONIC CHURCH

From the earliest days of radio, churches and denominations have used public airwaves to communicate the Christian message. The types of preaching heard on the media represented the whole range of theo-

---

23. Hunt and McMahon, *Seduction of Christianity,* use the term *placebo* to describe a counterfeit gospel (pp. 24–26).

logical opinion and communication styles. In recent years a new phenomenon has emerged. Religious broadcasting sponsored by churches and denominations has been superseded by aggressive, independent religious movements. These are predominantly Protestant and evangelical in theological position, and sensational, emotional in style. The enormous costs of television programming have tended to discourage church-sponsored use of this medium. Instead, a whole independent, market-oriented movement has arisen, big and powerful enough to serve its own interests apart from any ecclesiastical accountability.

The sermon as the formal preaching of the Word is gradually becoming less prominent in proportion to the total programming in religious broadcasting. Air time is increasingly filled with talk-show type interviews, musical entertainment, and personal testimony.[24] This format appears to be the most successful in terms of numbers of listeners and responses by telephone and mail. Preaching is done in an entertaining, enthusiastic, master-of-ceremonies style, since such an approach enjoys the best market response. It appeals primarily to the emotions rather than the intellect of the viewer. In short, this movement has adopted the model of the entertainment industry with its commercial orientation.

Successful programmers in the "electronic church" should be given credit for using these powerful media to witness to the Christian faith. The problem arises when the individual viewer permits the electronic church to substitute for the fellowship of a local body of believers. The problem is accentuated by some radio and TV preachers who never urge affiliation with a local congregation as a necessity in the Christian life. They may fear a loss of revenue from listeners who begin to support local churches. But media ministries should not be ends in themselves but channels of ministry for the church to fulfill her calling to proclaim the Word to the world. A relationship with an anonymous television audience can never be substituted for a congregation of real people who minister to each other in a redemptive face-to-face fellowship under the proclamation of the Word.[25]

24. "CBN's viewership has tripled since 1981, when Robertson switched from an all-religion schedule to a family entertainment approach, combining Christian shows with wholesome re-runs ('Flipper,' 'Father Knows Best'), westerns, old movies, and game shows." (*Time*, 17 February 1986, 67). Those religious broadcasters who are primarily Sunday programmers continue to emphasize preaching. As daily religious programming increases, preaching occupies proportionately less air time.

25. Eleven million more people listen to a radio or television religious broadcast each week than attend church in the United States. Cf. Holland, *Preaching Tradition*, 98.

## PREACHING AND BIBLICAL AUTHORITY

Our modern age is often characterized as anti-authoritarian. What is meant, of course, is that the traditional foci of authority are not respected as they formerly were. The authority of parents, teachers, public officials, religious leaders, and the institutions these figures represent is questioned, flaunted, and rejected. But authority is still with us as clearly as ever, since every act of human behavior and every decision made imply the right to be the "author" of an act or decision, or they appeal to some authorizing source. The question then becomes, By what authority is anything done, advocated, recommended, or claimed? A shift in the focus of authority should not blind us to the fact of its exercise. We must rather consciously expose the authority to which appeal is made. If a child refuses to recognize and shape his or her behavior according to the pattern of parentally established standards, the child arrogates authority to himself or herself or submits to the authority of a peer group for behavioral norms. Similarly, if the authority of a divinely inspired Scripture is not accepted as the basis of pulpit proclamation, the preacher implicitly comes with his own authority or appeals to his favorite theological peer group as basis for the claims he makes and the responsibilities he urges upon hearers. Or he may disclaim any authority at all and in good Schleiermachian tradition function as the interpreter of "religious experience" and leave each hearer to judge for himself or herself what implications can be drawn from it. Of course, there is the subtle intrusion of the claim that norms for faith and life emerge from existential religious experience, and there you have an appeal to another authority again. Even the principle of relativism cannot escape the authority claim, since if all is relative, that is, absolutely conditioned by its environment, the environmental circumstances are finally authoritative.

Preaching must be subservient to the authority of the Holy Scriptures as the Word of God. It must proclaim revealed truth as recorded in the Bible. To appeal to any other authority is to substitute human insights for the truth of God. Such a substitution would absolutize the relative and deny to people the good news of God's saving initiatives for the world. Fortunately, during the past few decades there has been preaching from many quarters that recognized the responsibility to Scripture as final court of appeal for faith and life. We turn now to consider some approaches from this stance.

## PREACHING THE BIBLE TOPICALLY

Topical preaching has been quite popular among well-intentioned evangelicals. Following the topical method of sermon construction, a preacher decides upon a particular topic and then proceeds to develop a "message" using biblical or extrabiblical material according to his own whim. The choice of topic is the preacher's prerogative. It is helpful to distinguish three types of topical sermons.

### GENERAL TOPICAL

In a general topical sermon a specific subject is arbitrarily chosen, such as anxiety or marriage conflicts or self-esteem, and the preacher proceeds to construct a sermon on the subject. If he happens to be so inclined, the preacher may consult the Scripture for what it has to say about the subject. But the method does not *compel* the use of Scripture. The tendency, rather, is to give one's own opinions in the matter and quote the Bible in support. This is, unfortunately, a common characteristic of contemporary preaching styles.

### TEXTUAL TOPICAL

In a textual topical sermon a topic is not arbitrarily chosen but is consciously derived from a specific text from the Bible. For instance, from the account of Joseph and Potiphar's wife, the topic of resisting temptation could be derived. But once the topic is determined, the preacher may proceed to develop the sermon as he pleases, without reckoning with the revelational intent of the passage at hand.

### BIBLICAL TOPICAL

The topic of a biblical topical sermon is usually of a general nature and is deliberately taken from Scripture, such as faith, prayer, conversion, etc. The preacher then proceeds to range widely throughout the Bible elucidating the topic from various passages. Again the method does not require careful in-depth exposition of any one passage. At best, it distills out of various passages material relevant to the broader topic.

The weakness of topical preaching is inherent in its nature.[26] Since it is the prerogative of the preacher to choose or find a topic, his private interests and personal observations tend to determine the subject chosen. Needs-oriented preaching is nearly always topical, since the preacher's own perception of people's needs determines sermon subjects.

Topical preaching has given birth to much "single theme" pulpit ministries in recent years. Consider the late Herbert W. Armstrong's persistent theme of the nature of the last days or Jimmy Swaggart and the holiness theme. Oral Roberts focuses on miracles and Carl McIntire on the communist conspiracy in church and state. It is the rare topical preacher who can maintain a balanced biblical range in preaching. The temptation to push one's own interests and crusade is too strong.

## NEEDED: TEXTUAL EXPOSITORY PREACHING

Simply stated, a *text* is a message unit of Scripture, or a self-contained unit of biblical revelation. Such an understanding can be construed to include a broad range of biblical material. The entire Bible is a self-contained unit of revelation, and it is perfectly correct to speak of the biblical *text* in the singular. Each book in the Bible is a text in this sense. But within these larger, written, documentary, textual forms there are distinguishable subunits that also present complete revelational thought units.

For example, Matthew 13 presents a series of kingdom parables and carries a common theme, the nature and preciousness of God's kingdom. The whole chapter is a coherent message unit of Scripture. Yet each separate parable is also a message unit, even as short a parable as Matthew 13:44. Just a single verse, it has an identifiable theme and supportive key elements by which the theme is unfolded. The practical situation a preacher faces is to choose a text that is rhetorically manageable—one that can be adequately expounded in a single sermon with sufficient detail and whose implications for the lives of the hearers can be clearly applied.

Professor Carl Kromminga of Calvin Seminary provides a good definition of a *text* in his homiletical class notes:

> A text for a sermon is a message unit of Scripture possessing a high degree of internal coherence, completeness, and intelligibility, ex-

26. James Daane, *Preaching with Confidence* (Grand Rapids: Eerdmans, 1980), 52–54. Daane provides a balanced critique of topical sermons.

isting in substantial distinction from its prior and following contexts, yet also partially shaped by these contexts with respect to its own structure and intention.

Sermonic loyalty to a specific text of Scripture is rooted in the nature of preaching itself. Preaching must be the proclamation of the Word. Preaching derives its authority not from the preacher or even his office but from the Word. The major responsibility of the preacher, therefore, is to convince the hearers that what is preached is in truth the authoritative Word of God to which obedient response is required. The sermon must demonstrate, from the Scripture, that what is proclaimed is God's Word. This can only be done convincingly through the exposition of a manageable message unit of the Bible, which serves as the guarantee of the truth proclaimed.

G. Campbell Morgan described his sense of allegiance to a text as follows:

> I read a text to my congregation. This is the message. This is the one thing that is absolutely and finally authoritative. My sermon has no authority in it at all, except as an interpretation or an exposition or an illustration of the truth which is in the text. The text is everything. That is the point of authority.[27]

Sidney Greidanus makes a convincing case for the indispensability of a specific text as the basis for biblically faithful preaching. He insists that it must be a unit, taken from one book, not a composite text.[28] Other valuable guides for textual expository preaching include Jay E. Adams, D. Martyn Lloyd-Jones, Haddon Robinson, and John R. W. Stott. Robinson makes an especially convincing case.[29]

Apart from careful attention to a specific text, the temptation in preaching is to make a point or state a position that is then proved by carefully selected references to scattered portions of Scripture. But listing fragments of Scripture out of context to prove a point is not preaching. At best it demonstrates the ability of a speaker to make a case for a

27. G. Campbell Morgan, *Preaching* (London: Marshall, Morgan, and Scott, 1955), 23.
28. Sidney Greidanus, *Sola Scriptura: Problems and Principles in Preaching Historical Texts* (Kampen: J. H. Kok, 1970), 218.
29. Jay E. Adams, *Preaching with Purpose* (Phillipsburg, N.J.: Presbyterian and Reformed, 1982), 16–20; D. Martyn Lloyd-Jones, *Preaching and Preachers* (Grand Rapids: Zondervan, 1971), 26–63; Haddon Robinson, *Biblical Preaching* (Grand Rapids: Baker, 1980), 15–29; John R. W. Stott, *Between Two Worlds* (Grand Rapids: Eerdmans, 1982), 211–27.

position, but it leaves doubt in the minds of hearers as to whether the position is truly biblical. Almost anything can be proved by choosing discrete statements in support of a preconceived idea. Textual preaching moves in quite a different direction. It faithfully expounds the text first, and then refers to parallel and related passages of Scripture illuminated in the light of the original text's teaching.

The relation of the text to the sermon can be viewed from several angles.

*Organically.* The text is the seed of the sermon. As the developed plant is potentially in the seed, so the entire sermon is potentially in the text. It is rooted and grows out from the text as its source.

*Mechanically.* The sermon is an expansion of the text. The text is unfolded and exposited in the sermon.

*Technically.* There is a positive identity of substance between the text and the sermon. The sermon reconstructs the truth of the text into a communicational package. The style and form differ, but the truth of sermon and text must have a relation of identity.

The text, then, is the message unit of biblical revelation upon which the liturgical address (sermon) is based as: (1) the exclusive source of its substantive content; (2) the absolute guarantee of its truth; (3) the plenary sanction of its ethic; (4) the divine warrant for its delivery.


## PREACHING THE WHOLE TRUTH TO THE WHOLE PERSON

Robert Metcalf of the Christian Studies Center in Memphis, Tennessee, once wrote an essay entitled "Pies, Docs, and Kuyps." In it he divided the Reformed Christian community into three groups suggested by his title. The "Pies" (pietists) emphasize personal holiness and the development of a faithful prayer life. Their orientation is toward a sincere emotional response in the religious life. The "Docs" (doctrinalists) emphasize confessional purity and orthodoxy. Their orientation is toward the intellectual comprehension of the truth. The "Kuyps" (Kuyperians) advocate and promote Christian organizations such as schools, relief agencies, professional organizations, and any other Christian institutional penetration of society. Their orientation is toward the reformation of all areas of life to bring to concrete expression the rule, or kingdom, of Christ.

Metcalf's identification of three camps in the Reformed community may help us to identify three parallel, narrow, one-dimensional types of preaching. For the pietist types, preaching focuses our attention on the emotional, moral response, and the sermon becomes an instructional device on how to become more godly, righteous, kind, and Spirit-filled—in short, more pious. The doctrinalist addresses the intellect, and for that type the sermon is a carefully crafted explanation of doctrinal issues so that orthodoxy may be maintained and heresy refuted. The Kuyperian type desires that the will be motivated to Christian action, so that the sermon becomes the means by which the hearer is stimulated to greater kingdom activity.

We certainly want all these things to happen as a result of good biblical preaching. Worshipers should leave a worship service motivated to be pious Christians. They should be instructed to understand the doctrinal implications of biblical truth. They should be stimulated to greater effort to bring all of life under the lordship of Christ. But none of these may be the primary focus or intent or purpose of preaching. The purpose of preaching must be seen in relation to the purpose of worship of which the sermon is a leading part.

Worship is the celebration of the mighty acts and deeds of our God by which He has demonstrated who He is and what we are in relationship to Him. The purpose of worship is to "proclaim the praises of Him who called you out of darkness into His marvelous light."[30] The gathered congregation of believers rejoice together in celebration of God's saving initiatives for the world. And it is in the sermon that God's redeeming acts are declared with greatest clarity and specificity. Preaching at its best, then, is the proclamation of God's redeeming work that He has accomplished in real planet-earth history as recorded in the Bible. When preaching as historical, redemptive proclamation is done faithfully, the expectations of the "Pies," "Docs" and "Kuyps" will all be realized; because declaring what God has graciously done to save the world always calls for a joyful, obedient response. That response will be emotional, resulting in more genuine piety; it will be intellectual, seriously desiring to know Christian doctrine better; and it will be volitional, motivating the believer to active kingdom service.

## BIBLICAL, THEOLOGICALLY SENSITIVE PREACHING

The importance of systematic theology in the theological enterprise can hardly be overemphasized. It is essential to have a vision of the

---

30. 1 Pet. 2:9, NKJV.

whole of Christian truth and to grasp that truth in its clarity and unity under the major headings of doctrine. But to preach the Word requires a biblical theological perspective. That simply follows from the nature of the Bible, the divinely inspired record of God's saving purposes in history. To preach the Word from a biblical theological perspective means preaching in the full awareness of the essential nature of Scripture itself.

For his contributions to the preaching task from a biblical theological point of view, we are especially indebted in North America to Edmund P. Clowney. His book *Preaching and Biblical Theology* presents the spirit and method of biblical theology as related to preaching.[31] That method begins with the recognition of the organic nature of the history of redemption. It approaches every passage of Scripture first with careful exegesis and then proceeds to identify connections and correspondence between the exegetical elements of the passage with figures, types, and symbols emerging in redemption history. It thus seeks to think God's thoughts after Him as the drama of redemption unfolds in the biblical record.

The Bible is unique as the inspired account of the God who reveals Himself as the world's Redeemer. It records the process of redemption in history, from bud to full flower, and every passage in the Bible has a specific place in that ongoing process. To preach responsibly on any text in the Bible requires the recognition of that text's unique place in the drama of redemption. It is also necessary to understand the relationship between that specific text and the larger context of biblical revelation. Several questions must be answered when a specific passage of Scripture is approached for preaching:

> 1. What did the Holy Spirit intend to reveal to the original hearers of the message? This is the *historical grammatical* question.
> 2. What is the relation of this particular unit of revelation to prior and later revelation, especially the supreme revelational event, the Lord Jesus Christ? This is the *biblical theological* question.
> 3. Why does God want us to know today, in the light of the cross, what was revealed to the original hearers? This is the *contemporary application* question.

The reason the third question above *may* be asked is that the human condition is the same, both in Bible times and now. Also the divine

31. Edmund P. Clowney, *Preaching and Biblical Theology* (Phillipsburg, N.J.: Presbyterian and Reformed, 1979).

initiative is the same, the God of grace calling a sinful world into redeemed fellowship with Himself. The reason the third question *must* be asked is that the proclamation of what God has done in salvation history calls forth an obedient response in our own unique historical situation. At this point the art of effective preaching is most tested. The contemporary, historically responsible situation is different from that into which God first intruded His revelational Word.

No sermon is complete even if it answers the questions of a text's meaning for the original hearers and demonstrates its meaning in the light of the peak revelational event, Jesus Christ. Up to this point the sermon may be an excellent exposition of Scripture, a fine Bible lesson. But the sermon must also have a contemporary purpose as its objective.[32] It must elicit a response. The response must engage the hearer at the point of the emotions, the intellect, and the will. That is to say, every sermon should call forth celebration of the saving initiatives of the God of all grace, increase knowledge of the truth, and stimulate will-full commitment to Christian service and devotion.

By virtue of the image of God he bears, a human being is a responsible creature, that is, response-able, or able to respond. It is unique to humans, among all that God has created, to be able to respond to the God who created them in His likeness. Trees and seas and stars and bees "declare the glory of God" (Ps. 19:1). They reflect as a mirror the grandness of the Creator. But they do so passively; it is not their conscious design to do so. With humans it is radically different. They are created as response structures,[33] able to respond to the divine address. In fact, they *must* respond either in joyful obedience or willful disobedience. The purpose of the sermon, then, is to call hearers to be fully human as God intended humans to be—His covenant partners. They are to celebrate His mighty saving works and ways, worship in the truth, and live as His faithful, obedient people. This is the response God expects from those who hear His word.

32. The most convincing case on this point is made by Adams, *Preaching with Purpose*, especially chaps. 3 and 4.

33. The term *response structures* is borrowed from Professor Troost of the Free University of Amsterdam.

$K$ierkegaard has "Climacus" say that Christianity is not for children. The reverse is true. It is for children and the child-like only. Jesus laid His hands on the children and said, "Of such is the kingdom of heaven." He is saying that to us of our children. In the Christ-centered home the child in the midst is not idolized but respected and loved, admonished and nurtured—in the Lord.

*Eutychus (and His Pin)* (1960)

# 10

# Christian Education:
# A Personal View of Three Decades

## Charles G. Schauffele

There is no subject more practical than theology. It is the basis for living in the image of God. However, in most seminaries practical theology is relegated to the last pages of the catalog with the fewest required hours, and in some respected "Reformed" institutions it is omitted from the curriculum altogether. The average pastor in the average church spends the major part of weekly time in counseling, recruiting, administering, teaching, and in the evangelism and Christian education of children, youth, adults, and families. It is strange, then, that these elements of ministry should receive such short shrift in the preparation of men for the pastorate.

Three decades in the career of Edmund Prosper Clowney demonstrate the practicality of theology in three areas. The emphases are seen in his ministries first in the Sunday school, then in the Christian day school, and finally in the theological seminary. Dr. Clowney was highly involved in each of these.

### THE SUNDAY SCHOOL

He was born into a Christian home in west Philadelphia at the close of World War I, the only child of Presbyterian parents. While he attended the public schools there, his major interests were in the Sunday school, the annual month-long vacation Bible school, and the other Christian education activities of Westminster Presbyterian Church. The

Sunday school of more than a thousand members in a church of more than two thousand was no mere adjunct activity. It stood on its own merit, with weekly sessions in summer and winter from half past two to four o'clock every Sunday afternoon. It grew out of the era of the great urban neighborhood Sunday schools such as Bethany Presbyterian, where John Wanamaker, the owner of Philadelphia's first department store, taught a men's class of fifteen hundred every Sunday afternoon.

These bastions of Sunday school orthodoxy were not without their critics and detractors. The Religious Education Association (REA) formed in 1903 was a professional and scholarly attempt to bring academic respectability and elements of modern biblical scholarship into an institution of longstanding devotion to biblical orthodoxy and the conversion of its students. While the REA was the "think tank" of reforming zeal, the International Council of Religious Education was the "hit team" to update the old materials and methods used so long and with such great influence upon American Christendom through the Sunday school. Most of the mainline denominations fell into line with professionally trained experts in curriculum building, child development, graded lessons, and all the newly acquired insights of progressive education. The hidden agenda was, of course, to get rid of the old "Uniform Lessons," the meat and potatoes of Sunday school diet since the National Sunday School Convention of 1872.

Young Ed Clowney learned many things during those early days under his pastor, Dr. Warren R. Ward, a friend of J. Gresham Machen from Princeton days. He learned that even with a formidable phalanx of larger-than-average Sunday schools (there were several in the presbytery), you may carry on a running battle with the liberals and progressives in denominational bureaucracies (such as Westminster Press, located in Philadelphia), but you don't win the war. He learned that students, both elementary and secondary, responded without complaint to the rigor of extensive memory work from the Bible and the *Westminster Shorter Catechism*. He learned that, if you keep at it long enough, you see beneficial results in the next generation. In the thirty-five year pastorate of Dr. Ward, no less than thirty-three young men and women entered the ministry or missionary service, four of them becoming seminary professors. He learned that a four-week vacation Bible school, patterned after the model of Dr. A. L. Latham's school in Chester, Pennsylvania, can be a reality, even in a hot and humid urban area like Philadelphia in the summer. He learned that in eight years of solid biblical and catechetical study, without the snacks and crafts of current

VBS, it is possible to construct a solid foundation of biblical values in young minds. He learned that the staffing of the Sunday school, vacation Bible school, and the various youth groups was a top priority among the pastor's tasks. Church life was not confined to the four walls of the building, but included open-air services in city parks, youth ministries at city missions, and youth area Bible studies on week nights. Above all, he learned faithfulness to biblical standards, commitment to promised tasks, personal devotion, and love for the Lord.

God continued to prepare Dr. Clowney for major contributions to the Sunday school through his life at Wheaton College, where he graduated with an A.B. in philosophy. Here he came in contact with an ecumenical group of students from various denominational and ethnic backgrounds. His extra-curricular energies were spent editing and writing for the college paper and being a leader in Alpha Delta, the campus journalism society, as well as the Excelsior Literary Society, a men's group that met Friday evenings for literary purposes.

Westminster Seminary was the next major input of basic biblical and doctrinal content, which became foundational for his subsequent service to the church at large. During the time of his student pilgrimage there not a single course in Christian education was offered in the curriculum. However, like that of several other graduates without an academic exposure to the subject, his preseminary experience with a first-rate Christian education program in a local church was equivalent to a seminary internship today. Dr. Clowney received his B.D. in 1942 and shortly after was ordained by the New Jersey Presbytery of the Orthodox Presbyterian Church (O.P.C.). He pursued further graduate study, leading to an S.T.M. degree, at Yale Divinity School while he was serving as church extension pastor in Hamden, Connecticut, from 1942 to 1946.

As far as the Sunday school was concerned, it had weathered the rise of the professionals on denominational boards, who were taking over from the laity the leadership that had long been theirs in the Sunday school world. The Wall Street crash in 1929 and the depression of the thirties had slipped the financial rug out from under the "new dealers" on the educational front so that further curricular revisions and organizational plans had to be put aside. In spite of a more closely graded format and more technical training courses led by the academicians, the national Sunday school enrollment figures in the mainline denominations declined far below those of the twenties.

Toward the end of the depression decade the Lord raised up a new force that would not only restore Sunday school enrollment but also give new luster to the whole Christian education movement. The National Association of Evangelicals was formed with Dr. Harold J. Ockenga of Boston as its first president. Evangelicals from all branches of the movement began to muster forces, and by 1946 the National Sunday School Association (NSSA) was formed with the Rev. Clate Risley as executive secretary. A force for infusing new life and power into the Sunday schools of America, it acted in the capacity of coordinator for more than forty denominations with a total constituency of over thirty million evangelical Christians. The NSSA set up three commissions: Research in Christian Education, the Youth Commission, and the Camping Commission.

Not only did the smaller evangelical denominations bring forth new energy to the Sunday school world but several independent publishers of Bible-based curricula moved in to fill the gap for these churches, as well as for many mainliners dissatisfied with the liberal elements in their denominational Sunday school lessons. One mainline junior take-home paper at this time devoted a page to Lincoln's record of social action with not a word about the place of the Bible in his life. On the opposite page, with his picture at the top, was Josef Stalin, who had freed the slaves in Russia from the tyranny of the czar and was leading his nation in the paths of social justice. They were shown as comparable heroes!

Since 1872 the David C. Cook Publishing Company has been printing biblical Sunday school materials; the company originated when the founder ground out weekly mimeograph sheets for Dwight L. Moody's ragtag Sunday school boys in the slums of Chicago. These lessons had made such inroads into the mainline churches that, at least in one major denomination, more churches were using the Cook material than that supplied by their own denominational board. At one point this supplier was sending biblically based curriculum into Sunday schools representing sixty-two different denominations. During the depression decade other independent suppliers, such as Scripture Press, led by Victor and Bernice Cory in Illinois, and Gospel Light, founded by Henrietta Mears in California, rose up to fill the need for Bible-based curricula. All three of these evangelical independents were significant supporters of the newly formed NSSA and helped to launch impressive national Sunday school conventions in major cities all across America. A flurry of postliberal curriculum material was at the same time emanating from the mainliners. The predominating theological complexion was unashamedly and proudly neo-orthodox. While it gave new life to the tired old liberal publications of the thirties, it was still no help to those churches in main-line denominations that wanted evangelical Bible lessons or to the flourishing younger fundamental denominations that would have nothing else.

It was at this time that the Christian Education Committee of the O.P.C. engaged Ed Clowney to write and edit a Great Commission vacation Bible school curriculum to be published for Presbyterian and Reformed congregations that wanted distinctly Reformed materials. The titles of these courses for juvenile learners give an idea of their content. The beginners' lessons were "Jesus, the Children's Savior" and "Our Home on Earth and Our Home in Heaven." For the energetic primary children there were "Stories of Fathers and Sons," "Soldiers for God," and "Stories of Men Who Loved Jesus." The juniors in the elementary grades studied "The Ten Commandments," "The Life of Christ," and "The Old Testament Prophets," while teenagers focused on "The Exodus," "Bible Survey," and "Paul's Missionary Journeys."

Dr. Clowney continued to work for the Committee on Christian Education by writing and editing the Sunday school curriculum, including the teachers' manuals, while pastoring a church in LaGrange, Illinois, until 1950. In May 1949 he was elected to the committee, which gave him a greater opportunity to guide in the educational task of the entire denomination. Today the Great Commission materials are used by 430 congregations in the Presbyterian Church in America and by 144 in the O.P.C., as well as 336 outside of those denominations. Revisions are taking place annually, and distinctively Presbyterian and Reformed, Bible-based curricula are available for training from infancy through adulthood. Clowney laid the foundation.

His move to be interim pastor at Westfield, New Jersey, did not diminish his writing and working for the Christian Education Committee. New units were added to the VBS curriculum until a three-year cycle was available. In comparing it with other Bible-based VBS courses on the market at that time, this writer observed that the Great Commission material had twice as much Bible content as the others. In place of long assembly periods, longer recess periods, and excessively expensive crafts, there was more time spent on Bible stories and memory work in the Great Commission series without slighting related crafts and activities to reinforce the lessons.

By the sixties the cleavage was even more marked between the Sunday schools run by the laity with Bible-based curricula and resulting conversions and those that were using the "character building" and "social consciousness" curricula of the mainliners. The Joint Educational Development was inaugurated in 1960 to produce a "shared approaches" curriculum, which would promise something for everyone according to one's theological taste. This was jointly sponsored by twelve denominations and commonly referred to as the JED curriculum. It offered "Knowing the Word" for those who wanted more Bible, "Interpreting the Word" for those who wanted more response to the Bible, "Living the Word" for those with more community consciousness, and "Doing the Word," emphasizing the social responsibility of God's children. So far, this innovation has not produced the expected revival or hoped for additions to Sunday school enrollment in those denominations, which were losing students by the thousands. In contrast, the Sunday schools of the Assemblies of God, Christian and Missionary Alliance, Conservative Baptist Church, and other orthodox groups are growing in numbers and influence with biblically based materials and committed teachers who want to see persons won to Christ and lives changed by the power of the Holy Spirit.

While real Christian growth depends on a Bible-based curriculum taught by dedicated soul-seeking teachers and leaders, many who have these indispensable assets still seek oblique ways to "bring them in." Fleets of buses, gifts of green stamps, fast food certificates, clutches of helium-filled balloons, awards for the largest family or farthest newcomer—all are being used to achieve the biggest, if not the best. Many attempted innovations have been made by those who lusted for "something new" in the Sunday school. Some changed the name to "church school"; others changed the time to a weekday afternoon, called the "Monday school." But none of these substituted for the unified enthusiasm generated on a Sunday morning with the whole family entering the church together. The children learned stories and verses from God's Word and sang His praises; the youth were diverted from discussion of last night's "blast" to more serious consideration of biblical instruction regarding their problems and conduct. The adults gathered to share and pray together and learn God's directions for "beating the system," using spiritual means rather than carnal.

This unifying of families in a society that has done its best to break them up is the motive behind a recent development, which should bring further excitement and growth to the Sunday school. The intergenerational pattern now used in different forms in several hundred schools across the country is gaining every day in acceptance. Negating the outworn theory that children and youth learn best when divided according to school grades, it is based on the indisputable results of social scientists' research that, for good or for ill, the home and the family furnish the greatest influence in the lives of its members. Thus, there is new interest in learning by modeling. Since this is so, why not conduct Christian education in that format—in family units with combined responsibilities of family and church for the learning process. Curricula are now available for teaching these intergenerational groups of three or four entire families with two or three singles in the same room with the same teacher(s) and the same lessons.

Other changes are being practiced to accommodate the acceleration of our fast-paced society and the growing short terms of commitment. Adult electives do not all have to be twelve weeks long. They can be four, six, or eight, whatever the subject requires or whenever the teacher is available. Teachers are no longer brought in for a "life term" but recruited annually. Sometimes and in some places the entire teaching staff is replaced by summer substitutes and a different type of curriculum is used. Some schools are sandwiched between two services of worship; other churches have two separate schools operated by two different teaching staffs when they have two or three morning worship services. The largest Sunday schools have all the accouterments of modernity, including computerized attendance records and reports, professional class visitation teams, constant enrollment campaigns and a church staff for the sole purpose of stimulating the nurture and growth of the Sunday school. While these remain the elite of the breed, the average size of the Sunday school is still within the 125 to 200 bracket, with volunteer lay workers, a pastor with little or no seminary training in Christian education, and insufficient space for effective teaching. The great national Sunday school conventions have now been superseded by over fifty city- or area-wide conventions around the country. One or two still stand out as the behemoths of the breed, but most operate on an annual constituency of one thousand to two thousand participants. These give the help and encouragement to the loyal laity who, from week to week, study, pray, and sometimes weep over their God-given tasks of being living epistles and teaching the Word with the goal of seeing lives changed by the power of the Holy Spirit.

Although a growing number of young men and couples are staffing the Sunday school classes, adult organizations, and the educational arm of the church, tribute must be paid to many capable and gifted women; they literally kept hundreds of Sunday schools alive during wartime when there was a shortage of male leadership and even in other times when they were the only interested, and often the only capable, persons in a congregation to give the administration and teaching required. If one were to investigate the origins of Bible-centered curriculum, one would also find much of it written by superbly educated and well-trained women who have a practical knowledge of both the Bible and student abilities. The future of the Sunday school, as we look to the year 2000, is as sound as its commitment to training students in obedience to Jesus Christ as Lord.

## THE CHRISTIAN DAY SCHOOL

The Christian education of the five young covenant members of the Clowney family was not confined to one hour a week in church on Sunday or even a two- or three-week vacation Bible school in the summer, but it included a day school experience where all truth is recognized as God's truth. Although the Christian day school was not a part of Dr. Clowney's own background, as conscientious parents of Reformed persuasion he and his wife, Jean, sought this kind of nurture for their growing family. All of the children attended Philmont Christian School in order of their seniority—David, Deborah, Paul, Rebecca, and Anne. Both parents were more active in the school than just being members of the Parent Teacher Fellowship. Jean taught in the music department of Philmont, while her husband served at least two terms as president of the board and as an active member for longer than that. Today the Philmont school occupies three campuses, enrolling over seven hundred students.

Christian day schools have their roots in the Reformation. The idea of the sovereignty of God and His providence over all His creatures and all their actions must necessarily affect all human endeavor in every field of enterprise. The early American schools of the colonies were decisively Christian in that they used Christian texts, were taught by Christian teachers, and had as their object the production of Christian men and women in politics, professions, business, industry, and the ministry. The secularization of American education began in earnest in the early 1800s, grew apace, and is still progressing. Not only did biblical knowledge disappear, but with it also went biblical values. Today our state system of public-supported education is not only secular but aggressively humanistic—and determined to stay that way.

The second decade of the Clowney pilgrimage saw an accelerated rise in the number of Christian schools in the United States and around the world. This developed not merely out of a growing dissatisfaction with state-run secular education with its fallout of lowering SAT scores, rising illiteracy among high school graduates, and violence and vandalism in the urban scene but out of an increased awareness that a biblical theology demanded a biblical praxis. Writers like Charles Silberman, in his *Crisis in the Classroom*, had written that the greatest need in education was to provide teachers with a sense of purpose and a philosophy of education. After a decade of trying to defend the public system, he concluded that the two best descriptive words for the enterprise were "mindless" and "joyless."

Thousands of Christian parents of all denominations, like the Clowneys, derived from Scripture their ideas of parental authority and responsibility for the education and nurture of their children. This idea had been affirmed often since the famous 1925 Supreme Court case in Oregon, giving parents the right to make educational choices for their children.[1] However, few took the initiative to do anything about it and passively accepted what the secular state handed out. Defenders of the public system in the 1960s again and again have accused the organizers of Christian schools of trying to avoid desegregation and busing to build their own elitism by hedging in their own educational domain. But Robert L. Smith of the Council for American Private Education shows that in more than half of the western states the proportion of minorities in private schools is *larger* than that in the public schools. In California alone, 41 percent of students in Catholic schools come from minority groups, while in public schools only 36 percent of students belong to minorities. In New York City, where one-third of all schools are nonpublic, minorities make up 60 percent of the student bodies of these nonpublic schools.

Opposers of the Christian school movement call it reactionary. Its positive characteristic is seen most strongly in the fact that between 1972 and 1977 over three thousand public grade schools closed across the country while Christian schools multiplied at the rate of two a day.

In his *Aims of Education* A. N. Whitehead said, "The essence of education is that it be religious."[2] True education is always religious; it is not a content-centered classical humanism or. an experience-centered permissivism but a God-centered balance, the way the revelation of God in His Word shapes the educational process. In Christian education humanity is seen as God's image, sinners needing redemption by sovereign

1. Pierce v. Society of Sisters, 268 U.S. 510 (U.S. Supreme Court, 1925).
2. Alfred North Whitehead, *The Aims of Education* (New York: Macmillan, 1929), 23.

grace with a mandate to inculturate and bring every area of life under God's dominion. It is an educational process with a starting point and an objective in conformity with the godly ideals and ideas of church and home. In a pluralistic society it allows for patriotic loyalty in place of a bland acceptance of a dreary status quo. It brings a semblance of free-market competition to education (even though some parents have to pay twice to get the education they can use once). It has given a burst of enthusiasm to the founding ideals of the republic. Dwight D. Eisenhower said: "Without God there could be no American form of government, nor an American way of life. Recognition of the Supreme Being is the first—the most basic—expression of Americanism. Thus the Founding Fathers of America saw it, and thus, with God's help, it will continue to be."[3] Christian schools produce citizens who recognize God's authority in the state, who are conscientious and vocally loyal to government, and whose thinking about civic matters is based on a vital, God-centered life-and-world view.

Defenders of the public secular system often complain about a "new" form of education being foisted upon the American public and threatening the tradition of the melting-pot society, which our schools were supposed to promote. They forget that from the early 1600s to about 1835 there were over two hundred years of Christian community-operated, family-governed, Protestant schools in the United States, while from 1835 to the present we have had about 150 years of state-controlled, secular, and bureaucratic education. In our country, then, Christians are simply returning in a philosophic way to a system in which families utilize their God-given rights to educate their children in the nurture and admonition of the Lord. The Christian school movement is founded on absolute truth from God as opposed to the relativism of Dewey and his followers. Christian schools are effectively training more young people over a longer period of time than ever before in our national history. They are willingly financed by parents and benefactors who acknowledge their standards and beliefs with passion and conviction. They are not financed by string-attached government funds, thereby escaping any present threat to their freedom to teach under the dictates of God rather than the opinions of the "experts." Christian schools are generally doing a better job with less money, less materials, and less manpower, thereby discrediting the claims of the humanist schools that they could produce better students if they had bigger budgets.

3. Cal Thomas, "Face the Facts," *Fundamentalist Journal* (April 1983):10.

Christian schools are producing God's quality people. Success of the system is not indicated by higher achievements alone. We would normally expect such results from students who come from Christian homes and have praying parents and praying teachers who love while they teach. Producing obedient servants of Jesus Christ is the bench mark of those who are thus privileged. As Machen expressed it, "It is this profound permeation of every human activity, no matter how secular the world may regard it as being, which is brought about by the Christian school, and the Christian school alone."[4]

Not only in the United States but abroad as well, the movement and acceleration of Christian schools is running apace. In our own land over thirty-four thousand non-public schools are listed in the telephone directories of the fifty states, comprising about 125,000 teachers and over 2,000,000 students. In Korea there are many schools of over 1,000 students, and in Seoul two of more than 5,000. The world's largest, with 12,000 students, is in San Salvador. In poor Haiti, where nearly every evangelical church cradles a Christian school, over 600,000 students are enrolled.[5]

It was in this system with these foundational principles that the Clowney family invested hours, days, weeks, months, and years of administration, teaching, and the bone-wearying task of day-to-day participation with a family of five children.

## THEOLOGICAL EDUCATION

Even with all the intense activity and concentration that a Christian school family requires, Dr. Clowney was now instructing at Westminster Seminary, where he was to spend thirty years of his life in effective service, sixteen of those as president. While serving as interim pastor at Westfield and writing teachers' manuals for the Sunday school series of the Christian Education Committee, he was lecturer in practical theology at Westminster Seminary. His subjects included homiletics, homiletic practice, public worship, and public speaking. Today this would constitute a full teaching load for a full-time professor. While theological education must have basic cognitive information for its foundation, Dr.

4. J. Gresham Machen, "The Necessity of the Christian School," *Annual Report of National Union of Christian Schools* (August 1934):15.

5. Paul Kienel, *Christian School Comment* (Association of Christian Schools International, Whittier, Calif.) 16, no. 3:1.

Clowney realized that effective communication must also be taught. At this time as well, he was writing the third cycle of the vacation Bible school curriculum, a communicant's course, and a handbook for the *Westminster Shorter Catechism.* In the next two years he was to add to his seminary teaching courses in ecclesiology, church polity, poimenics, Christian education, church government, missions, history of preaching, methods in Christian education, Christian faith and healthy personality, local evangelism, homiletical hermeneutics, and ethnic religions. These are more courses than some seminaries offer with a division of practical ministry consisting of three or four members. In 1954 Dr. Clowney was made assistant professor of practical theology, while at the same time, for the Committee on Christian Education, he managed to produce a catalog consisting of twenty-six pages for a mailing of five thousand copies. The catechism handbook was now handed over to Dorothy Partington, who developed it into the popular *Bible Doctrine Workbook* series.

Student involvement in the teaching-learning process was beginning to gain ground at this time in seminary education, and the natural place for it to start would be in the practical theology department. The movement of "adult education" was just beginning to be accepted as a teaching-learning model at the university level, but it would be a long time before conservative seminaries would deviate from the old Princeton style of classes and classroom methods of teacher-centered, transmissive, cognitive learning. Charles I. Cragg of Harvard University wrote: "The assumption that young men of intelligence would be able to function after a series of lectures and readings rests on another decidedly questionable one: namely, that it is possible by a simple process of telling to pass on knowledge in useful form. This is the great delusion of the ages. If the learning process is to be effective, something dynamic must take place in the learner. This becomes more apparent when the learner approaches the inevitable time when he must go into action. No amount of information, whether theory or fact, in itself improves insight and judgment or increases ability to act wisely under conditions of responsibility."[6] The androgogical principles of Malcolm Knowles and others, the idea that adult education is different from pedagogy (the training of children), had been ever so slowly finding their way into the classrooms of graduate schools. But only now and then did they get in

6. Charles I. Cragg, "Because Wisdom Can't Be Told," in *Reshaping Evangelical Higher Education,* ed. Marvin K. Mayers, Lawrence Richards, and Robert Webber (Grand Rapids: Zondervan, 1972), 67.

under the door of the seminary classroom. This turning away from pedagogy and utilizing the proven methods of androgogy would not be an easy or welcome change in the day-to-day operation of seminary courses. Since more than 35 percent of the education in the church involves adults, it becomes increasingly important that the leaders and ministers be trained as adults and in adult methods rather than those of pedagogy. In fact, this is one of the great lags in adult Bible classes, small groups, seminars, etc., in the local church; the "schooling" model is still being used, because we teach as we have been taught. The seminaries are the last to break out of the pedagogical shell into the adult world of androgogy.

Dr. Clowney's pilgrimage at Westminster from lecturer to instructor to assistant professor to associate professor reached its apex when in May 1966 he was elected president and inaugurated in October of that year. This appointment is singular in itself. The trustees did not choose a systematic theologian, an expert in church history, an outstanding Hebrew or Greek scholar, but a person who all his life had been doing practical theology. While the totem pole of academia was suddenly turned upside down, at the foundation of all the "doing" was the systematic theology, the church history, the languages, and particularly the crafts that had been his teaching responsibilities over the years. When Wheaton College awarded Dr. Clowney a Doctor of Divinity degree in August 1966, his commencement address was entitled "The Spirit of Christian Education." His philosophy of Christian education was enunciated when he said, "The spirit of Christian education is the spirit of liberty in creation, in community, in calling."[7] In that address he talked much about the Creator Spirit who is the dynamic of all true Christian education. He spoke of the Spirit's leading into servanthood to fulfill the Great Commission, which is to make disciples. "Every Christian calling is spiritual and every spiritual calling has the focus of the mission of the Spirit. Christian education is vocational in the highest sense. . . . Education for Christ is education in service and for service." These words from that address characterized the administrative philosophy Dr. Clowney carried on at Westminster for fourteen years in the classroom and for sixteen years as its president.

During his administration many changes were taking place in seminaries across the country. Enrollment was decreasing in liberal schools while increasing in theologically conservative ones. As a matter of fact, en-

7. Edmund P. Clowney, "The Spirit of Christian Education" (Commencement Address at Wheaton College, Wheaton, Ill., 12 August 1966).

rollment at Westminster increased from 84 in 1954 to 478 in 1984. Not many students were coming straight from college; now the majority was coming after eight to ten years in business or professions elsewhere. The average age was ten years older than in the previous generation.

This fact again presents a major reason why seminary education should follow androgogical principles of teaching-learning rather than pedagogical. These mature adults now entering seminary after a career of eight to ten years are beginning an educational experience. Learning is for them a means to an end. Children and youth are required to go to school; adults choose to go. The adult takes the initiative to learn and therefore assumes the responsibility for it. He or she makes the decision of what is to be learned, a decision that ought to be shared in the classroom and in the individual course as well. The adult student should be involved in the process to the highest possible extent. After setting one's own goals as to what outcomes are to be expected, the adult should certainly evaluate whether he or she achieved these goals in the process.

A still further plank in the androgogical platform is that this young adult in seminary brings a considerable amount of experience to advanced learning—possibly sixteen years of formal education and many more than that of informal training. This all provides a landing pad on which new learning finds connections. Since adult learning in a Christian context should be cooperative (instead of competitive, as is encouraged by our current grading system), this resource of previous learning should be available to the whole group in that particular learning situation. The teacher becomes a facilitator to point to resources available to meet the goals of the persons in the group. Some previous experiences may have to be unlearned before new experiences can be assimilated. Individuals will learn in their own context, so that regimentation is not the goal but direct personal development of one's own goals and objectives. The mature young adult will learn in meeting his or her own developmental tasks. The student may be single seeking a partner, married to a working spouse, a parent with a family to support, burdened with older parents needing help, keeping one foot in a business while in school, or characterized by a host of other possibilities. Whatever the case may be, the learning will take place in that particular context. In one entering class of seminaries I observed the age spread from twenty-nine to sixty-two. This would include not only the mature young adult but the harried middle-aged adult and the preretirement older adult as well. Each of these has his or her developmental tasks to which to relate.

Another difference between the pedagogical learning of children and youth and the androgogical learning of adults is the immediacy of its application. Children and youth are preparing for eons of time in the future. For the adult in seminary the future is now. There isn't that much time left to get started on whatever the Lord is calling to be done. There are physical needs and resources to be considered, family needs to be met, cultural demands to satisfy, and spiritual aspirations that have arisen to meet God's higher goals. These differences between the way children and adults learn give point to Paul's admonition in 1 Corinthians 14:20 where he says, "In your thinking be adults."

If the evangelical seminary is going to be a useful instrument in preparing men and women for ministry today, it will have to intentionally and aggressively begin a serious transitional phase of adapting the teaching-learning experience to self-directed patterns and a lifelong process of education. The changeover from merely cognitive informational input to the addition and integration of experiential learning will have to be accelerated a great deal if the church is to have an adequate number of persons to serve in the various ministries now required. The seminary as it now exists cannot do the job. Theological Education by Extension holds promise of more adequately meeting the needs of the church of the future than anything now on the drawing boards. The great advantage of training persons on the job has been seen in other countries for a number of years. Right now it is being done in our own country with considerable success and appears to be expanding significantly in the near future. Shifting curriculum around in our present seminary situation or putting in more Christian education and counseling courses will not meet the needs. That is like rearranging the deck chairs on the *Titanic*. As far as the future is concerned in the field of seminary education, a radical departure from traditional models is needed if there is to be survival at all.

A plethora of articles and papers currently exists on the future of seminary education. One of the best publications is *Missions and Theological Education in World Perspective.*[8] Several outstanding chapters suggest the need for substantial changes for conservative seminaries. The best one is Dr. David Kornfield's "Seminary Education Toward Adult Education Alternatives"; another is that of Dr. Ted Ward, "Servants, Leaders and

---

8. Harvie M. Conn and Samuel F. Rowen, eds., *Missions and Theological Education in World Perspective* (Farmington, Ill.: Associates of Urbanus, 1984).

Tyrants." A very interesting model comes out in John Frame's essay, "Proposals for a New North American Model." Younger, more aggressive lay trustees of conservative seminaries will have to take the initiative, using androgogical principles and computer technology to enable seminaries not only to exist into the twenty-first century but to thrive in creative and effective ways. The goal is not changed, but the means must be.

Three decades have seen developing improvements in Sunday schools, Christian day schools, and evangelical theological seminaries. For one person to have so effectively influenced the lasting quality of each of these movements is a privilege as well as an opportunity. It is not an exaggeration to state that our sovereign Lord had his hand on Edmund Clowney from childhood to maturity for such a time as this. History now has one more example of how one individual, under God, can forward kingdom enterprises dedicated to evangelism and nurture.

*L*ove for the Lord will motivate elders to imitate the care of the Good Shepherd. God directed his people as a flock, leading them through the wilderness. So, too, Jesus leads his sheep, going before them. The elder-shepherd is not a cowboy, driving his flock like cattle. He leads them as a shepherd would, walking on ahead. Central to the work of the shepherd (and of Christ the Shepherd) is the feeding of the flock. . . . God protects his flock. His rod and staff defend his own; he carries the lambs in his bosom; the sheep with their young are safe with him.

*The Message of I Peter* (1988)

# Reflections on the History
# of Biblical Counseling

## Jay E. Adams

*F*irst just a word about my friend Ed Clowney. For a number of years we worked together in the practical theology department at Westminster Theological Seminary. I have known him as a man of great integrity and devotion to Christ, coupled, in rare combination, with amiability, humor, creative vision, and absolute loyalty to the Scriptures.

Add one more ingredient: Ed is a genius. This quality perplexed and vexed us. Often we left meetings determined to consider a particular matter only to return next time to find that while we had traveled a mile or two from the point of our last departure, Ed had sped along for what seemed light years ahead of us. His genius pulled us through many difficult circumstances as a seminary. But it was not always easy to live with. It was a bit disconcerting to find that after having thought that we tacked down a rug securely, Ed had pulled it loose and was thinking about a rug of a different color. His mind poured forth oceans of ideas. I often thought this must have been a problem for him as well. But perhaps the most disconcerting fact of all was that when you disagreed with him, he was almost always right.

He acquitted himself well as first president of Westminster Seminary, and under his leadership it grew from one to two viable institutions bearing that name today. My impression is that Ed endured much in that position and would rather have been lecturing, preaching, or speaking at an Inter-Varsity conference. In these areas he not only excelled but was brilliant.

Ed's great passion is to preach Jesus Christ and to teach others to do so. In this he himself sets an unattainable example students sometimes think easy to emulate but rarely, if ever, can. In preaching Christ his personal devotion undergirds all he says, giving his preaching a quality of its own. He has had valuable things to say about biblical theology that go far beyond the technical information he so securely has in hand.

Ed has been my colleague, friend, mentor, and fellow conspirator in practical theology. I can only thank him for allowing me free reign to develop the nouthetic counseling movement virtually unhampered by any restrictions. He took a chance on me, and while I am sure I have not lived up to his expectations, I trust that I have not disappointed him.

In closing these personal comments, let me say, Thanks, Ed. Thanks for so much more than in your humility you would ever let me say to your face. I wish you the Lord's best in the new work to which He has called you and in whatever yet lies ahead in your efforts for Him.

Fortunately, the concerns of this book have to do with the three decades that most closely parallel the teaching career of Edmund P. Clowney. I say "fortunately" because it is precisely those years in which the most activity in the history of pastoral counseling has occurred. On the other hand, given the bulk of material, the limitations of space in the volume do not allow for anything like a thorough discussion and analysis of all that has taken place. That is why I have delimited my concern to "reflections" on the period.

## HISTORICAL ROOTS OF PASTORAL COUNSELING

Prior to the Reformation, not only was counseling done in an unsystematic manner (except in certain specialized areas, largely having to do with the confession of sin and church discipline) but it was not often identified as a distinct ministerial task. That is not to say, of course, that pastors did not counsel. Faithful ministers of the Word met with members of their flocks, dealt with problems, wrote manuals concerning counseling issues such as melancholy (now called depression), and, in general, through letters and personal conference, carried on an embryonic, unsystematic form of counseling. The term *cure of souls* (*seelsorge*, which is still the identifying title in Germany) gradually emerged as the first and most enduring name for that branch of pastoral work that has to do with helping people deal with the problems of life from a pastoral perspective. Yet to this day in Europe, where it is often heard, that term is imprecise and refers to differing responsibilities according to the person using it.

Calvin was the first to distinguish sharply counseling (the term he used was *admonition*, a translation of the biblical Greek word *noutheteo*) as a regular, formal obligation of the pastor. As a result, he "is justly famous for devising and establishing in Reformation Geneva a system of pastoral visitation of daily life that aimed to reconcile every aspect of human affairs with the Sovereign God's revealed law."[1]

Calvin wrote:

> What would happen if each is allowed to do what he pleases? Yet that would happen if to the preaching of doctrine there were not added private admonitions, corrections and other aids of the sort that sustain doctrine and do not let it remain idle. (*Institutes,* 4.12.1)

Where did Calvin get such notions and, more precisely, what was he talking about? His view of counseling (admonition or nouthetic confrontation) came from the Scriptures. He believed such work was an absolute obligation of the minister of the Word. This belief came from his exposition of Paul's sermon to the elders at Ephesus (Acts 20). Commenting on that passage he noted that Paul refused to hold back anything that might be beneficial to the Ephesian church as he preached publicly; further Paul also insisted on these truths becoming a part of life, individually adapting biblical principles "privately, as every man's necessity did require." In his commentary Calvin continues, "Common doctrine will ofttimes wax cold, unless it is holpen [helped] with private admonitions [the word used in the Greek of Acts 20:31 is *noutheteo*]." Indeed, he goes so far as to chide those preachers who "having made one sermon, as if they had done their task, live all the rest of their time idly; as if their voice were shut up within the church walls," calling such behavior "inexcusable." Moreover, he calls this private ministry of the

1. William A. Clebsch and Charles R. Jaekle, eds., *Pastoral Care in Historical Perspective* (New York: Harper Torchbooks, 1967), 224. This book contains perhaps the most useful compilation of writings of various thinkers in the field over the ages. Luther also believed in and practiced pastoral counseling. In his *Babylonian Captivity of the Church* he wrote, "For a bishop who does not preach the gospel or practice the cure of souls—what is he but an idol in the world (I Cor. 8:4), who has nothing but the name and appearance of a bishop?" And, in the same book he spoke of his own counseling: "Now suppose I counseled her to procure a divorce from his husband. . . . Then I would further counsel her. . . ."

Word a "necessary duty" of the pastor. Here, as in so many things, if succeeding generations had only followed up the truly advanced insights of the Reformation, pastoral counseling might well have become long ago a vital factor in the life of the church, systematized and functioning in a biblical way.

The Puritan emphasis upon "cases of conscience" was an adaptation of the Reformation concern for counseling. But it was largely deflected from concern for the life of the believer when it frequently degenerated into a discussion of the problems of salvation with which many Puritans busied themselves. A schematic approach emerged in which they attempted to analyze and program conversion in a manner unknown to Scripture (breaking it down into definable steps or stages). Those Puritans who became involved in the preparationist teachings that grew out of this, like many psychologists at the present time, themselves probably unwittingly created most of the "cases of conscience" with which they subsequently dealt. Such Puritans (not all engaged in the activity) were the first Protestant psychologizers of religion, and the effects of their efforts were not unlike those confusing effects currently seen among evangelicals busy mixing psychological schemes of problem solving with the pure teaching of the Word of God. An in-depth study of this matter in Puritanism might have a salutary effect on the contemporary problem.

In addition to the book cited in footnote 1, three other volumes are especially important to a study of the various periods of pastoral counseling.[2] But while they tell us much about the history of pastoral counseling through the years, when these studies reach the modern period, they fail to take any note whatsoever of the emergence of the counseling movement in the evangelical churches. For that reason I shall try to fill in the gap.

## PASTORAL COUNSELING IN THE LAST THREE DECADES

The modern pastoral counseling movement in America is of recent origin and may be said to have begun with the publication of an article

2. John T. McNeill, A History of the Cure of Souls (New York: Harper and Bros., 1951); E. Brooks Holifield, A History of Pastoral Care in America (Nashville: Abingdon, 1983); H. Richard Niebuhr and Daniel D. Williams, The Ministry in Historical Perspectives, rev. ed. (New York: Harper and Row, 1983). Note that only the last two chapters of Holifield's book deal with the period we are treating in this essay; and, unfortunately, what he had to say pertains entirely to liberal Christianity, totally ignoring counseling in the evangelical church.

entitled "Challenge to Our Seminaries" by Anton Boisen, which appeared in *Christian Work*, (1926). It stressed the need for instructing pastors in pastoral counseling. Boisen set forth the thesis that "in mental disorders we are dealing with a problem which is essentially spiritual." Ten years later in *The Exploration of the Inner World*, Boisen argued (against Freud) that mental disorders arise from a bad conscience occasioned by real guilt rather than inner conflict over "false guilt."

Had the pastoral counseling movement developed along the lines suggested by Boisen, its subsequent history might have been considerably different. Although a liberal in theology (he held the moral influence theory of the atonement), Boisen saw clearly that this area, which increasingly was slipping away from the church into the hands of the psychiatrists, should be retrieved and made the object of theological discussion. He was right in claiming that counseling about life problems was the province of the church. His call, if heeded, might well have returned evangelicals to their Reformation moorings.

But instead of heeding this challenge, the pastoral counseling movement—even among Bible-believing churches—soon was redirected into Freudian channels and early succumbed to the idea that the pastor's major task is to defer and refer to the psychiatrist. Ministers of all theological descriptions bowed to the unending stream of propaganda published and disseminated under the aegis of the mental health movement, which insisted upon the medical model advocated by Freud and others. According to this model, counselees must be considered mentally ill, their problems the result of sickness rather than sin. This medical model removed responsibility from the counselee, who was now considered a victim rather than a violator of his conscience, and necessitated referral by the pastor, who was considered incompetent to counsel persons suffering from difficulties more severe than a psychic scratch.

With no biblical perspective on the matter and no imperative such as that which Calvin saw in Acts 20, ministers in liberal churches easily adapted to the propaganda and even began to spread it. Many of them, wishing to help others, saw psychiatry as the great answer to our needs that would replace the faith they themselves had abandoned. They studied psychology and psychiatry with a vengeance, incorporating its teachings into their preaching and doing counseling based upon its supposed findings. Early in the period we are discussing, Norman Vincent Peale, in conjunction with psychiatrist Smiley Blanton, developed a counseling center. Perhaps the first of its kind, it incorporated the views of those psychologists and psychiatrists with whom they agreed as part and parcel of the ministry of the Marble Collegiate Reformed Church in America. This unnatural wedding was a statement of the supposed compatibility of psychology with Christianity while acknowledging the separate but equal territories of the pastor and the psychotherapist. A number of pastors and prospective ministers (including Carl Rogers) went over completely into psychotherapy, abandoning the church and becoming psychologists or psychiatrists instead.

Such capitulation by liberals is understandable, but how was it that conservative, Bible-believing ministers and institutions alike did much the same thing? Could they not see what Boisen, himself a liberal, saw? There were circumstances that do not excuse, but do explain, the nearly wholesale capitulation of the evangelical church to the mental illness viewpoint—a capitulation that was almost total by the 1950s. These circumstances clouded the picture so that Christian leaders failed to understand what was happening. With far lesser reason, many to this day are still engulfed by that cloud.

During the period when psychiatry and counseling psychology were gaining strong foothold, the church was fighting a battle that took almost all of the time and resources it had. This was the battle for the Bible and the faith being waged against unbelieving science and liberalism in the church. Many evangelical churches and institutions had been taken over by liberals. Consequently, the airwaves, publishing houses, schools, and buildings built by evangelical money were all falling into their hands, and Bible-believing people were fighting for their very existence.

Great blows had been struck at the church. Evolution had all but destroyed belief in the doctrine of creation for many. Adam was considered but a mythical character, and the fall of man was denied. Christ's death had become an embarrassment and a problem. Few wanted to eliminate Him from the picture altogether, but His ministry and death had to be redefined. Higher criticism declared the words of Scripture untrustworthy so that each person, according to the latest "findings of the experts," was free to accept or reject what he or she wished. This made it possible to regard the Jesus of one's own preferences to be the "Jesus of history" behind the gospel records. Such attacks had to be answered.

As a result, many important matters were wrongly relegated to a position of low priority. Much teaching about the Christian home, for instance, was totally abandoned for abstract doctrinal discussions. Moreover, with supplies, personnel, resources, and strategic positions all in the enemy's hands, evangelicals found themselves faced with the mammoth task of rebuilding a church that had crumbled. Critics jeered, Samaritans sniped, vast amounts of energy were consumed in battles for the faith, and even capitulating Christians (of which the woods were full) heaped discouragement upon the faithful few who undertook the task. The infighting had been exhausting; the opposition, bold and ruthless. But in spite of everything, today a new church built out of the ruins of the old is perhaps better and stronger than the one that fell. Yet, much was lost during the fighting and rebuilding—particularly in the field of counseling. Rather than developing as a definite task of the minister of the Word in true Reformation fashion, counseling was handed over lock, stock, and barrel to the psychotherapists.

As a result of its understandable but faulty prioritizing during the last three decades, the church easily succumbed to influences that destroy the home and make a mockery of the relationship between Christ and His church that Christian marriage is to reflect. Similarly, the church's place in the broader counseling enterprise, so clearly enjoined by Scripture, as Calvin pointed out, was simply overlooked. Overburdened pastors, often with relief, accepted the propaganda that assured them they were not competent to handle "mental illness." Under such circumstances it was easy to ignore added burdens. It was easy to refer.

At the same time there grew up within the Bible-believing church a self-appointed caste of practitioners who encouraged "mental health" ideas of pastor incompetence and counseling as the province of psychology. All over the evangelical map, counselors trained in psychology rather than theology began to call themselves "Christian counselors" and hung out their shingles in competition with the church. Such people also found their way into seminaries, where they convinced a large proportion of the ministers now serving evangelical churches that the Reformation emphasis upon counseling as the task of the minister was wrong.

Chief among those evangelicals who have taught eclectic views are Donald Tweedie, Vernon Grounds, Clyde and Bruce Narramore, Gary Collins, Tim LaHaye, James Dobson, Frank Minirth, Paul Meier, and Larry Crabb.

An exception is Henry Brandt, whose counseling and writing go back to a period almost as early as Clyde Narramore's (their work began in the '40s and became well known in the '50s). Trained as a psychologist, Brandt soon realized that, in practice, his training was both ineffective and unbiblical. Discarding this training, he made an intensive study of the Bible to discover what God said about human problems and His solutions to them. When he began to apply Scripture in counseling, God blessed his efforts and he became an effective counselor, helping many. Brandt has published a number of books and booklets for laymen, but he has never systematically set forth his counseling principles and practices in writing for the benefit of counselors.

Founder of a counseling institution located in Rosemead, California, speaker on an ongoing radio broadcast, and author of a steady stream of books and pamphlets, Clyde Narramore has done more to establish eclectic counseling among evangelicals over the years than anyone else. His radio program, for many years called "Psychology for Living," sets the theme: in serious difficulty, one turns to psychology—or more to the point, to psychologists—for answers. Following a trichotomistic view, Narramore parceled out the body to the physician, the spirit to the preacher, and the soul to the psychologist. In his books one finds a strange mixture of fundamentalist belief side-by-side with Freudianism or some equally objectionable viewpoint. In his work there is little systematization of thought and an amazing tolerance of inconsistency.

Donald Tweedie early advocated an adaptation of Victor Frankl's logotherapy approach, in which the pursuit of meaning (*logos*) is the foundation for all counseling. His views during the '50s and '60s were rather influential but have not been widely accepted, and his influence has waned.

Vernon Grounds, Christian statesman and former president of the Conservative Baptist Seminary of Denver, was another prime mover during the '50s and '60s. His eclectic, Freudian-based writing and lecturing early seduced a large portion of evangelicalism into such thinking. His approach is best summarized in his article on "Christian counseling" in *Baker's Dictionary of Practical Theology*.

Clyde Narramore, Brandt, Tweedie, and Grounds were the principal spokesmen for counseling in the evangelical church during the '50s and '60s. Since Brandt's contributions were largely as a practitioner and not as a theoretician, his views failed to spread, while the efforts of the others yielded so large a return that they set the course of mainstream evangelical counseling down to the present time. Since the '60s others, such as Collins, Bruce Narramore, LaHaye, Dobson, Minirth, Meier, and Crabb, have gained prominence.

## FROM THE '60S TO THE PRESENT

Gary Collins of Trinity Evangelical Divinity School, Deerfield, Illinois, unlike most of those mentioned above, mainly writes and teaches about, rather than practices, counseling. His writings as much as those of any other individual represent the continuation of the movement begun by Clyde Narramore in the '40s.

Bruce Narramore began the Rosemead Graduate School of counseling under the auspices of his uncle Clyde Narramore in conjunction with the Rosemead Foundation. This school later joined forces with Biola University of La Mirada, California. The school's orientation is avowedly eclectic, emphasizing a more scholarly, academic approach. Together with John Carter, Bruce Narramore founded *The Journal of Psychology and Theology,* which reflects their position.

Tim LaHaye, while pastor of the Scott Memorial Baptist Church and president of Christian Heritage College in El Cajon, California, through several books, popularized a modern adaptation of the old Greek temperament theory of the four humors set forth by Hippocrates and, more recently, by O. Hallesby. LaHaye originally acknowledged the pagan origin of the system, which he expanded to include combinations of the original four temperaments, but later "found" the big four temperaments set forth in an obscure passage in Proverbs.

Much stronger in their impact at this time are James Dobson, Frank Minirth, and Paul Meier, who through their books and radio shows regularly promote psychological views throughout the church.

Larry Crabb, writer, lecturer, and teacher, has expressed a desire to divorce himself from the mainstream evangelical-eclectic movement in favor of establishing a cognitively based "biblical counseling" system. So far he has failed in the attempt, because he continues to tie tightly the foundational principles and practices of this approach to Adler, Freud, Ellis, and Maslow. As in the case of others mentioned above, there is little exegesis. The Bible is used to support positions arrived at apart from Scripture, and biblical material is molded to fit views and practices the Bible itself does not teach.

All in all, one can say that in the evangelical church theology and exegesis have had little to do with the positions and viewpoints adopted and taught. This is largely because most of the principal promoters of the eclectic view have little or no training in theology and exegesis, but much training in psychology. The (faulty) assumption seems to be that a Christian who is a counselor thereby automatically becomes a Christian counselor, regardless of the beliefs and practices inherent in his or her counseling.

The problem is that while these practitioners themselves for the most part are Christians, their counseling is anything but. It was, and largely still is, true of such counseling that the counselor's Christian orientation only served to confuse and delude the Christian counselee, who uncritically imbibed pagan thought and advice, thinking it was Christian. For instance, Vernon Grounds quotes Quentin Hyder as saying:

> The actual psychotherapy I had given him was not significantly different from that which he would have gotten from a non-Christian psychiatrist. However, there were three factors which were different. First, he felt more easily able to express his problems in biblical terms and knew that I understood what he was trying to say. Second, being reassured that I was myself a committed believer, he was much more readily able to accept my explanations and respond to my suggestions. Third, I was able to read a few relevant passages of Scripture to him and we often concluded our sessions with prayer together.[3]

Significantly, Grounds comments, "It is this stance and spirit that most Christian counselors appear to identify with today."[4] Notice that Hyder considers neither the Scriptures nor prayer to be part of the psychotherapy as such; such matters seem to constitute little more than trimmings, which create more acceptable conditions for psychotherapy. By these Christian accouterments the counselee was led to let down his or her guard, being assured of the Christian commitment of the counselor and, accordingly, as Hyder notes, found it easier to accept the non-Christian explanations and suggestions given. Such "Christian counseling," in which Christianity is only in the packaging, Grounds describes as typical.

## THE RISE OF NOUTHETIC COUNSELING

Only during the 1960s has a belated challenge to such counseling been issued. At Westminster Theological Seminary, under the impetus of Cornelius Van Til's insistence that every movement be examined presuppositionally according to the Scriptures, basic questions were asked concerning the foundations of the pastoral counseling movement and the teaching and practices forming an integral part of it. Plainly, it was shown that the Reformers and Boisen were right: counseling deals with

---

3. Vernon C. Grounds, "Christian Counseling: Who Has the Answer?" *Eternity* 26, no. 1 (January 1975): 19.
4. Ibid.

changes in people having to do with their values, behavior, beliefs, and attitudes. The task involves changing and improving relationships— to God and our fellow human beings, as Christ explained when He declared that the Bible could be summed up in the two commands to love God and our neighbor. Therefore, the school began to treat counseling as a theological matter. Man could not be viewed as he was by Freud, Rogers, Skinner, or other unbelieving theorists and still be helped. Their teachings and practices are not neutral; they were shown to be nothing more or less than bad theology. The counselor's anthropology must be biblical. Moreover, sin, guilt, and the fruit of the Spirit are all theological matters that bear directly on counseling and, therefore, could no longer be ignored. The place of the Scriptures not as trapping but as integral to the process of change itself and, in this regard, the work of the Holy Spirit in and through the ministry of the Word were emphasized.

Thus, a new movement, sometimes known as nouthetic counseling, grew up, calling for a return to counseling by pastors (as a life calling) and Christians in general (in more informal ways) within the church according to biblical principles. The necessity for a systematic approach to biblical counseling, built upon biblical principles and presuppositions, was acknowledged, and such a system has been under development since 1965.

Books in a steady stream have been published during the last fifteen years setting forth various aspects of the system; courses and audio and video tapes have been produced. The movement has spread across America and Europe, where three national associations of biblical counselors have been set up for purposes of certifying and networking, and nouthetic counseling works have been translated into thirteen different languages. Centers for counseling and training counselors have been started in churches, and conferences are held regularly in various parts of the world to teach the biblical viewpoint. Seminaries and Bible colleges in increasing numbers now provide training in biblical counseling. Doctoral work in biblical counseling can be taken at Westminster Theological Seminary. Principal among the various influences that have formed and molded this movement is the Christian Counseling and Educational Foundation located in Philadelphia, Allentown (Pa.), Princeton, and San Diego.

Briefly stated, nouthetic counseling sees the work of pastoral counseling as part of the work of sanctification, a ministry of Christ's church in which one Christian helps another to put off old, sinful life patterns and to put on the new biblical responses required by God in their place (cf. Eph. 4:22–24). This work of ministry must be done in the power of the Holy Spirit, who in His way honors His Word as it is ministered faithfully. Unbelievers are not counseled but precounseled (i.e., evangelized). Such verses as Galations 6:1, Colossians 3:16, and Romans 15:14 depict counseling as the obligation of believers in general, whereas Colossians 1:28, Acts 20:20, 31, and similar passages describe nouthetic confrontation as the work of the pastor in particular. Thus, there are such activities as informal and formal counseling. The latter, the work of the eldership of the church, involves the official and authoritative ministry of the Word.

The word *noutheteo*, singled out by the Reformers as relating to the counseling of individuals from the Word about their lifestyles, has no adequate English equivalent. It embraces three ideas: (1) the *confrontation* of a Christian whose attitudes, beliefs, or behavior must be (2) *changed* by appropriate verbal means (3) out of *concern* for him. Rather than a harsh sort of confrontation (as some wrongly suppose), this third element is especially prominent in the Word, and such concern never loses the familial connotations firmly adhering to it.

All nouthetic counselors worthy of the name strive to help people to solve life's problems God's way from His Word. Moreover, they see Paul's words in 2 Timothy 3:16–17 as a description of the process of change that God effects by means of His Word ministered in the power of the Spirit by a "man of God" (minister). They will find that the Scriptures "fully equip him" for every task of changing people to which God has called. They see no need, therefore, to "integrate" biblical counseling with those counseling systems which present alternative patterns of living that compete with God's. When God has said that peace, joy, and other blessings are the fruit of the Spirit, biblical counselors cannot conceive of these qualities of life as equally the fruit of Rogerianism, Freudianism, or other schools of thought. They plainly recognize that integration is impossible since the Bible teaches God does not bless His competition. Moreover, they point out that for over nineteen hundred years prior to the birth of Freud, the church was not without the resources to help its members make those changes which please God!

Of course, the findings of legitimate (noncounseling) psychology may indeed prove useful, though never necessary, to biblical counseling. But competitive *counseling systems* and *methods* designed to attain the goals of those systems can never be integrated with biblical teaching.

Moreover, since the outset, nouthetic counselors have worked hand in hand with physicians, provided they stay in their own province (treating the body and not trying to tell their patients how to relate to grandmother). Nouthetic counselors have advocated the establishment of a significant relationship with Christian physicians so that they may work in tandem.

According to 2 Timothy 3:16, biblical counseling proceeds from scriptural *teaching* as the standard of faith and practice, to a *conviction* of failure to conform to that standard, moving next to *correction* of sinful ways by confession and forgiveness, and finally to the putting on of God's new ways through *disciplined training in righteousness.* That is not to deny that in the simpler forms of counseling the mere impartation of information or the encouragement of the counselee is all that is needed. However, in 2 Timothy 2, Paul looks at the process of *nouthesia* (nouthetic counseling, or admonition and correction) and not at these simpler tasks, which are performed under such biblical labels as *encouragement* and *teaching.*

Biblical counseling demands counselor involvement, taking counselees seriously about their sin, prayerful use of the Bible, discipline, teaching, the fellowship of the flock, and the worship of the church—all in the context of the activity of the Holy Spirit, who is the Paraclete. In its broadest sense, *paraclete* means "assistant, one who comes alongside to help." The help may be of any form, but when specified as of a particular type in the New Testament, it is "comfort," "counsel," or "advocacy." As the Paraclete in counseling, the Holy Spirit is *the* counselor. But He is also the one who convicts and comforts.

The biblical counseling movement has made an impact on evangelical churches and drawn the line between the two sorts of counseling approaches now in use. According to Collins, who is no advocate of nouthetic counseling, "few others have been courageous or creative enough to attempt . . . to build a counseling system which begins with and is built on Scripture." He admits that "there is no alternative system which is as clearly biblical."[5] There is a great difference between (a) building a system from biblical presuppositions and principles and then developing practices out of these, that are consistent with them at every point, and (b) stuffing biblical material into the pigeonholes of a system

5. Gary Collins, *How to Be a People Helper* (Santa Ana, Calif.: Vision House, 1976), 169.

built from nonbiblical materials. There is a great deal of the latter. Collins has the insight to see that apart from the nouthetic system, the former does not exist.

The nouthetic approach is yet incomplete. Unlike many other systems narrowed to the thinking and experience of men, nouthetic counseling is based upon the limitless Word of God. It is an open system; but unlike other open systems, it is open only to God's Word. Thus, as new biblical insights are developed, they may be added without upsetting those discovered previously. Such is not the case with other open systems, where opinions of men are replaced by more opinions, none of which is complete. In saying this, nouthetic counselors do not deny that they may have wrongly or incompletely understood the Scriptures at various points or claim that everything in the system as now construed is complete or perfectly reliable. It would be sheer arrogance and stupidity to say any such thing. But they do affirm that insofar as they have accurately understood and construed the Scriptures in relationship to human problems, their system can be amplified by true biblical insights without significant alteration. Because nouthetic counselors work with the inerrant Word of God, whenever they are correct, they build unshakably for the future.

This leads to one more factor—the effect of the counseling system upon the counselor. Whatever a counselor spends his or her efforts, time, and energy thinking about and using day by day will affect that person as well as those counseled. Indeed, such principles and insights probably affect the counselor far more than any individual counselee, since the counselor is exposed to them for a much longer period of time and in a more intensive and thorough way. Thinking regularly about people and their problems as Adler, Ellis, and Maslow do, and building a worldview and lifestyle around their pagan presuppositions is dangerous, not to say discouraging. But the biblical counselor, confined to the limits of the Scriptures alone, spending time in the exegesis and application of the Bible to the problems of people, is continually blessed by the work itself.

The extent to which the infiltration of pagan ideas into evangelical circles has now progressed can be seen in two recent publications: William Kirk Kilpatrick's *Psychological Seduction* (Nashville: Nelson, 1983) and Dave Hunt and T. A. McMahon's *The Seduction of Christianity* (Eugene, Ore.: Harvest House, 1985). Furthermore, in a recently published book, *The Biblical View of Self-Esteem, Self-Love and Self-Image* (Eugene, Ore.: Harvest House, 1986), I have demonstrated how the evangelical church has become filled with Adler-Maslow teachings that threaten to revolutionize the church of tomorrow if not successfully met and overthrown.

The period under study has been an exciting one, but full of confusion, experimentation, and (as two of the aforementioned volumes note) seduction. Yet, out of it all God has raised up, for the first time since the Reformation, a viable biblical counseling movement in which biblical principles of counseling have not only been put into practice but also codified in the form of a working system. As Collins indicates, this is unique. Practical theology has been the stepchild of the seminaries and the church. But it is a Johnny-come-lately that has come!

While most other aspects of Christian ministry, doctrinal and ecclesiastical, have for many years been determined by creedal affirmations and denials, those pertaining to preaching and the work of counseling have not. Today, the church is becoming aware of the great dangers of the infiltration of its ranks by those who advocate psychological doctrines—many of which are every bit as bizarre as those held by the most extreme cults. My hope is that the church in the near future will not only cleanse itself of such teachings but will for all time set down its abhorrence of, and warning against, them in doctrinal statements about the work of the minister and that such statements will eventually issue in generally agreed-upon creedal forms. This is the lesson about pastoral counseling the church should learn from the last three decades. If it fails to do so, who knows how many decades of disaster may lie ahead?

The sovereign, triumphant grace by which Christ draws men to himself puts its demands upon us who are trophies of that grace. Christ's total power in heaven and earth assures his disciples of the success of their mission but it also binds them to that mission. "Go ye therefore . . ." What the disciples are to teach as they go to the nations are the meaning and purposes of that very kingdom in which Jesus is exalted.

"The Missionary Flame of Reformed Theology" (1976)

# 12

# *Evangelism*

## *Roger S. Greenway*

The past three decades have witnessed a virtual explosion of interest in Christian evangelism among Reformed and evangelical Christians in North America. More books and articles have been published, courses taught, and sermons preached on the subject of evangelism in this period than ever before. Besides, there has been a proliferation of mission agencies and evangelism programs, all of which make appeals and receive support from the Christian community. Judging on the basis of the amount of words and ideas being communicated and the number of activities performed in the area of evangelism, we can safely conclude that we have progressed tremendously in the past thirty years in our understanding of and commitment to the Christian work called *evangelism.*

As part of my research in preparation for writing this chapter, I conducted a survey among twenty-five leaders in evangelism within the Reformed and Presbyterian community of North America. I asked each of them four questions:

1. How would you compare your thinking today about evangelism with your thinking on the subject thirty (or so) years ago?

2. What authors and books have done most to give shape and substance to your thinking on evangelism in the last three decades?

3. In your opinion, what today distinguishes Reformed evangelism from the emphases found in Catholic, liberationist, fundamentalist, or Mennonite traditions?

4. Where do you think Reformed evangelism should direct its major attention in the next decade? What would you like to see happen in Reformed missiology and practice?

My purpose in conducting the survey was to find out from these leaders where they perceived missiology to be today, at least as far as North
Americans are concerned. Is it still possible and legitimate to speak of
Reformed evangelism as an approach distinguishable from that of other
Christians? Have we changed substantially from where we were three
decades ago, both in theory and practice? Who is shaping Reformed
thinking and activity in evangelism and missions today? Where are we
probably heading in the years ahead?

The answers I received, in my opinion, were very interesting, and in
the first section of this chapter I report and reflect on the best of them.
We have obviously moved a long way since the time when writers on
the subject labored hard to convince the churches of their duty to reach
out to the unsaved with the gospel and tended to define Reformed evangelism largely in terms of the sovereignty of God and the familiar "five
points" of Calvinism.[1] The old emphases have not been abandoned and
they continue to provide the underlying presuppositions. But Reformed
leaders obviously have moved ahead in their understanding of Scripture,
and they are applying its teaching and implications in wider and more
challenging ways.[2]

## HOW PERSPECTIVES ON EVANGELISM HAVE GROWN

Everyone agrees that there has been tremendous progress in our perception of the nature and scope of evangelism as revealed in the Word
of God and applied to human conditions. Unquestionably, most of us
have made a quantum leap in this area.

Progress has taken various forms. On the one hand, we have learned
important lessons concerning the demand of Scripture for consistent
Christian living and the witness of the home, family, and neighborly
relationships in conjunction with the verbalization of the gospel mes-

1. E.g., see the standard work on Reformed evangelism of a generation ago, *Reformed
Evangelism: A Manual on Principles and Methods of Evangelization*, compiled by the Grand
Rapids Board of Evangelism of the Christian Reformed Churches (Grand Rapids: Baker,
1948). Note particularly "The Fundamental Principles of Reformed Evangelism" by Martin Monsma (pp. 13–40) and "The Reformed Approach" by D. H. Walters (pp. 71–89).
2. The following leaders in Reformed evangelism contributed valuable insights for the
preparation of this chapter: Paul Bergsma, Harvie M. Conn, Edmund P. Clowney, Dirk
Hart, Paul Long, Paul McKaughan, C. John Miller, Timothy Monsma, Sidney Rooy, Eugene Rubingh, Addison Soltau, Paul Schrotenboer, and Dick L. Van Halsema.

sage. The importance of demonstrating compassion for those who suffer and are in need and of diaconal ministries in and through the church receives universal acknowledgment. At the same time, there is a deepening awareness of the importance of preaching, of kerygmatic evangelism apart from which the good news of salvation is not heard and believed.

## THE MISSIONARY SPIRIT AND DEMONIC OPPRESSION

The Holy Spirit as the prime mover and enabler of evangelism has received increased attention in the past thirty years. The Spirit according to Scripture is the missionary Spirit whose impulses continue to drive the church to recognize its responsibility before God to evangelize the world. Connected to this is a growing recognition of the gifts of the Spirit as "equippings" God provides so that the church can be and do all that it requires. Fresh emphasis on the person and work of the Holy Spirit is seen as the prerequisite for inner renewal and outward ministry.

Related to this, there is surfacing a clearer recognition of the demonic in the lives of individuals and of society. The biblical teaching about Satan and demons is receiving fresh attention. Satan is seen to be very real. He is no longer regarded as belonging largely to some far-off orbit, but his presence and influence are recognized in the world's affairs and in opposition to divine truth and righteousness. In short, there is a fresh emphasis on the immediacy of God and the Holy Spirit and of Satan and his cohorts. The one brings comfort and strength to God's servants, and the other is the archenemy of evangelism.

## RENEWED EMPHASIS ON THE CHURCH

The organized church has received increased attention in connection with evangelism. The church growth school of missiology, particularly the writings of Donald A. McGavran, Peter Wagner, and Win Arn, have had an immense impact. They call attention to the fact that a great deal of time, money, and effort are spent on types of evangelism that do not lead to measurable church growth. But the kind of evangelism the Scriptures describe, say McGavran and his associates, is evangelism that plants, multiplies, and develops vital churches. This renewed emphasis on the organized church stiffly challenges those forms of evangelism which tend to ignore the question of the church. It also appears threatening to some conservatives who feel it places too much emphasis on numbers and outward success, running the risk of doctrinal compromise.

While there appears to be an enhanced concern for planting and developing churches, denominational loyalty and distinctive identity seem to be declining. Those who are most deeply involved in evangelism are primarily concerned to see converts gathered into living congregations where they can be nourished in the faith and share Christian fellowship. Whether or not the congregations are affiliated with the evangelist's own denomination is not as important as it once was. In the face of growing secularism and the force of non-Christian religions, the highest priority is given to personal faith in Christ, fellowship with His body, and consistent life and service rather than denominational loyalty and growth. Maybe the history of the church in China during the past thirty years is forcing us to rethink certain things.

## HOLISTIC EVANGELISM

Also increasing is the realization that biblical evangelism requires a holistic approach. Holistic evangelism proclaims the whole Christ, by word and deed, as Savior and Lord, Redeemer and King. It is first of all the church that needs to hear this, for from this message springs the missionary mandate in all its breadth and challenge. Holistic evangelism avoids the mistake of dividing human needs into neat compartments, such as spiritual, material, and psychological, but proclaims the indivisibility of the human person in the redemptive purpose of God. Consequently, word and deed in holistic evangelism are kept closely together. The proclamation of the divine Word is central in the mission of the church, but it is never disassociated from ministry in Christ's name to the multiple hurts and needs of the human family.

Connected to the holistic approach is an increased awareness of the fact that in the work of evangelism we must be sensitive to the sociocultural, political, and economic dimensions of the world as they affect the task before us. The people we address and seek to serve in the gospel are all wrapped up in their own contexts. To ignore these contexts can spell disaster for communication. For that reason, studies on crosscultural communication, counseling, and cultural anthropology are important for Christian evangelists, and courses in these areas have in recent years been added to the curricula of seminaries and missionary training schools.

## EVANGELIZING AN URBAN WORLD

The past quarter century has witnessed tremendous demographic changes throughout the world, and this is reflected in a growing appreciation for the fact that the future of world evangelization lies in cities. In the decade of the eighties alone, one billion people will make the trek from rural life to city living. When most church and mission leaders received their formal education, there was little awareness of the demographic changes that were occurring, and mission work was thought of in terms of jungles, mountains, and South Sea islands. That has changed, however, and a whole new era has been ushered in which focuses on urban evangelism, both in North America and Europe, and in most other parts of the world.

Alongside this, there is a new awareness that despite the fact that nearly 33 percent of the people on this planet call themselves Christians, approximately two billion people have never heard, and probably will never hear, the gospel through the ordinary channels now available within their countries. They are separated from gospel proclamation by visible and invisible barriers, including language, culture, religion, class or racial segregation, or by barriers created by the very situations in which they live. For that reason they are called "unreached" people, because they are not hearing the gospel and no churches are planted and growing among them. While it is true that there are Christians in all 223 countries of the world, unreached people groups of various size exist almost everywhere. This fact has become a major preoccupation for all who are concerned about evangelism.

Added to the number classified as unreached are millions of people who may describe themselves as Christians, but by their lack of regular attendance at worship, their lifestyle, and religious beliefs, they show themselves needing to be evangelized in almost the same way as those without any association at all with Christianity. In this category are more than 200 million people in Latin America and large portions of the population in North America and Europe. Depending on one's definition, they may be regarded as "reached" or "unreached," but by anyone's standard they need to hear the fresh call of the gospel. This is yet another reality that has been driven home forcefully to evangelists and missiologists in the past three decades. It has prompted large, new evangelistic efforts in Europe and Latin America, as well as continual efforts to present Christ and His word to Canada and the United States.

## AUTHORS AND BOOKS OF GREATEST INFLUENCE

Our survey indicates that today's leaders in missions and evangelism, at least in Reformed and Presbyterian circles, are drawing fresh ideas from a fairly wide spectrum.

Among the Reformed missiologists most often mentioned are J. H. Bavinck, whose *An Introduction to the Science of Missions* (1960) and *The Church Between the Temple and the Mosque* (1966) head the book list. Also mentioned frequently are Harvie M. Conn's *Evangelism: Doing Justice and Preaching Grace* (1982); Harry R. Boer, *Pentecost and Missions* (1961); Johannes Blauw, *The Missionary Nature of the Church* (1962); Richard R. De Ridder's *Discipling the Nations* (1975); Roger Greenway's *Apostles to the City* (1978); R. B. Kuiper's *God-Centered Evangelism* (1961); Carl Kromminga's *Bringing God's News to Neighbors* (1975), and J. Verkuyl's *Contemporary Missiology* (1978). On the practical side, D. James Kennedy's *Evangelism Explosion* (1970) and C. John Miller's *Evangelism and Your Church* (1980) are often mentioned. Somewhat surprising is the fact that several leaders in Reformed mission circles did not mention a single Reformed writer in their list of authors whose books had done the most to give shape and substance to their thinking on evangelism in the past three decades.

Among the other writers on missions and evangelism, the works of Donald A. McGavran top the list, particularly his book *Understanding Church Growth* (1970). Following McGavran, Peter Wagner's titles, too numerous to mention, are apparently being read. Eugene Nida's *Message and Mission* (1960) has made quite an impact, as well as Robert Coleman's *The Master Plan of Evangelism* (1963). The symposium edited by Ralph Winter and Steven Hawthorne, *Perspectives on the World Christian Movement* (1981) is providing almost everyone with guidance and inspiration. Charles Kraft's books are mentioned by several, particularly *Christianity in Cultures* (1979). J. Russell Hale's *Who Are the Unchurched?* has made some do hard thinking, as have George Sweazey's two books, *The Church as Evangelist* (1978) and *Effective Evangelism* (1953). Older, out-of-print books by John R. Mott, Hendrik Kraemer, and Samuel Zwemer continue to be read by those fortunate enough to have copies. Symposiums and anthologies do not seem to get much attention; with the exception of the one large volume compiled by Winter and Hawthorne, none is mentioned. We might expect titles such as *Reaching the Unreached* (1984) and *Discipling the City* (1979) to have received at least some notice.

Perhaps too soon to have made the circle are the recent titles *Eternal Word and Changing Worlds: Theology, Anthropology and Mission in Trialogue* (1984) by Harvie M. Conn and *Unleashing the Church* (1982) by Frank R. Tillapaugh. There is no end to worthwhile books on evangelism, church growth, and world mission today. The problem most of us face is finding time to read and digest them all—and the energy to put their good ideas into practice.

## COMPARING THEOLOGICAL TRADITIONS IN RESPECT TO EVANGELISM

Generally speaking, what today distinguishes Reformed evangelism from the emphases found in Catholic, liberationist, fundamentalist, or Mennonite traditions? That is a hard question, for there are a dozen exceptions to almost everything one may say. Traditional Catholicism is rigid, tradition-bound, sacramentarian, closed, and defensive vis-a-vis Protestantism. But that too has changed in a number of ways, and the charismatic movement has opened up new avenues in Catholicism where the gospel is proclaimed and new life appears. In the face of secular humanism and atheistic communism, evangelical Protestants sometimes find themselves more closely aligned with Catholics than any of us would have dreamed possible a few decades ago.

Liberation theology is still fairly new, and no fixed "tradition" has yet developed. There are as many liberation theologies as there are writers addressing social and political issues using the hermeneutic methods characteristic of the movement. Generally speaking, in liberation theology the biblical idea of salvation is equated with the process of liberation from oppression and injustice. Joining with the oppressed against the oppressors is said to be what evangelization is all about—solidarity with God and His people against injustice and exploitation. Old biblical and theological terms such as *conversion* and *new birth* are given radically different meanings. All communion with God is predicated on opting for the poor and exploited classes, identifying with their plight, sharing their pain, and finding among them the kingdom of God. It is obvious that liberation theology's agenda for evangelism is very different from that of traditional Christianity.

Fundamentalism in most cases avoids those issues the liberationists put highest on their agenda. "Otherworldly" is the term usually associated with fundamentalism. Fundamentalism tends to be superficial in its dealing with intercultural missionary questions. It avoids the tough issue of contextualization and fails to produce an integrated kind of discipleship that does justice to the comprehensive demands of Christ's lordship. The prevalence in many places of fundamentalist-style evangelism leaves Christians vulnerable to the liberationists' charge that in evangelism we gloss over the evils of structural injustice and oppression while focusing our attention on those lesser evils which are more the results than the causes of society's problems. It is over the issue of the poor and the questions of how Christians should respond to the enormous injustices in society that fundamentalists reveal the characteristics that most set them apart.

Mennonite tradition, like the others, is hard to capsulize. Some are conservative to the point of being isolationists, while others have outstanding records of word-and-deed evangelism around the world. Mennonites today are at the forefront of many of the best movements in world evangelization.

## A CONVERGENCE OF POSITIONS ON EVANGELISM

Among most of its leading North American proponents, Reformed evangelism maintains its commitment to historic theological positions regarding God's sovereignty, the total depravity of sinners, the doctrines of grace, Christ's lordship, the church and sacraments, and the work of the Holy Spirit in regeneration and the Christian life. At the same time it recognizes that a kind of convergence among Reformed and non-Reformed thinkers is occurring on a number of issues. This is reflected in the books making the greatest impact in mission circles, the speakers and writers at mission gatherings, and the remarkable similarities found in positions taken on various issues. Clearly, the kind of integral biblical thinking that leads toward a world-and-life view centering in Jesus Christ, His saviorhood, and lordship, and requiring that everything in life be subject to the scrutiny and authority of His Word is no longer restricted to a few isolated groups.

Many definitions of Reformed evangelism are offered, and none of them says it all. But essential to any definition is this thought: Reformed evangelism calls for whole-person-conversion on the one hand and whole-person-involvement-in-society on the other. The aim of evangelism is the establishment of God's complete *shalom,* perfect peace and reconciliation through Jesus Christ, involving restored relationships vertically between God and redeemed sinners and horizontally between people. *Shalom* means well-being as a whole, body and soul, time and eternity. Between Pentecost and Christ's second coming, the church is both the chief agency of evangelism and the showcase of restored relationships, of righteousness and peace with God. For that reason evangelism must aim also at the incorporation of all who are reconciled into the visible body of Christ, the church.

A large portion of the Christian world seems to be moving toward such a position on evangelism as described above, and this makes the present era very exciting. At this point it may seem to be better to refrain from speaking about *Reformed evangelism* and move to the term *biblical evangelism,* which would broaden the platform for discussion and make non-Reformed people who share a common loyalty to Scripture feel more comfortable.

## IS REFORMED EVANGELISM POSSIBLE?

There have been interesting discussions on this point recently in Christian Reformed circles, with the argument made that elements in Reformed tradition not demanded by God's Word may, because of our style of clinging to them, become hindrances to Reformed evangelism. Inviting people into the body of Christ, it is argued, should be an open invitation with only biblical boundaries. In an article entitled "Is Reformed Evangelism Possible?" Hendrik Hart proposes a broader approach.

> A more evangelistic Reformed tradition may need a more open Reformed tradition. To be all things to all people is a good biblical style of evangelism. This would require us to distinguish truly biblical requirements in the Reformed heritage from traditions that may be changed in order to be more hospitable. Our broad kingdom perspective and the continual call for reformation characterize what is beautifully biblical in being Reformed. Our vision has wide horizons. A discussion to evaluate unnecessary barriers of traditions in the light of God's Word would be "Reformed" in its best

sense. I have in mind an open discussion within the bonds of an agreed submission to God's Word. This could promote the development of a genuinely Reformed style of evangelism.[3]

There is no essential conflict, as I see it, between Hart's proposal and the strong defense of Reformed distinctives in evangelism as set forth in Morton H. Smith's booklet, *Reformed Evangelism*.[4] Smith is arguing for a message that springs from Scripture and the Reformed and Presbyterian confessions and for methods consistent with those standards. Insofar as some have slid away from those doctrines, Smith's book deserves reexamination and continued reflection. But nothing in Hart's analysis would necessarily circumvent the standards. Hart is addressing a different issue, traditions-beyond-Scripture, those traditions which the church invariably accumulates in the process of time and which easily become hindrances to evangelism. Honest submission to the authority of God's Word involves a continued process of reform and renewal, and this is bound to cut at times at hallowed traditions that are not biblically required.

I think we must be alert to a negative factor that has often characterized conservative thinking on evangelism—an attitude of over-cautiousness that goes so far as to become nonresult oriented. It holds in serious doubt every thought and methodology not born and raised within its own tradition and context, and it assumes that success in evangelism is sure proof of doctrinal compromise. Such narrow traditionalism is a deadly hindrance to progress. With all that is happening in the area of evangelism, this is a good time to reaffirm our belief that the Holy Spirit is still guiding the church to know and do the truth. And until Christ returns no chapter on evangelism will be the final word.

## AGENDA FOR TOMORROW: WHERE SHOULD WE BE GOING IN EVANGELISM?

The mission leaders whom I surveyed presented an amazing list of responses to the question, Where should we be going in evangelism in the next decade?

3. Hendrik Hart, "Is Reformed Evangelism Possible?" *The Banner* 121, no. 17 (5 May 1986): 8–10.
4. Morton H. Smith, *Reformed Evangelism* (Clinton, Miss.: Multi-Communication Ministries, 1975).

- Reformed evangelism should incorporate into its thinking many of the insights of the church growth movement and adapt them to its own theological perspective.
- We must emphasize church renewal, including the renewal of systematic theology in the church and the seminaries; for without renewal, interest in evangelism is bound to dwindle.
- Evangelism must wrestle with the problems of the city, the issues of poverty, injustice, and what it means to be a disciple of Christ and His church in an urban and suffering world.
- Mission leaders would do well to take seriously the five issues raised by Gerald H. Anderson in his address at the International Association for Missions Studies at Harare in 1985: the threat of nuclear war, authoritarian regimes, evangelism and social justice, and the loss of conviction on the part of many major churches. If leaders in evangelism don't deal with these issues, who will? What do we have to say to a world on the verge of self-destruction?
- All evangelism in the next ten years should be aimed at unreached peoples in the large cities and wherever they are found.
- Third World leadership must be recognized, encouraged, and listened to seriously, because there lies the future of world evangelization.
- New methodologies must be sought, particularly in the developing countries, that will reach the masses, the poor, and the working classes. Our Western strategies have not done much to penetrate the masses in most countries.
- The Holy Spirit has to be given more attention in our theory of evangelism, our prayer for evangelism, and in evangelistic methodology. We must emphasize reliance on the Holy Spirit and be open to power encounters. In theology and in practice we still are deficient in our understanding of what it means to be freed by the Spirit from Satan's bondage; this liberty is the key to the abundant life and fruitful evangelism.
- Christ possesses culture, and the implications of that truth must be explored and applied. It is subject to elenctic judgment, but not all negative; above all it is a transformational truth.
- Muslims and international students must receive a great deal of attention.
- In overseas work, we must stop being ashamed of being Reformed and of emphasizing Reformed distinctives. Because we are so oriented to servanthood, we've been reluctant to come out strongly for what we believe in particular areas. Because we are so strongly committed to the autonomy of the national church, we have held back from imposing what might be viewed as our own

culturally conditioned theology. We have just taught the Bible, assuming that eventually the national churches would become Reformed in doctrine and practice. But the result is that other groups, not as modest, strongly influence the fledgling churches by literature, radio, and aggressive propaganda, molding them in all sorts of un-Reformed ways. They are always putting us on the defensive, and we end up trying to straighten out the confusion caused by outsiders. We who are engaged in evangelism must be bold to establish churches consciously and confessionally Reformed before we can expect them to carry on the task of "ever reforming."

• The doctrine of the kingdom of God must be studied in relation to missions and evangelism. Here we have a concept big enough for a world of great cities and of horrendous human problems.

• We need to learn from the Pentecostals what power and enthusiasm really are and to pass this on to our church members. Reformed people need to become less reflective and more active.

• Both the rethinking and rewriting of Reformed theology in light of the church's mission and the context of contemporary crises in church and society are needed. This would include fresh exegesis of Scripture, a historical perspective on theological development, plus humility and openness to the worldwide operations of God's Spirit and love.

Each one of the above suggestions has merit, and I hope each receives attention in the years ahead. There are two related areas I want to comment on.

## KINGDOM EVANGELISM PROCLAIMS THE LORD WHOM WE SERVE

The first point has to do with what Edmund P. Clowney calls "kingdom evangelism." In a chapter by that title, Clowney reminds us that to deepen our understanding of evangelism requires us to deepen our understanding of the gospel, the evangel.[5] Particularly in Reformed theology, the importance of the kingdom message has received considerable attention. Enriched in recent years by the writings of Geerhardus Vos and Herman Ridderbos, Reformed scholars have underscored the fact that in

5. Edmund P. Clowney, "Kingdom Evangelism," in *Pastor-Evangelist*, ed. Roger S. Greenway (Phillipsburg, N.J.: Presbyterian and Reformed, 1986).

evangelism we proclaim the kingdom. We announce to the world who the King is, and we ask people whom they want to serve.

The following quotation from the South African missiologist David J. Bosch highlights how far-reaching the implications of the kingdom can be for evangelism. Speaking appreciatively of Andrew Kirk's position on the kingdom, Bosch says:

> If it is indeed the gospel of the *kingdom,* and if the kingdom is "the detailed expression of God's caring of the whole of life," then we are concerned *in our evangelism* with a God whose "nature as king is to intervene to *satisfy every basic need of man, to uphold justice and equity,* to *watch over the circumstances of strangers, widows and orphans* and to *liberate the poor and prisoners.*" The kingdom is, after all, "the complete reversal of all the consequences of man's evil: death, disease, plagues, enmity, famine, hate, greed, exploitation, idolatry, oppression, violence, culpable ignorance, prejudice and empty religious practices" (Kirk, 1980:131–32). Evangelism is communicating the gospel of the kingdom, and the goal of God's kingly rule is nothing less than "the complete reclamation and reconstitution of the created universe."[6]

The implications are as exciting as they are awesome. Nothing lies outside the kingly claims of Jesus Christ. When He is lifted up and His saving power announced and unleashed, earth's mighty ones have to tremble and satanic strongholds know they will fall. God's work of reclamation has indeed begun. Evangelism is its means.

## KINGDOM EVANGELISM IN A WORLD OF CITIES

When we take this kingdom perspective and apply it to cities, what do we find?

First of all, the challenges are the greatest in the history of mankind. In the next decade or two we will see the proliferation of hundreds of megacities (populations of one to four million), many supercities (under ten million), and a surprising number of supergiant cities (ten million or more inhabitants). The problems facing these cities will be as enormous as their size.

6. David J. Bosch, "Evangelism," *Mission Focus* 9, no. 4 (December 1981): 65–74. His quotations are from Andrew J. Kirk, "The Kingdom, the Church and a Distressed World," *Churchman* 94, no. 2 (1980): 126–44.

Second, the task of evangelism itself becomes exceedingly complex. This world of cities has already taken on a more complex image as far as the ethnic, linguistic, and religious composition of each city is concerned. The fact is that the world's cities have begun a radically new era of multiracial, multiethnic, multilingual, and multireligious pluralism unprecedented in the entire history of the world. To illustrate this, Paris is now 14 percent Arab and Berber; the English cathedral city of Leicester is 20 percent Gujarati, 10 percent Pakistani, and 5 percent West Indian; Japanese sects including Soka Gakkai and Tenrikyo are found in African cities; Chinese Buddhists are living in staunchly Catholic Dublin; and Los Angeles is expected to become 60 percent Hispanic by A.D. 2000.

What does it mean to proclaim the saviorhood and lordship of Christ in cities of such size and complexity, cities whose populations represent all the *ethne* of the human race and all the religions people profess? Christian evangelism's greatest challenges lie immediately before us, and they will be found in cities.

David B. Barrett, the distinguished mission researcher from England, has given his analysis of this challenge in a recent book, *World-Class Cities and World Evangelization*. To clarify the task and provide some means by which to measure past and present accomplishments, Barrett makes a basic distinction between the following terms: (a) the biblical idea of *discipling* (Matt. 28:19), which he interprets to imply evangelism-that-results-in-churches, and *evangelizing* (Mark 16:15), which he takes to mean proclaiming or spreading the Good News, evangelism-whether-or-not-it-results-in-churches so long as people are made aware of the Christian message; and (b) *evangelization*, a word derived semantically from *evangelism* but much broader connotatively than *church planting*. Evangelization includes the entire outreach of the Christian world beyond the boundaries of the established churches; it stands for the total outreach, producing an adequate awareness of the gospel, and the entire influence of Christ and the Christian faith on the world.[7] I feel that Barrett is coming close to describing kingdom evangelism in seminal form.

Barrett calls for an evangelism strategy that will give adequate attention to both the major components of obedience to the Great Commission: evangelizing and disciple-making, spreading the gospel and multiplying churches. The unfinished task, he says, demands "megamin-

7. David B. Barrett, *World-Class Cities and World Evangelization* (Birmingham: New Hope, 1986), 9, 10, 23, 24.

istries." Such mission work will call for a clear understanding on the part of the evangelizers of what it means for a city to have "adequate access" to the gospel and for special strategies of outreach that target the unevangelized areas, peoples, and cities, with a view to giving them adequate exposure to the Christian message. Megaministries, Barrett adds, requires megamissionaries, persons specifically trained, set aside, and commissioned for full-time work in such ministries. [8]

The size of the populations, cities, and problems facing workers in evangelism in the years ahead exceeds anyone's ability to comprehend, much less to prescribe solutions. Within the lifetime of children already born, 80 percent of the world's population will be urban dwellers, and 80 percent of these will live in the Third World. World travel and communication will be fast and available to many, with great potential for the propagation of both good and evil, of the kingdom of God and the kingdom of Satan.

Gone forever are the days when neat distinctions could be made between local "evangelism," which was directed toward straying Christians and delinquent covenant youth, and "missions," which meant crossing the oceans to reach animists and worshipers of foreign gods. The whole world now stands at our doorstep, and the issues once raised in regard to cultures and faiths in distant places now demand attention right at home. The church is surrounded by a vast mission field everywhere it stands.

In view of this, no responsible Christian can regard evangelism lightly and as the concern alone of a small group of specialists. Christian schools and seminaries in every land must regard themselves as war colleges for the King's army. These are exciting days to be alive and serving the Lord Jesus. And who can forecast what challenges lie ahead for those who will have the privilege of engaging in evangelism into the twenty-first century!

8. Ibid., 28.

$T$ he gospel is the message of God's redeeming love in sending his own Son into the world. Those who understand that love will be driven to share it. They will not only rejoice to sit down with other redeemed sinners in heaven's feast: they will seek other sinners in Christ's name to call them home. As Christ was sent, so he sends them, and the dynamic of mission is the heart of the love of God. Again we see that missions is not an addendum. Rather, it is evidence that the church understands the gospel. The love that fulfills the law, as Jesus taught in the parable of the Good Samaritan, is the love of compassion, love modeled on the love of God.

"The Biblical Theology of the Church" (1987)

# 13

# The Evolution of Evangelical Mission Theology

## Arthur F. Glasser

One of the unhappy consequences of the squabbles among "separated" Presbyterians in their efforts to be "faithful" members of "faithful" churches in the decade immediately prior to World War II was the polarization within even these circles and a tendency to mutual caricaturization.

Because of this unfortunate polarization, I only gradually became aware of Edmund P. Clowney and his unique contribution to the service of the church. I guess it was the report of his excellent course on Reformed theology and the Christian mission that first made me desire to meet him. Then came the rumor that he had studied under Professor Hans J. Hoekendijk at Union Theological Seminary, New York, and as a result was one of the few evangelicals abreast of the theological debate within the World Council of Churches (WCC) on the church and its mission. This heightened my desire to meet one who apparently didn't fit any of the caricatures impressed on me in seminary. Well, in time we did meet, and I found that the half had not been told me.

During the years following graduation from seminary, I became increasingly involved in the amorphous, growing reality that defies precise definition—evangelicalism. Max A. C. Warren (1962) of the Church Missionary Society came closest to an adequate definition when he spoke of "a particular balance" of a cluster of ingredients: (1) unquestioned submission to the authority and trustworthiness of Holy Scriptures as the Word of God; (2) the essentiality of the atonement of Christ if one is to be made fit for the presence and fellowship of God; (3) an existential saving encounter with the Holy Spirit; and (4) a concern for the proper use of the sacraments. Most evangelicals would add the obligation to evangelize non-Christians and do so on a worldwide basis. Evangelicals subscribe to no unifying creed; neither do they have any particular church order or precise theological orientation (whether Reformed, Lutheran, or Arminian).

With the passage of time, however, I became restless within this broad context and began to hunger anew for my rootage in the Reformation, particularly Presbyterianism. After all, its precise definitions and rigorous consistencies have an abiding appeal. At the same time my missionary involvement—communicating the gospel cross-culturally and its demand that I be receptor oriented in my preaching—made me pause before giving unquestioned recommitment to the Reformed faith. How universal were the tenets of a theology shaped by the Westminster divines of the seventeenth century?

It was during this period of inner turmoil—those troubled 1960s—that I met Edmund Clowney. We were separately, though concurrently, involved in teaching the Bible to informal groups in private homes in suburban Philadelphia. He was a professor of theology and I a mission administrator. When I began to take the full measure of this man of God, I envied his theological coherence—his deep and confident commitment to the Reformed faith—despite his wide exposure to the theological diversity within the Christian movement, particularly within the growing World Council of Churches.

During those days I was hard pressed to provide the sort of intellectual leadership my mission colleagues had the right to expect of me. The old colonial era of missions had abruptly ended with World War II. But many of its patterns of mission work lingered on and held back, rather than furthered, the work of the Holy Spirit in the churches. All of us in Asia were caught up in a confusing transitional period amid rapid social change, and too many churches seemed unwilling to move forward into the bracing and demanding uplands of a still largely undefined future. They simply could not cope with the diversity surrounding them. What particularly seemed bothersome was "the ecumenical problem"—what to do with those people who professed Jesus Christ, calling Him Lord, yet with whom evangelicals seriously disagreed? Should such people be consigned to outer darkness, or ignored, or what?

About this time I began to meet Professor Clowney in his writings on the church, its ministry, and what he called "the politics of the kingdom of God." There was a maturity to his understanding of the theological currents of the day. Soon I found myself eager to walk in his steps. This meant obtaining a leave of absence, going to Union Theological Seminary in New York, and exposing myself to the secularized and socialized missiology of Hoekendijk and his call to the church to get lost in the world. One just had to face honestly the turmoil of the 1960s and grapple with the serious questions the churches were asking as they confronted the anguish of the postwar world. Did not our Reformed tradition exhort us to ponder "the embodiment of the divine thought" not only in the phenomena of nature but also in "the general constitution of the human mind, and the facts of experience or history"?[1] The Scriptures cannot be studied in a vacuum. Nor should one be content with merely mastering the answers that the Bible gave to those who addressed questions to it in earlier centuries. Like Professor Clowney, I found it both a stimulating and appalling experience. It is one thing to take the full measure of the issues the world is pressing on the church in our day. But it is quite another matter to do so in a seminary context where it was widely argued that the great postulates of the historic Christian faith were no longer relevant. The Bible was said to be too time-conditioned and too flawed to provide adequate answers.

I emerged from this experience, which included close exposure to a black church in Harlem committed to the Reformed faith, convinced that the evangelical approach to the worldwide mission of the church needed considerable overhauling, even though its movement worldwide was growing by leaps and bounds. Sheer growth in members, important though this is, is not necessarily an essential sign of the presence of God in the midst of His people. On the other hand, a church that is not growing should engage in serious self-examination to inquire why this is so. All things being equal, churches are expected to grow.

Ed Clowney senses the appropriateness of reviewing the past. On one occasion he gave a brilliant address on the contribution of Dr. Cornelius Van Til to the ongoing theological debate within Reformed circles. In it he made a memorable "aside" that was nothing less than a review of the vicissitudes of millennial thought during recent centuries. This evidence of his wide-ranging competence was, and is, impressive. So then, I would like to share the record of evangelical reflection on the mission of the church since World War II, believing that he would regard such a review as salutary. Alas that Professor Clowney is not undertaking this task himself. We'd all be much better informed.

1. Louis Berkhof, *A Manual of Reformed Doctrine* (Grand Rapids: Eerdmans, 1933), 26, 27.

In this chapter I will seek to trace the postwar evolution of evangelical perspectives on the theology of the Christian mission. "Evolution" of evangelical theology? I've already intimated the complexity involved in defining the word *evangelical*. And when have evangelicals ever admitted that their theologizing reflects "evolution" (that very bad word)? Peter Beyerhaus discerns at least six different kinds of evangelicals.[2] But even he would be hard put to judge where the midstream of their theologizing exists, whether among the separatistic dispensationalists, or the traditional orthodox, or what he terms the neo-evangelicals.

Hence, while I beg your indulgence, I will attempt to indicate successively the shifts in thought and emphasis that seem (to me, at least) to have characterized the evangelical debate on mission theology since 1947, when, according to Max Warren, those who met at Whitby, Canada, for the first postwar gathering of the International Missionary Council (IMC) were quite hopeful "that the most testing days of the Christian mission, at least in our generation, lay behind us."[3]

## AFFIRMING THE GREAT COMMISSION
### (PLUS "FOLLOW UP")

The only significant student gatherings on the mission of the church in the first decade after World War II were triennially convened at the University of Illinois (Urbana) by the InterVarsity Christian Fellowship (IVCF). In the late 1940s and early 1950s their mission theology had but one burning theme: the Great Commission as defined in Matthew 28:18–20. Indeed, for a long time thereafter Urbana speakers continued to identify the Christian mission with the commission Christ Himself received and modeled for the church (John 20:21 with Luke 4:18–19). Even though the worldwide political scene drastically changed during this period, none of the leaders of these gatherings saw fit to broaden this biblical focus. Colonial empires were breaking down, communists were triumphing in East Asia, and the Korean War was trying the West, but no matter. All this contributed to Max Warren's solemn summarization of the best thought of many IMC-related mission leaders at the IMC gathering in Willingen, 1951: "We know with complete certainty

2. David J. Bosch, *Witness to the World* (Atlanta: John Knox, 1980), 30.
3. M. A. C. Warren, "The Christian Mission and the Cross," in *Missions Under the Cross*, ed., Norman Goodall (London: Edinburgh House, 1953), 40.

that the most testing days of the Christian mission in our generation lie just ahead."[4]

However, evangelicals remained unmoved. Although they sought to heed Jesus' word that they not be alarmed by deteriorating world conditions (Matt. 24:6), they failed to respond to His injunction to be creatively responsive to "the signs of the times" (Luke 12:56). They still largely perceived the missionary task in terms of evangelism. So far as they were concerned, the world had yet to be fully evangelized. Their personal, experiential encounter with Jesus Christ and their commitment to His lordship gave them but one desire: to share Him with all those making up their generation. They regarded this desire as God-implanted. Had not the Lord commanded that they "make disciples of all nations"? I can still recall how the Bible addresses at those IVCF student gatherings were largely taken with personal discipleship, not with anything approximating a comprehensive mission theology. And as for the revolutionary changes upsetting the status quo of the world, the typical comment was "So what? Hasn't the world always been in a mess?" Then would follow the clincher: "What Christ has commanded we must obey! No disciple of His can be indifferent to the missionary mandate!"

Nothing seemed to catch the imagination so much as the individualism reflected in Edward M. Bounds's memorable salvo: "Men are God's method. The church is looking for better methods; God is looking for better men."[5] Obviously, an elaborate theology of mission was not felt necessary. What counted was personal discipleship—the sort of devotion to Christ that made one a faithful witness to His gospel, particularly in those places where He was largely unknown.

This emphasis on discipleship was greatly strengthened and popularized by the Navigators. During the war many American service personnel came under the spell of Dawson Trotman and this movement with its vivid focus on "follow up." Billy Graham began using its personnel and methods in his postwar crusades to establish new converts in the faith. Soon it became increasingly apparent to even Graham's most relentless critics that, through the Navigators, permanent results were indeed being achieved in his evangelistic crusades. However, this rigorous Navigator additive only confirmed to many the truncated and highly individualistic nature of evangelical Christianity. Something else was needed.

4. Ibid.
5. Edward M. Bounds, *Power Through Prayer* (Grand Rapids: Baker, 1963), 5.

## DISCOVERING CHURCH GROWTH
## (PLUS THE ANTHROPOLOGISTS)

My own missionary experience as a member of a large multinational and interdenominational society (the China Inland Mission from 1945 to 1951) followed by four intense years teaching a growing number of missionary volunteers (Columbia Bible College from 1952 to 1955) was largely shaped by the emphases just described. Our preoccupation was with ardor rather than method, and the texts we used stressed Christology and soteriology more than ecclesiology. In China my evangelistic activity was initially among the Chinese and only marginally related to the deliberate outreach of local congregations. I had never heard anyone discuss the need for devising plans to increase the membership growth of existing congregations or to multiply the number of congregations in populous areas. Such strategizing would have been regarded as unspiritual. Our concern was to focus the energies of Christians on their own spiritual development so that they might be more vigorous and authentic in their witness to Christ. We did not critically evaluate our work. We tended to tolerate the sort of ministry that was indifferent to measurable results. After all, God alone gave what increase we enjoyed (1 Cor. 3:6).

Later, I found myself in the midst of a tribal people movement in which the emergence of new congregations was a significant reality. But no one suggested that we analyze the reasons for this phenomenon. All were agreed that it too was totally of God. God worked in answer to prayer, and the best missionary method we could follow was to give ourselves to the work of prayer.

Donald A. McGavran raised serious questions about this in 1955 with his epochal work, *The Bridges of God*. Slowly at first, but increasingly, evangelicals began to talk of "church growth." This stimulated the beginnings of evangelical theologizing. True, many had read Roland Allen, Johannes H. Bavinck, Robert H. Glover, Adoniram J. Gordon, and others, but it was McGavran who pressed us to "think church." He argued that the key to worldwide evangelization was the multiplication of churches, not the multiplication of evangelists. Yet, even though he eventually made a massive impact on evangelicals worldwide, as late as 1976 his perspectives were still struggling for acceptance. In that year *Christian Missions in Biblical Perspective* appeared, written by a highly respected evangelical, J. Herbert Kane. It soon became a widely used text in evangelical schools worldwide. Strangely, Kane devoted only ten pages to the role of the church, and even these pages are devoid of any specific discussion of its essence, structure, or functions in terms of mission outreach.

Those who began to listen to McGavran, however, started to concentrate on the growth and multiplication of local congregations. This was God's will, a chief and irreplaceable element in mission praxis. At first the focus was almost entirely methodological, but eventually this stimulated the beginnings of reflection on the church as a reality in its own right. The new thesis was: when any particular church ceases to grow in an area where other churches are growing, something fundamental has been lost in its very essence as the people of God in the midst of the nations. Increasingly, the Great Commission came into focus. Converts must not only be "taught to observe" all that Jesus had commanded. They must be baptized—and this pointed in the direction of their entrance into the life, worship, witness, and service of the local congregation.

Evangelicals both within and outside WCC-oriented churches flocked to hear McGavran. The church growth movement began to take shape, and multitudes began to struggle with the new terminology: *homogeneous units, Class II leaders, people movements, transfer growth, resistance-receptivity axis, redemption and life, harvest theology,* etc. The list keeps growing.

A new stream of input came into the midst of this church growth ferment through a journal subsidized by the American Bible Society, *Practical Anthropology.* Growing numbers of evangelical anthropologists began using it as a vehicle for promoting cultural sensitivity and exposing the mono-cultural stance and cultural blindness of the missionary movement. Charles Kraft, Eugene Nida, Kenneth Pike, William Reyburn, William Smalley, and many others slowly awakened missionaries to the possibility of receiving help from the social sciences in their efforts to understand the nature of culture, the startling principles of cross-cultural communication, the cruciality of leadership selection and training, the possibilities latent in revitalization movements, and the like. Looking back, one can confidently affirm that in the three decades since McGavran's *Bridges of God* appeared, evangelicals have been increasingly using these insights to probe every aspect of the church—its decay as well as its growth.

However, the church growth movement soon became vulnerable to criticism because of its professed "fierce pragmatism" (whatever produces more church members must be ordained by God). Some highly respected evangelicals began to question the recourse to pragmatism in laying the foundations to so fundamental a theme as the cross-cultural communication of the Christian faith. They argued against divorcing means from ends, for this can all too easily get one into serious trouble. True, they thereby exposed themselves to many ardent "McGavran-ites" who defended consecrated pragmatism by appealing to the apostle Paul's claim, "I have become all things to all men so that by all possible means I might save some" (1 Cor. 9:22). Actually, this theoretical debate was overshadowed by a larger, more serious interchange that arose over McGavran's emphasis on "homogeneous units." He had written: "Peoples became Christians faster when the least change of race or color is involved" (1955), and "Men like to become Christians without crossing racial, linguistic, or class barriers."[6] Critics reasoned that an overemphasis on this pragmatism could easily result in the deliberate establishment of "segregated churches." Was this not in sharpest contrast to the multicultural character of apostolic congregations (Acts 13:1–3)? Many thought so. True, much of the criticism did not come from field missionaries, who felt that the homogeneous unit emphasis was a good evangelistic ploy. Why should they not work through family connections and produce many small house congregations in much the same way the apostle Paul did? Field missionaries readily granted that these beginnings of emerging homogeneous congregations by no means represented the ultimate ideal for Christian interrelatedness. In their growing maturation all congregations should move toward the heterogeneous unity for which Christ prayed (John 17:20–23). But few critics were mollified.

So then, over the years serious scholars have increasingly asked tough questions, exposed evident flaws, and in other ways contributed significantly to a better understanding of the primary issues inherent to the church growth perspective on the Christian mission. One cannot but call attention to the two masterful sets of essays that Wilbert R. Shenk compiled from the writings of David J. Bosch, Harvie Conn, Orlando Costas, Albert Krass, Rene Padilla, Robert Ramseyer, John H. Yoder, and many others.

Indeed, since 1955 a significant literature has been produced on church growth as well as mission anthropology. Some missionaries even began to tackle the task of developing an integrated mission theology that was consistently biblical. Johannes Blauw gave unexpected impetus to this with his 1962 survey of the biblical theology of mission, *The Missionary Nature of the Church*. But it wasn't until much later, with the

6. Donald A. McGavran, *Understanding Church Growth* (Grand Rapids: Eerdmans, 1980), 223.

appearance of Charles Van Engen's massive study, *The Growth of the True Church* (1981), that evangelical professors of missiology became convinced that the central postulate of the church growth movement was absolutely true: the yearning of the church to grow and its actual growth are tests whereby its faithfulness to God is truly demonstrated. The writings of such evangelicals as Peter Beyerhaus, Harry Boer, David Bosch, Orlando Costas, Richard De Ridder, John Stott, and Johannes Verkuyl helped along the way.

## CHALLENGED BY ECUMENISTS (AND BY THE CHINA WITHDRAWAL)

At the beginning of the 1960s evangelicals were only marginally interested in the ecumenical movement. They were uniformly distressed over the dwindling commitment of its member churches to evangelism as biblically defined and to mission as traditionally understood. In contrast, they heartily endorsed Lesslie Newbigin's great line, "In the places where there are no Christians, there should be Christians."[7] As a result, evangelicals were less than curious as to what was emanating from Geneva. Furthermore, the radicalization of the WCC in the 1960s, paralleled by signs of the growing vigor of evangelicals, seemed to indicate to many that evangelicals were on the right track. But were they taking the full measure of what was happening in the world? I was personally baffled over the lack of interest of many in the sober lessons I thought God was seeking to teach evangelicals, arising from their encounter with communism in China and subsequent expulsion from that country (1949–53). Not a few ex-China missionaries in mainline churches seemed to care, although I became rather impatient with those who wrote off the whole China mission as a massive failure—nothing less than the judgment of God. But what provoked me more was their suggestion that the whole missionary movement come to an end, the sooner the better.

In the midst of the growing radicalization of the 1960s, evangelicals began to receive new insights, and these came from surprising quarters. Pope John XXIII and Vatican II shattered the long-held stereotype that Rome was incapable of change and that it would never encourage its members to study the Scriptures. On the other hand, the radicalization

7. Lesslie Newbigin, "Mission and Missions," *Christianity Today* 4, no. 22 (1 August 1960): 23.

of the WCC (Geneva 1966, Uppsala 1968, Bangkok 1973) confirmed the darkest thoughts evangelicals had of its future.

Yet not entirely. Although the probability is that evangelical publications are largely only read by their own constituencies, many evangelical leaders were increasingly reading the literature of their opposite numbers in the WCC. They know something about such writers as Wilhelm Andersen, Gerald Anderson, José Miguez Bonino, Ferdinand Hahn, Johannes Hoekendijk, Kosuke Koyama, Paul Loeffler, Hans Margull, Paul Minear, Stephen Neill, Lesslie Newbigin, Eugene Smith, Bengt Sundkler, John Taylor, Georg Vicedom, and Max Warren. And they are somewhat knowledgeable of such Roman Catholics as Gustavo Gutiérrez, Hans Küng, Aylward Shorter, Thomas Stransky, and others. These lists are merely representative. But it was through these authors that some evangelicals began to sit up and take notice, for not a few of the authors wrote with genuine evangelical concern. Furthermore, they often showed themselves remarkably at home in the Scriptures, and the passages they used were often those that evangelicals tended to overlook. A case in point: when the WCC's Commission on World Mission and Evangelism delegates met in Melbourne (1980) under the rubric "Your Kingdom Come," they used passages from the synoptic Gospels. When evangelicals met a few weeks later in Pattaya, Thailand, their motif was "How Shall They Hear?" and their focus was on the Pauline Epistles. This dichotomy and polarization seemed strange: Gospels vs. Epistles! Was it theologically necessary? Actually, during the 1960s some evangelicals were beginning to wonder whether or not they were really listening to the total witness of Scripture. Had they been preoccupied with an "evangelical canon" within the larger corpus of revealed truth?

## STRUGGLING FOR A HOLISTIC GOSPEL (AND LISTENING TO THE MENNONITES)

When I joined the faculty at Fuller Theological Seminary in the fall of 1969, I found the atmosphere anything but tranquil. War in Vietnam, the civil rights movement, and the confrontational tactics of the students all challenged evangelical preoccupation with evangelism, discipleship training, and church growth. Among those who welcomed me was one who conveyed the "official" suggestion that I do what I could to "get some Bible into that church growth movement!" Although administrative duties largely absorbed my time, I felt I should review all that evangelicals had written on mission and social responsibility. This largely drew a blank. The evangelical "right" was fearful of publishing anything that might be interpreted as even a whiff of the long-discredited "social gospel." An innocuous article I wrote in *Freedom Now* (January 1969), stressing the importance of evangelical social concern, was dismissed as "favorable toward this deadly menace" by a prominent Baptist leader.

Understandably, the evangelical consensus had long since dismissed the old liberal theology and ethic as bankrupt. Its political and social philosophy had not stood the test of time. It had proved itself both naïve and impractical. Its mission theory reduced the gospel to a social message and the church to a mere social institution. This resulted from its nonrecognition of the Fall and its unwillingness to accept the absolute necessity either of Christ's vicarious atonement or of the new birth—if one is to see, much less enter, the kingdom of God.[8]

The only consistent expression of relevant evangelical insight into social responsibility seemed to be coming from the public witness and hard-working pens in the Mennonite tradition. They alone seemed to have escaped an encapsulated, individualistic evangelicalism as well as the reduction of the gospel to a vapid "Christian" humanism. But why did the writings of Guy Hershberger, Paul Peachey, and John Howard Yoder not include creative approaches to evangelism and church growth at home and abroad? Only later, with the appearance of the journal *Mission Focus* in 1972, did we begin to sense the breadth and depth of their missionary concern. In contrast, the writings of Reformed theologians continued to stress the lordship of Christ over all of life, yet seemed only marginally concerned with the urgency of the unfinished evangelistic task.

At this point, evangelicals here and there began to fall back on what proved to have acceptable missiological credentials, if one was to judge by the standards of Gustav Warneck (1834–1910). He believed that the *Kulturbefehl* should have a central place in mission thought and practice.[9] Among others, I had been preaching and writing on the growing interest of evangelicals in this theme ("The Cultural Mandate").[10]

8. See Edwin Walhout, "The Liberal-Fundamentalist Debate," *Christianity Today* 7, no. 11 (1 March 1963): 519–20.

9. See Hans Kasdorf, "Gustav Warnecks Missiologisches Erbe" (D.Miss. diss., School of World Mission, Fuller Theological Seminary, 1976), 54–67.

10. Arthur F. Glasser, "Confession, Church Growth, and Authentic Unity in Mission Strategy," in *Protestant Crosscurrents in Mission*, ed. Norman A. Horner (Nashville: Abingdon, 1968), 178–221.

My major contention was that evangelicals were remiss in their handling of Scripture if they neglected what it had to say about life in this world. The Bible is not solely a revelation of redemption. Actually, two streams of obligation course through its pages. One is rooted in the creation story and reflects God's concern for this world—all its social patterns and political institutions. To participate in the renewal of human civilization and to seek the amelioration of all its destructive tendencies is pleasing in God's sight. The other stream of obligation is rooted in God's redemptive concern that comes to a climax in the salvific work of Christ—His death, resurrection, issuance of the Great Commission, and sending of the Holy Spirit. Both of these mandates are clearly stated as response to the question, What does the Lord require of His people, but "to do justice, and to love kindness, and to walk humbly with your God?" (Mic. 6:8; Matt. 23:23).

At first it seemed that the acceptance of responsibility for both mandates provided evangelicals with a holistic gospel. But in the early 1970s some began to realize that this neat equation did not solve the issue of priority. Which came first, evangelism or social responsibility? Then came Billy Graham's massive 1974 Lausanne "houseparty"—The International Congress on World Evangelization consisting of four thousand guests. It wonderfully affirmed the validity of both mandates in its covenant (especially paragraph 5). Evangelicals almost immediately thereafter began to divide over the issue of priorities. To some the answer was obvious. Others disagreed. This debate continued throughout the 1970s.

But some at Lausanne stood taller and saw further than the rest. They voiced the concerns of the Mennonites and those serving the long-exploited peoples of Latin America. In no uncertain terms they spelled out the theological implications of a radical discipleship that embraced the total biblical obligation. They exposed the triumphalism and arrogance of evangelicals, their ethnocentrism and unwillingness to condemn societal and institutionalized sin, especially that of racism. In their eyes evangelicals all too often promoted "a fascist form of nationalism in the name of Christ" (to borrow Clowney's perceptive phrase).[11] Indeed, they excoriated all who would attempt to drive a wedge between the gospel and social responsibility and, thereby, mute the prophetic voice of the church.

---

11. Edmund P. Clowney, "The Politics of the Kingdom," *Westminster Theological Journal* 41, no. 2 (1979): 310.

## LISTENING TO THE "THIRD FORCE" (AND MAKING YOUR MISSION THEOLOGY TRINITARIAN)

One of the great signs of hope during the entire postwar period has been the growing vitality and size of the "Third Force" (Henry P. Van Dusen's phrase). Until the 1970s Pentecostals and the mainline charismatics tended to pursue their own goals for world evangelization. They largely ignored the evangelicals despite the high level of theological agreement and personal commitment they had with them. Unfortunately, certain segments within evangelicalism either openly criticized their exegetical conclusions or tacitly despised their social roots. Then these ardent spirits started to invade evangelical seminaries. Fuller's provost, the late Glenn W. Barker, used to say: "Twenty years ago we were not sure they would make it. Now they are running away with all the prizes!" The charismatics began doing what evangelicals could only envy. They were not only multiplying churches all over the world but bringing significant renewal to mainline congregations. Here was something separatistic dispensationalists thought impossible.

Moreover, these joyful Christians were initiating all sorts of lay evangelistic movements and launching a variety of significant mission societies. Although unashamedly evangelical in their high view of Scripture and their enthusiasm for evangelism and church growth, they tended to draw back from involvement in interdenominational evangelical enterprises prior to the 1970s. Following Lausanne (1974), however, they came into their own and caused many noncharismatics to sit up and take notice. Stereotyped impressions and entrenched prejudices began to give way. In no time at all new light was beginning to be gained on the previously baffling and divisive question of mission priorities. It came about because of their introduction of the subject of spiritual gifts.

By the mid-1970s Pentecostals and mainline charismatics had everyone talking about spiritual gifts, their diversity, and their exercise in ministry. The lists in various parts of the New Testament (Rom. 12; 1 Cor. 12; Eph. 4; 1 Pet. 2) cannot but mean that God does not force His people or their congregations to adopt any one "authorized" agenda. Spiritual gifts make possible a congregation's obedience to both the cultural and redemptive mandates. Since all Christians are the recipients of the Holy Spirit's indwelling presence and enablement for confessing Jesus Christ "by word and deed," each congregation must be seen as primarily a confessing and serving presence in society. In the full exercise of the gifts Christians have individually received, there will always be those involved in the general apostolate, serving as God's envoys to the non-Christian world. There will always be others involved in the prophetic calling, reminding churches and Christians of their societal responsibilities. And there will always be those whose concerns are pastoral, assisting local congregations in their worship, nurture, study, and mutual helpfulness (1 Cor. 12:28–31). What this means is that one cannot establish biblically the thesis that evangelism should be the priority of all Christians, although all are under obligation to bear witness to Jesus Christ.

Whereas the evangelical encounter with the Third Force proved to be mutually enriching, new problems began to surface. Somehow, the recourse to spiritual gifts brought other things to the fore. Evangelicals were now being confronted with glossolalia, words of knowledge, prophecy, healing, and exorcism. Furthermore, they were being told that their popular understanding of evangelism was inadequate. Biblical evangelism allegedly involved more than presence (being there) plus proclamation (bearing witness to the gospel) plus persuasion (issuing the call to receive Jesus Christ as Lord and Savior). What brought evangelism to fullness was "power" evangelism (that which conditions people to believe). The argument was that when Christians are filled with the Holy Spirit, there is the possibility of "signs and wonders" being wrought in His name. And this really "works" in that wherever it takes place, the church really grows. Just look at those pragmatic charismatics!

Not all evangelicals agreed. Some said that the emphasis on spiritual gifts all too often caused Christians to disparage what they were by parentage, personality, intelligence, training, and life experience. The Holy Spirit is seen at work through Christians almost independently of what they were as created human beings. This resulted in a misplaced emphasis on the supernatural and a failure to take seriously the creatureliness of people. Were Christians to regard themselves as "lifeless instruments that serve God, sometimes without or even against their wills?"[12] Hardly!

Another internal debate arose over this reemergence of the issue of pragmatism: "signs and wonders" must be of God because of the growth of the churches within the charismatic movement! But is it as simple as this? What of those evangelicals who are troubled over the extravagant claims made by those preoccupied with the miraculous? They call attention to what is perceived as psychological manipulation and the recourse to magical formulae. And they rightly ask many questions: What steps

12. Arnold Bittlinger, *Gifts and Ministries* (London: Hodder and Stoughton, 1974), 18.

are being taken to guard against "deceiving spirits" and "doctrines of demons" (1 Tim. 4:1; 2 Tim. 1:14)? Are the spirits being tested "to see whether they are from God" (1 John 4:1–4)? What of Christ's warning of "false prophets" and of their "signs and wonders" (Matt. 7:15; 24:24)? Why the excitement over church growth when it is not accompanied by any testing of the spirits? And why is it that those most preoccupied with physical and demonic realities appear little interested in responding to the demanding ethical and social issues of our day? After all, the ultimate focus of the New Testament is ethical, not charismatic.

Even so, evangelicals are grateful to the charismatic movement for reminding them of the role of the Holy Spirit in the mission of the church. Reformed theology had almost forgotten this! We worship and serve a trinitarian God, and all three persons of the Trinity are one in the missiological task. They particularly work through the leadership of the church. A case can be made (in part) for what the Reformers and many others subsequently believed—that the Great Commission was primarily given to the apostles. In Acts 1:2 Luke pointedly states that prior to the ascension, Jesus gave a commandment "through the Holy Spirit . . . to the apostles whom He had chosen." This means that in their leadership of the emerging church, they were particularly responsible to see that the constant focus of all congregations must be on making disciples of all peoples. And so ever since. Because of the "sentness" of the church, all Christians must be reminded by their leaders to give high priority to the sending forth of those gifted for evangelism and outreach to the regions beyond, where Christ has yet to be named (2 Cor. 10:16). God is concerned that His people be constantly reminded of the need for apostolic advance into neglected areas and among unreached peoples. And significantly, there has yet to emerge a vital mission-oriented congregation whose pastor has been indifferent to the central priority of the Great Commission.

## REAFFIRMING THE KINGDOM OF GOD (AND ENTERING THE ECUMENICAL DEBATE)

How can the church be liberated to evangelize this generation? If it confines itself to maintenance activity, to "churchly" affairs, it becomes preoccupied with religious behavior and with its own kind of people. It feels itself threatened by the world and retreats from positive interaction with it. But when it becomes kingdom oriented, a buoyancy of spirit takes over. The priority becomes broad, for kingdom activities include all human concerns and this world as well. As Howard Snyder correctly affirms:

> When Christians catch a vision of the Kingdom of God, their sight shifts to the poor, the orphan, the widow, the refugee, the wretched of the earth, to God's future—to the concerns of justice, mercy and truth. Church people think about how to get people into the church; Kingdom people think about how to get the church into the world. Church people worry that the world might change the church; Kingdom people work to see the church change the world. . . . If the church has one great need, it is this: To be set free for the Kingdom of God, to be liberated from itself as it has become in order to be itself as God intends. The church must be freed to participate fully in the economy of God.[13]

Evangelicals here and there are increasingly coming to sense that the kingdom of God motif provides what Verkuyl has called "the hub around which all of mission work revolves." He adds, "If it be true that we who practice mission must take the Kingdom of God as our constant point of orientation, it is imperative that we pay close heed to the whole range of burdens and evils plaguing mankind."[14] If God's tomorrow means the end of exploitation, injustice, inequality, war, racism, nationalism, suffering, death, and the ignorance of God, Christians must be "signs" today of God's conquest of all these "burdens and evils" through the cross and resurrection of Jesus Christ. No longer can evangelicals confine themselves to the single priority of proclaiming the knowledge of God among the nations and settle for the status quo of everything else. Of course, Christians shall not establish the kingdom, much less bring it to fullness. Any trinitarian theology of mission worth its salt will show that God alone will accomplish this. The consummation of human history and the manifestation of the kingdom in power and glory will be the work of God alone. But this does not mean that Christians today dare indulge the luxury of indifference to the moral and social issues of today. Only those are "blessed" who are the merciful, the peacemakers, the persecuted for righteousness' sake: "theirs is the kingdom of heaven" (Matt. 5:7–12).

13. Howard A. Snyder, *Liberating the Church* (Downers Grove, Ill.: InterVarsity Press, 1983), 11.

14. Johannes Verkuyl, *Contemporary Missiology*, ed. and trans. Dale Cooper (Grand Rapids: Eerdmans, 1978), 203.

One theme remains. If evangelicals are to develop an adequate trinitarian mission theology based on the kingdom of God, they must face up to the implications of the ecumenical problem: What must we do with those whose confession of Jesus Christ we must take seriously, yet whose perspectives on the Christian mission differ markedly from our own? Are they to be consigned to outer darkness—excommunicated or ignored—because they "know only in part" and "see through a glass darkly" while we evangelicals possess all truth in perfect balance?

The tragedy is that no Christian's life embodies in fullness the understanding of truth he or she claims to possess. Evangelicals should never forget that the truth they possess is not for themselves alone but for all the people of God. This means that evangelicals have no alternative but to enter the arena of public debate on the mission of the church in our day. They must expose their insights to the scrutiny of others. They must listen as well as speak. Only thereby will they make any significant contribution to the maturity of the church. To retreat from this obligation is to impoverish themselves as well as others. It goes without saying that such encounter is essential to the renewal of the church. And where in Scripture are Christians told to separate from other Christians simply because they disagree with them?

One final word. After almost forty years of wilderness wandering, evangelicals convened Wheaton 1983, their first international conference on the nature of the church. And they made sure that the keynote address was on the kingdom of God! Were they now ready to enter the Promised Land? Many thought so at that time. Actually, however, since 1983 the debates within the evangelical camp have surprisingly produced a variety of new issues and new tensions. For instance, not all are agreed on how to cope with the pressures precipitated by the realities of religious pluralism in the West. What about the uniqueness and finality of Jesus Christ, "the Savior of the world" (John 4:42)? And despite the lessons of the 1960s and 1970s many remain unconvinced of either the rightness or the benefits to be derived from entering the ecumenical debate. Better to work for the renewal of the churches at the grass-roots level through "prayer and the ministry of the Word" (Acts 6:4). Involvement at high-level conferences may be a valid service for some, but most evangelicals still regard it as time-consuming and relatively nonproductive. They only heed the strong and persuasive voices that call for the concentration of all evangelical strength only on evangelism: "People need to be born again. If not, they will wish they had never been born at all!" And this sounds scriptural to many evangelicals still, especially the growl, "Down with all this talk about holistic mission—whatever that is!"

Even so, evangelical leaders throughout the two-thirds world are asking for help in matters that go beyond evangelism. They feel they must move ahead with the urgent task of contextualizing theology so that it is truly shaped by the thought forms of one's own people. In a very real sense all theology is contextualized theology. However, the forms in which the gospel has been proclaimed and understood up until now are too Western and, hence, not fully intelligible or meaningful to non-Western peoples. But the big problem is how does one go about this task and still remain completely loyal to Scripture? "Come over and help us!"

Then too, what about the growing urbanization of the world? These leaders are increasingly asking for assistance in penetrating their massive cities with the gospel. How does one research the city, discover its crucial elements, and then provide insight into strategizing its evangelization? Within the next few years the evangelical movement will probably undergo a massive shift from working in rural areas to becoming an urbanite movement. This shift will enlarge significantly the number of problems they will face. Indeed, throughout the urban world of the last decade of the twentieth century, the evangelical church will find itself as never before among the devotees of the great ethnic faiths— Buddhism, Hinduism, and Islam, as well as secularism. It shall also be in contact with the first object of God's unfailing love—the Jewish people. The big test of its faithfulness to Christ and to Scripture will then be whether or not the church seeks to reach this troubled people with the one who was named Jesus that He might "save His people from their sins" (Matt. 1:21). Indeed, may all evangelicals be filled with anticipation as they face the future as "fellow workmen for God" (1 Cor. 3:9).

As Christians we must not only tolerate our fellow-men in a negative fashion, we must positively love them. We must love them enough to spend hours in prayer for them, to treat them kindly, binding their wounds, helping them in their hours of need. If our love is met with scorn, or blows of hatred, we must reply with more love. But above all we must manifest our love by proclaiming to them the truth, the only truth, the saving Gospel of our risen Christ. We do not tolerate or love them if we tolerate the lies and errors which are destroying their souls.

"Tolerance" (1946)

# 14

# The Church and Authentic Dialogue

## Bruce J. Nicholls

*I*ncreasingly, practical theology, even in the schools of the United States, finds itself part of a global community. Issues that in the past were characteristic of the non-Western church find themselves on the study agenda of the Western curriculum. American churches find themselves across the street from Hindu temples and Muslim mosques. Christians live next door to Buddhists and Sikhs. The question of interreligious dialogue is no longer simply the narrow concern of the missions professor.

Out of concern for this aspect of the globalization of practical theology, I focus in this chapter on the question of the world's religions in dialogue, with particular emphasis on the place of the Christian community in that dialogue.

## MY CONTEXT

I am the pastor of a Hindi-speaking congregation of the Church of North India in the satellite town of Gurgaon, thirty-five kilometers from the center of the capital city of New Delhi. A career missionary seconded by a mission agency to the Diocese of Delhi, I was appointed by the Bishop of Delhi and am accountable to him, as is every other presbyter in the diocese. In our State of Haryana only one in one thousand of the population belongs to the Christian community and in some places only one in ten thousand. Our local church of seventy families and the Roman Catholic Church of the same size are the only structured congregations in a town of perhaps 400,000 people. Thus the Christian community is a very small and insignificant community in the midst of a plurality of communities, some of which are antagonistic to us. Our natural tendency is to retreat into our own ghetto, keeping to ourselves the limited benefits we possess and viewing with suspicion outsiders who want to join us. In such a context dialogue with other communities becomes a struggle for both communal harmony and our call to evangelism and church planting. These are no academic issues for the Christian church. They are matters of life and death. [1] In the turbulent flow of our national life, the church is either moving upstream in the struggle against principalities and powers or drifting downstream towards self-destruction. The question before the evangelical Christian is not whether our goals and methodologies are biblical but whether they are biblical enough or big enough to encompass the whole of biblical revelation. Do we as churches have a biblical wholeness in our understanding of the gospel and the function of the church in the world?

In the hermeneutical process of working through these issues, it is legitimate to begin at any point, provided that in the dialogue between text and context we maintain the dynamics of working from an authoritative text to a relative and changing context. Dialogue is a two-way process of listening and speaking, speaking and listening. In this consideration we have chosen to begin our discussion with the context. [2]

## DIALOGUE IN COMMUNITY

Communities are defined by the grouping of culturally identifiable people. They are integrated people groups with a common world view, common set of values, and a common understanding of the functions of the institutions of society. They share common customs and behavioral patterns. The Christian community in North India is a small and fragmented community struggling for identity and survival, and yet called by God to witness to the plurality of communities that are ever attempting to absorb us. One of the most characteristic elements of Indian society over the past five thousand years is its capability to harmonize and absorb the ideologies, beliefs, and lifestyles of any opposing community. The classic example is the reabsorption of Buddhism into the Hindu

1. James P. Alter and Herbert Jai Singh, *The Church in Delhi* (Nagpur: NCC, 1961), 81–115.

2. Bruce J. Nicholls, *Contextualization: A Theology of Gospel and Culture* (Downers Grove, Ill.: InterVarsity Press, 1979), 48–52.

fold. To some degree the Muslim community has successfully resisted this eclecticism and to a lesser extent the Christians have done so. In the area where I work thousands of Christians reconverted to Hinduism after national independence in 1947 through the evangelizing efforts of reformed and militant Hindu communities and the subtle pressure of economic and educational benefits offered to those who declared themselves to be Hindu *harijans* and outcastes, from which communities most of the Christian converts came.

We agree with Paul Tillich that "religion is the substance of culture and culture is the form of religion."[3] If we include ideologies that are generally substitutes for religion, then this dictum is abundantly evident across Asia. It is true of the mosaic of cultures and communities that make up the nation of India, which until forty years ago included the present Pakistan and Bangladesh.

The local church I pastor is itself a plurality of subreligious cultures. Some of the members have a high church Anglican heritage, others come from Presbyterian or Methodist or Baptist communities, each with its own approach to worship, witness, and service in the world. In our local church worship we use Hindi, Urdu, and English, and we sing the Psalms in Punjabi. Most other religious communities in our town conduct worship in one language only and are generally homogeneous in lifestyle.

In the eyes of the other communities in our town, the Christians are not just disciples of Jesus, for many non-Christians also claim to follow Jesus alongside the other gods and gurus they accept. Rather, they are people who have been baptized and have thereby separated themselves from other communities. In the eyes of the other communities, baptism is the mark of belonging to the Christian community. More than receiving Christ as Savior and Lord, baptism may be an enormously disruptive step. It marks the transferring from one community to another. It has been stated that seven out of ten converts from Islam to Christianity in our subcontinent return to the faith of their fathers, embittered and disillusioned that the new community from which they hoped to receive so much support has not accepted them as full members or been willing to share the benefits of their community with them.

In all Asian cultures the unit of the community is not so much the individual as the family and kinship group. Decision making is rarely a private affair. The community is all-important. Decision making in mar-

3. Paul Tillich, *The Protestant Era* (Chicago: University of Chicago Press, 1948), 57.

riage arrangements is primarily a negotiation between families. Love marriages are seen as threatening communal harmony. In this context it becomes painfully evident that hit-and-run evangelism by parachurch groups with little accountability to the church bears little lasting fruit and rarely leads to visible church growth. The ghetto mentality has to be broken from the inside.

Our local church in Gurgaon is thus one definable community living day by day in the midst of the majority and dominant Hindu communities and the minority communities of Sikhs and Muslims, each with its own clearly definable worldview, values, social institutions, and customs. In addition to these religiously centered communities, the families of our local church live in and mix with other types of communities. Some communities are work oriented. Patterns of behavior and relationship of those working in the factories surrounding our towns are very different from those of the people who serve in local schools and hospitals or in government offices. In our caste-controlled society few of our people own businesses or work in retail shops. None hold public offices in the municipality of our town. Economically, most of our Christians are lower middle class with their own homes, though a few are so poor that they are unable to afford an electric light connection.

Our town ranges from communities of rich families to slum dwellers to a leper colony. Some families continue to live in a village lifestyle in a densely populated urban neighborhood; others are urban born. However, none of the communities, including the Christian community, are static. Families are constantly moving up and down economically and socially as they move from one employment to another or to unemployment. A few are becoming very rich while perhaps half of the population is becoming noticeably poorer. Other factors facilitate rapid change, such as death in the family, natural disasters of floods and droughts, and changes of ruling political parties in local and national politics. Our Christian community tends to vote conservatively to maintain the status quo.

The crisis of Christians in India, as elsewhere, is one of identity. Individuals, families, and church communities are struggling with their identity as Christians in the midst of people of other faiths and with their identity as culturally Indian. While in all other communities religion and culture are harmonized, Christians have little definable and distinct culture of their own. This is both a strength and a weakness. Our Christians are struggling with what it means to be unashamedly Christian and at the same time to be culturally Indian. "Indianness" is an elusive concept. Many educated and observant Hindus continue to view Christianity as a foreign religion with foreign allegiances.

Dialogue in community becomes our starting point for all other expressions of dialogue including evangelism. The theological consultation on Dialogue in Community held at Chiang Mai, Thailand, April 1977, brought together eighty-five Protestant, Orthodox, and Roman Catholic theologians to reflect on some of the issues raised in situations such as I have described.[4] The statement adopted by the consultation is perhaps the most biblically conservative statement to come from this subunit.[5] It gives valuable insights into the nature of dialogue between communities and a valuable critique of syncretism. The issues of the relation of God's universal action in creation to His redemptive action in Jesus Christ, the work of the Holy Spirit outside the church, the nature of God's self-disclosure to people of other faiths, and biblical criteria for dialogue—all were referred for further study. For evangelical Christians these issues are vital to our understanding of dialogue and cannot be postponed.

What then is the role of the Christian community in its day-to-day relationship with people of other communities? Christians have a unique opportunity to be peacemakers in the midst of communal conflicts. Our failure to be so in Northern Ireland, the Middle East, Sri Lanka, South Africa, Nicaragua, and elsewhere is one of the tragedies of our time. It is a denial of the gospel and a stumbling block to others coming to faith in Jesus Christ. Never has the need for peacemakers been greater than today. In India communal riots are regular and predictable. Daily killings by terrorists in the Punjab show little sign of abating. For some engaged in dialogue, peace is the negation of conflict, the inward withdrawal from involvement in the stress of daily life. But for others dialogue means reconciliation and working together in harmony for the good of all people.

In the midst of the destruction of life and property that takes place in communal rioting, Christians have a unique opportunity to be apostles of peace to all who suffer, through compassionate service and rebuking those who perpetrate injustice and oppression. In the carnage that followed the Hindu-Sikh riots in New Delhi after the assassination of Mrs.

4. At this consultation sponsored by the subunit on Dialogue with People of Living Faiths and Ideologies of the World Council of Churches, the writer and a handful of other self-confessed evangelicals attended as full participants.

5. *Faith in the Midst of Faiths, Reflections on Dialogue in Community*, ed. S. J. Samartha (Geneva: WCC, 1977), 134–49.

Gandhi in 1984, some local churches won the respect and confidence of the bereaved Sikh families by their sacrificial service. Dialogue must be a way of life for all men and women of good will.

For the Christian partner, dialogue is taking up the cross daily and following Christ. This compelling dialogue of love and compassion must also characterize the Christian lifestyle in times of natural disasters. In the severe drought of 1987, Prime Minister Rajiv Gandhi appealed to voluntary agencies to come forward and offer their help. Unfortunately, few churches responded.

Dialogue in community is also a commitment to overcome the misunderstandings that have built up between our religious communities. Some misunderstandings relate to past colonial rule when churches received state protection and some missionaries were imperialistic and insensitive to those values and customs which Hindus, Sikhs, and Muslims cherish. At the same time the church must rise above its own indigenous character and welcome partnership with other Christian communities worldwide. The church then becomes a powerful witness to a caste- and class-ridden society that reflects the spirit of apartheid.

Other misunderstandings are theological and hermeneutical. The difficulty for Muslims overcoming their prejudices and understanding the Christian view of Jesus as the Son of God is a case in point. So far most local churches have failed to take the initiative in inviting dialogue with the people of the temple, the *gurudwara*, or the mosque. The way forward may be structured meetings of local and national religious leaders after the pattern of the round-table conference initiated by the missionary evangelist Stanley Jones a generation ago.[6] At the same time unstructured meetings in the round of daily work in the market place or at the level of the village *panchayat* (council) are to be encouraged. Christian involvement will be costly if progress in overcoming misunderstandings is to be achieved. Jesus urged His disciples first to be reconciled with those who held something against them and then come to offer their gifts (Matt. 5:23f.) Participation in true dialogue begins for the Christian partner at the cross.

Dialogue in community for communal harmony is a prerogative for every church. Those churches which limit their ministry to evangelism may reject this perspective on missions. Such churches may appear to experience rapid church growth but may quietly wither and die because they have no roots in the community and no identity with the suffer-

6. E. Stanley Jones, *Christ at the Round Table* (London: Hodder and Stoughton, 1928).

ings and oppression of the people. They want the fruits of the cross without the demands of the incarnation. Their gospel does not include the kingdom of God coming on earth. They love God without loving their neighbor.

A more biblical understanding of mission will include the search for good neighborliness and communal harmony as well as evangelistic activity and the planting of new churches. These ministries, though distinct, belong together. They belong to the gospel of the kingdom of God. In his discussion on the centrality of mission, David Bosch takes up H. W. Gensichen's distinction that everything the church is and does must have a missionary *dimension*, though not necessarily a missionary *intention*. [7]

Since mission belongs to the very nature of the church, all the church's ministries must have a missionary dimension. Worship and the ministry of the sacraments have a powerful evangelistic effect, though this may not be their intention. Often Hindus will attend our church services because they want to see if the Christians are really in communion with the living God. Likewise, the church's ministry to be peacemakers in the midst of communal terrorism has enormous evangelistic potential, though this is not their primary intention. The missionary dimension of the church is the base for its missionary intention.

Much of the contemporary debate on the primacy of evangelism over social service misunderstands the relationships of the intention and dimension of the church's mission. It reduces theology to ideology and the church as the community of the people of God to the individualism of salvation for life after death. True dialogue in community calls the churches neither to manipulate or deceive their partners in dialogue with a hidden agenda nor to hide the truth of the gospel and its evangelistic intent for fear of giving offense. My own experience in such dialogues with representatives of other religious communities is that openness and integrity in declaring our missionary intention is the only acceptable basis for the mutual respect of each other's values and human dignity.

If dialogue in community is a way of life, then central to the Christian's participation in dialogue is the ongoing.renewal of the church. Integrity, authenticity, and accountability—three essentials of any meaningful dialogue—can only flow from a church living according to its nature and mission. The sixteenth-century Reformers spoke of the

7. David J. Bosch, *Witness to the World* (Atlanta: John Knox, 1980), 198–201.

*ecclesia reformata semper reformanda* (the reformed church continually being reformed). Renewal is a call for continuous reforming of doctrine, worship, and ethical behavior according to the Scriptures and the purifying and empowering of the church for mission in the world by the Holy Spirit. Only a renewed church can withstand the deceitful attacks of the devil and effectively relate dialogue to the totality of the church's ministry.

Christ calls His church to be both a model of the new messianic community and His agent to change the world. He calls His church to be in the world but not of the world. He calls it to be both light and salt, witnessing to the gospel and yet penetrating the whole of society with divine goodness. Only a church sanctified by the truth and protected from the evil one can be faithful in dialogue with other religious communities. True dialogue is the lifestyle of the church.

## DIALOGUE IN THE BIBLICAL AND THE ECUMENICAL CONTEXTS

### DIALOGUE IN THE BIBLE

John Stott reminds us that "the living God of the biblical revelation himself enters into a dialogue with man. He not only speaks but also listens. He asks questions and waits for the answers."[8] God respects the human dignity and freedom of the men and women He created in His own image, despite their willful sinfulness and rejection of the law. " 'Come now, let us reason together,' says the Lord" (Isa. 1:18). God's incredible patience with His people suggests that dialogue lies at the very heart of God. Significantly, in His preaching and teaching Jesus Christ gave central place to question and response, whether in dealing with individual inquirers, like Nicodemus and the woman at the well, and with His critics, the lawyers and Pharisees, or in making use of the parabolic method. He almost always invited discussion. The one exception was His confrontation with demonic powers. He rebuked Satan and commanded the evil spirits to depart from those possessed by them. He never reasoned with Satan.

Christ's encounter with seeker and critic is a model for the Christian dialogue with people of other faiths. The early church followed the same pattern. Paul engaged in dialogue in the synagogues (Acts 17:2, 17;

8. John Stott, *Christian Mission in the Modern World* (London: Falcon, 1975), 61.

18:4, 19), in the market place in Athens (Acts 17:17), and daily for two years in the lecture hall of Tyrannus (Acts 19:9); in each case *dialegomai* means "to discuss or reason with a view to persuade." The proclamation of the gospel and conversion to Christ was always explicitly or implicitly the goal of Paul's dialogue with Jew or Gentile.

In classical and Hellenistic Greek the noun *dialogos* was used for reaching the truth through the dialectical method developed by Socrates, Plato, and Aristotle. Truth was the goal of the process and not the presupposition for dialogue. There is no exact equivalent to this method in the New Testament.

## THE CHANGING ROLE OF DIALOGUE IN THE ECUMENICAL MOVEMENT

Dialogue has been a concern of the ecumenical movement since the Jerusalem conference of the International Missionary Council (1928) where the "values" of non-Christian religions dominated discussion.[9] However, up to the time of the New Delhi Assembly of the World Council of Churches (1961), the idea of dialogue was set within the framework of Christian communication. The New Delhi Assembly referred to "dialogue as a form of evangelism which is often effective today."[10]

New Delhi was a turning point for the WCC. On one hand, it was the high watermark of "biblical theology." On the other, it marked the beginning of the process of the secularizing of theology and of salvation as true humanization. In the context of witnessing to the cosmic Christ present in all of life, the contemporary idea of dialogue took shape. Interest shifted from dialogue in evangelism to dialogue in God's saving work in people of other faiths. The "discontinuity" of Hendrik Kraemer and the Barthian era gave way to a new understanding of the continuity of spirituality common to all faiths. Christ is present in all search for truth. Karl Rahner popularized the idea that seeking non-Christians should be thought of as anonymous Christians, while Raymond Panikkar argued that Hinduism has a place in the universal saving providence of God. He states, "The good and *bona fide* Hindu is saved by Christ and not by Hinduism, but it is through the sacraments of Hinduism, through

---

9. Carl F. Hallencreutz, *Dialogue and Community* (Geneva: WCC, 1977), 21–34.

10. *New Delhi Report* (London: SCM, 1961) sec. 3; cited by S. J. Samartha, "Dialogue as a Continuing Christian Concern," in *Mission Trends No. 1*, ed. Gerald H. Anderson and Thomas F. Stransky (Grand Rapids: Eerdmans, 1974), 248.

the message of morality and good life, through the *Mysterion* that came down to him through Hinduism, that Christ saves the Hindu normally."[11]

The new emphasis in dialogue became evident in the series of dialogues sponsored by the WCC: Kandy 1967, Zurich 1970, Ajaltoun 1970, Broumana 1972. The era of direct dialogue with people of other faiths had begun. Following several consultations the meeting of Christians at Zurich (1970) prepared a statement on new attitudes and relationships for interreligious dialogue for the meeting of the Central Committee at Addis Ababa (1971). Interim guidelines for dialogue were proposed. At this important meeting a separate subunit on dialogue was established by the WCC.

While brief reference to dialogue had been made in the documents of the Uppsala Assembly (1968), the first real development took place at the Salvation Today meeting of the Commission on World Mission and Evangelism at Bangkok (1973). Here the contribution of dialogue to the theme of the consultation was seriously considered.

This proved to be a curtain raiser for a major debate on dialogue at the Nairobi Assembly (1975) in the section "Seeking Community: The Common Search of People of Various Faiths, Cultures and Ideologies." Five members of other faiths were present as guests: a Jew, Hindu, Sikh, Buddhist, and Muslim. The chairman, Metropolitan Gregorias (Paul Verghese) of India, called for a common search for world community and not a debate on dialogue. The concern for the unity of mankind was given new priority. Dialogue as total openness was advocated by some delegates. Raymond Panikkar stated in the preparatory document that the Christian "goes unarmed and ready to be himself converted. He may lose his life; he may also be born again." This statement was endorsed by Samartha at the press conference following the debate.[12]

As already stated, the theological consultation on Dialogue in Community held at Chiang Mai, Thailand, two years later was a generally more acceptable statement to evangelicals, even though little reference was made to evangelism and many key theological issues were not discussed. It appears that since Chiang Mai this more balanced emphasis has continued in ecumenical thinking. Evangelism is once again on the

11. Raymond Panikkar, *The Unknown Christ of Hinduism* (London: Barton, Longman and Todd, 1964), 54.
12. Bruce Nicholls, *Nairobi 1975: A Crisis of Faith for WCC* (Taipei: Asia Theological Association, 1976), 20–24. The author was present as an observer.

agenda. Evangelical criticism from outside the movement, the appointing of more theologically conservative staff to the WCC, and the growing influence of the evangelical voice worldwide are having their effect. The WCC Sixth Assembly in Vancouver (1983) stated, "Dialogue is not a device for, nor a denial of, Christian witness. It is rather a mutual venture to bear witness to each other and the world in relation to different perceptions of ultimate reality."[13]

However, the question must be raised as to whether dialogue as developed in ecumenical circles has a significant role for the future. If it means only elite scholars of different faiths all skilled in the language of cross-cultural relationships meeting together and producing reports, then its value is questionable. Dialogue must get beyond textbook religion to the actual religious life as experienced by ordinary believers, for it is here that communal prejudices are strong and intercommunal rioting takes place.

Today the major religions are experiencing the revival of religious fundamentalism and fanaticism. The hope of achieving peace through ecumenical dialogue is fading. In the context of mounting poverty, injustice, and oppression, it is not surprising that concerned Christians are turning away from dialogue and embracing the political ideologies and practices of liberation theologies. Political theology is overshadowing dialogical theology.

Is there a better way to the more effective use of dialogue? We believe there is. A more faithfully biblical understanding of dialogue must be recovered. Dialogue must once more be set in the context of evangelism. The proclamation of a message of forgiveness and hope, of peace and justice, undertaken in a spirit of authenticity, humility, integrity, and sensitivity (to use John Stott's categories)[14] is essential to dialogue's becoming an effective agent of change in an increasingly violent world.

David Hesselgrave's challenge to evangelicals to "demonstrate a new kind of bravery" in entering into a true dialogical relationship with people of other faiths is still largely unheeded.[15] Similarly, Vinay Samuel and Chris Sugden have called evangelicals to dialogical mission in the context of religious pluralism and social injustice.[16]

13. *Gathered for Life, Official Report, VI Assembly of WCC*, 40; cited by Paul Schrotenboer, "Inter Religious Dialogue," in *Evangelical Review of Theology* 12, no. 3 (1988): 211.
14. Stott, *Christian Mission*, 71–73.
15. David J. Hesselgrave, *Communicating Christ Cross-Culturally* (Grand Rapids: Zondervan, 1978), 227–40.
16. Vinay Samuel and Chris Sugden, "Dialogue with Other Religions: An Evangelical View," in *Sharing Jesus in the Two-Thirds World* (Bangalore: PIM, 1983), 177–204.

## UNVEILING HIDDEN ASSUMPTIONS IN DIALOGUE

Advocates of ecumenical dialogue rightly condemn hidden agendas in dialogue and any attempt to manipulate for evangelistic ends those who have received help through social service. The "Chiang Mai Statement" warns, "We soundly reject any idea of 'dialogue in community' as a secret weapon in the armoury of our aggressive Christian militancy."[17] This warning needs to be heeded by all Christians—Protestants and Catholics alike. True dialogue calls for transparent openness and integrity between partners in dialogue but without compromise or eclecticism. My observation is that non-Christian partners expect this kind of integrity from Christians. They may be offended and angry when they are told that they are already saved by the hidden or anonymous cosmic Christ. The resurgence of religious fundamentalism could be in part a reaction to the hidden agendas of Christians, which are interpreted as signs of arrogance and imperialism.

In contemporary ecumenical dialogue, theological assumptions are often left undiscussed for fear of being divisive. Of these, we will limit our discussion to three areas that need open reflection: the nature of truth, the universalism of the people of God, and the work of the Holy Spirit outside the church.

First, we begin by asking, "Is religious truth always relative or is there a finality of truth that can be known and experienced?" This issue turns on whether revelation is always relational or whether it is also propositional. Dr. S. J. Samartha, the former director of the WCC unit on Dialogue with People of Living Faiths and Ideologies, clearly states his position: "Since truth in the biblical understanding is not propositional but relational . . . dialogue becomes one of the means of the quest for truth."[18] His successor, Dr. S. Wesley Ariarajah, holds a similar position. He states, "Rightly understood, all theology is 'story-telling.' It is the framework within which one seeks to give expression to one's experience and faith. . . . The danger and temptation are to hold that one 'story' is more valid than the others."[19]

The issue is a hermeneutical one. Evangelicals who affirm their confidence in the Bible as the authoritative and infallible Word of God hold to a gospel that is nonnegotiable, because they believe in the finality of Christ in whom all Scripture finds its ultimate fulfilment. The relational

17. *Faith in the Midst of Faiths*, 144.
18. S. J. Samartha, *Courage for Dialogue* (Maryknoll, N.Y.: Orbis, 1981), 11.
19. S. Wesley Ariarajah, "Towards a Theology of Dialogue," *The Ecumenical Review* 29, no. 1: 5.

and relative view of truth undergirds the existential interpretation of the Christian faith, which owes much of its inspiration to Martin Buber, Emil Brunner, Paul Tillich, and Rudolf Bultmann.

The dialectical process is basic to the methodology of ecumenical dialogue. For Hegel no idea has fixed meaning or unchanging validity. In the dialectical principle of thesis, antithesis, and synthesis, truth is never final. It is always relative, always becoming. Truth is always inclusive. This creates an expectation in dialogue that opposing and mutually exclusive understandings of reality can ultimately be reconciled and harmonized. Hence the unity of mankind has become an attainable goal.

To this assumption is added the process theology of Alfred North Whitehead and the evolutionary goals of Pierre Teilhard de Chardin. It is then a short step to turn from spiritual and theological categories to those of sociology and politics. The genius of the Indian theologian M. M. Thomas lies in his capacity to utilize the Marxist dialectical method to synthesize divergent lines of thought and action in terms of the process of secularization and to synthesize salvation as humanization. Since the Nairobi Assembly, Thomas has forcefully advocated "a Christ-centered syncretism." Paul Knitter, the American Catholic theologian, has more recently developed the unitary principle as a new model of truth for dialogue.[20] He sees all religious traditions as talking about the same reality.

Second, the universalism of the people of God has become an assumption of many engaged in dialogue. If special revelation is only a providential evidence of God's general and universal revelation, and salvation history is the salvation of human history itself, then "the people of God" become co-extensive with humanity. In this context, the shift in emphasis from the unity of the church to the unity of mankind becomes significant as the goal of dialogue.

This leads to the view that the universal Christ is present in all religious dialogue and that Christianity is only one of many ways to God. As Ariarajah concludes: "A theology of dialogue should take the human community as the locus of God's activity. There is nothing particular about the Christian community except that it has come to accept the event of Jesus Christ as a decisively significant event in the whole history of humankind."[21] Undoubtedly, universalism in salvation is the central assumption in much of ecumenical dialogue today. In a pluralis-

20. Paul F. Knitter, *No Other Name?* (Maryknoll, N.Y.: Orbis, 1985).
21. Ariarajah, "Towards a Theology of Dialogue," 1of.

tic world, it is assumed to be true, but it is rarely "unpacked" and openly discussed. Is it not a subtle form of manipulation?

This incipient universalism is frequently couched in terms of a common pilgrimage. The "Chiang Mai Statement" called Christians to participate fully in the mission of God (*Missio Dei*). It states, "To this end we would humbly share with our fellow human beings in a compelling pilgrimage."[22] It then adds that as disciples of Christ we come to know Him more fully as we engage in His mission in the world and enter into dialogical relationships of service with other human communities. From my own experience, I have found this to be true. In dialogue, the issues of continuity and discontinuity, of judgment and hope, have been sharpened, enriching my own theological understanding. My commitment to Christ has been strengthened. As pilgrims we are exhorted to live godly lives (1 Pet. 2:11).

However, to others at Chiang Mai "a compelling pilgrimage" meant a common search with people of other faiths to find the truth and experience salvation. This view is unacceptable to us and a denial of the grounds of Christian assurance. For the Christian, peace with God is the beginning of the road, not its goal. Salvation is by grace through faith, not the reward for any self-denying quest (Eph. 2:8–10). A compelling pilgrimage is a compelling discipleship of the Lord Jesus Christ. Christology is the central issue in dialogue. Jesus' question "Who do you say that I am?" is the central question.

Third, the question of the Holy Spirit outside the church is an increasingly compelling issue in our pluralistic world, in which great communities of people are without a clear understanding of the gospel demands. This is no academic matter. I am the pastor of one of sixteen congregations of the Church of North India in the State of Haryana with its sixteen million people, and we are the strongest church in the state! The spiritual and eternal lostness of people outside of Christ calls us to new faithfulness in discipleship.

While some theologians have advocated a cosmic or anonymous Christ present in every community, others have framed their response in terms of the universal work of the Holy Spirit outside the church community. The Orthodox Metropolitan George Khodr, in his well-remembered address at the Addis Ababa meeting of the WCC (1970), spoke of the economy of the Holy Spirit in a universal Pentecost. He suggested that "non-Christian religions may be considered as places where his [the Holy Spirit's] inspiration is at work. All those visited by

22. *Faith in the Midst of Faiths*, 143.

the Spirit are the people of God."[23] Khodr added that the man of faith must wait patiently for the coming of the Lord and "secretly be in communion with all men and the economy of the Mystery within which we are moving slowly towards the final consummation, when all things will be gathered up in Christ." Once more universalism in salvation is the assumed premise of this position.

## THE HOLY SPIRIT ON THE FRONTIERS OF THE KINGDOM

The Holy Spirit is God's missionary to the world.[24]. He is sent by the Father into the world as the Spirit of truth (John 14:16). He was in the world from the divine act of creation, "hovering over the waters" (Gen. 1:2). He energizes nature and controls history (Ps. 104:29f.; Isa. 34:16). The Spirit of God in the Old Testament is God active in the whole of life and culture. He guided the children of Israel and used the rulers of the pagan nations as His servants. He prepared the people of Nineveh to turn from their evil ways at the preaching of Jonah. At Pentecost the Holy Spirit came upon God-fearing Jews and proselytes who were worshiping in Jerusalem. God has not left Himself without a witness in the changing seasons of nature (Acts 14:17). He prepared the Gentile Cornelius to respond to the Word preached to him (Acts 10:44–48), and He opened the hearts of some of the educated pagans of Athens through Paul's dialoguing with them (Acts 17:16–34).

God the Holy Spirit is always ahead of the church's witness. He goes before and prepares the hearts of those who will respond to the Good News. He is in the frontiers of the kingdom as the Spirit of truth— penetrating the kingdom of Satan, the father of lies and the ruler of this world. An awareness of and sensitivity to the prevenient grace of the Spirit is foundational to a biblical understanding of dialogue. It creates a spirit of expectancy, delivering us from aggressive behavior born out of

23. George Khodr, "Christianity in a Pluralistic World: The Economy of the Holy Spirit," in *Living Faiths and the Ecumenical Movement* (Geneva: WCC, 1971), 140.

24. Evangelicals took up the issue of the work of the Holy Spirit in the world with special reference to evangelization at a consultation at Oslo in May 1985 sponsored by the Theology Working Group of the Lausanne Committee for World Evangelization and the Theological Commission of the World Evangelical Fellowship. Dr. David Wells was commissioned to write a book based on the material presented and the discussion of the consultation. See David F. Wells, *God the Evangelist: How the Holy Spirit Works to Bring Men and Women to Faith* (Exeter: Paternoster, 1987).

insecurity or overzealous, self-generated responsibility. We know that salvation is of God, and we can trust Him to work.

Dialogue is a way of life, an attitude of mind as well as a verbal defense and proclamation of the gospel. The testimony of the fruit of the Spirit in our lives is more important than debate or verbal persuasion. The Spirit enables us to listen as well as speak and to discern what God is already doing in the lives of the partners in dialogue. The great poet and hymn writer of western India, Narayan Vaman Tilak, a Brahmin convert, claims to have come to Christ over "the bridge of Tukuram."

The Hindu saint of the sixteenth century, Tukuram, the worshiper of the god Vithoba, had a Spirit-filled hunger for God. In one of his poems he cries out,

> As on the bank the poor fish lies
>   And gasps and writhes in pain,
> Or as a man with anxious eyes
>   Seeks hidden gold in vain,
> So is my heart distressed and cries
>   To come to Thee again.

Tilak shared this hunger but found satisfaction in Christ, which began in a dialogue with a missionary on a train journey. Christ fulfills all spiritual search. The noted Islamic scholar J. N. D. Anderson wrote, "I have found that converts from Islam never regard the God whom they previously sought to worship as wholly false, but rather rejoice that they have now, in Jesus Christ, been brought to know and have fellowship with that God as he really is."[25]

As the image-bearers of God, all human beings have an insatiable longing for God or spiritual reality. Agnostic secular humanism and atheism only mask this hunger. Marxism as an ideology is no match for the spiritual power of the world's religions—be it Christianity, Islam, Hinduism, or Buddhism—as the history of Marxist Europe and Asia is now unfolding. Those religions which offer a holistic view of life are having the strongest appeal.

Every day millions of people in India repeat the prayer recorded in the Brihadarayaka Upanishad:

> From the unreal lead me to the real
> From darkness lead me to light
> From death lead me to immortality.

25. Sir Norman Anderson, *The World Religions* (London: Inter-Varsity Press, 1975), 236.

The renewal of the Hindu way of life, fuelled by national TV serials on traditional religious epics, is the most powerful force in Indian society today. That ten to fifteen million pilgrims could bathe in the Ganges (during the Kumbh Mela at Allahabad) on one day (6 February 1989) auspicious for the washing away of sins is visible evidence of this fact. This spiritual search creates an atmosphere of openness conducive to genuine dialogue, but only when the Holy Spirit is in our midst. Therefore prayer is an essential component of living dialogues.

However, we must not lose sight of the reality of satanic presence in every dialogue. All human beings are fallen beings, and we are ever rebelling against God and rejecting His law. Sin pervades the whole of life and taints and perverts all of culture. All people and all societies are idolatrous in all their acts, whether the symbols are visible and material, as in Baal worship or Hinduism, or spiritual and relational, as immorality and covetousness (Col. 3:5).

The rebellious worshiper creates God in his or her own image and then seeks to manipulate deity through symbolic or magical rituals and *mantras*. Forsaken by God, the idolater becomes a slave of his or her own creation. Paul's account of this process (Rom. 1:18–32) is a salutary reminder that serious dialogue is an engagement with evil as well as good. Thus dialogue is warfare as well as reconciliation and peace. Judgment precedes hope, discontinuity is inseparable from continuity, and we should not shrink from either. The Holy Spirit convicts the world of guilt in regard to sin and righteousness and judgment (John 16:8), as well as guiding into all truth (John 16:13) and the way of peace and discipleship (John 20:21f.).

## CONCLUSIONS

In the light of the issues discussed in this chapter, a number of conclusions are suggested.

First, dialogue is only authentic when the Holy Spirit is present, convicting of sin and leading into all truth. We dare not go ahead of Him; we must let God do His own work. As Christian partners, we are called to patience, to transparent honesty and openness, and to a sensitivity to the work of the Spirit in others as well as in ourselves. We go into dialogue in the resting confidence that God the Holy Spirit is in our midst.

Second, Christians in dialogue must be Christ-centered. They must know Him in whom they have believed and have the inner witness of the Spirit of their own salvation in Christ. The Christian partner must with humility and grace confess that there is no other name by which salvation comes.[26] We acknowledge that the gospel itself is not negotiable, though others may help us to see our own misunderstandings of the gospel. A Christ-centered approach to dialogue will involve a costly identification in the sufferings, hurts, and fears of others and obedience to the way of the cross in self-denial. The finality of Christ precludes a false universalism in salvation.

Third, dialogue is the lifestyle of the community. If the church is to maintain an effective openness and witness in dialogue, it needs to be constantly transformed in all its life, theological understanding, spirituality, ethical behavior, unity and structures, and commitment to mission in the world. *Ecclesia reformata semper reformanda.* The structure of the church must be constantly renewed to maintain the primacy of the church's function. In the economy of God the church is God's agent for change. It lives on the frontiers of the kingdom in a hostile world.

Finally, effective dialogue demands that the church live on the frontiers of mission, meeting genuine needs whenever and however they may arise. This may mean meetings with leaders of other faiths, to overcome misunderstandings, joining with other communities in time of national crisis or disaster to reduce human suffering, being peacemakers in times of violence, working together for the betterment of the wider community life.

It will also mean rebuking corruption and oppression in every area of living, attacking the evils institutionalized in social structures. But it will also mean faithfulness in witnessing to salvation in Jesus Christ, recognizing that "if our gospel is veiled, it is veiled to those who are perishing" (2 Cor. 4:3). True dialogue belongs to the mission of the church in the same way that God enters into dialogue with the world He created and in Christ redeems. Everything the church is and does has a missionary dimension, but everything does not have a missionary intention.

---

26. See W. A. Visser't Hooft's *No Other Name* (London: SCM Press, 1963) for a valuable discussion on the dangers of syncretism and the nature of Christian universalism.

# Part Three

# Projections

*I*t is time for judgment to begin in the house of God. Let the church break with the deadening customs that have stifled its living service of the Lord. Let it put into practice the politics of the kingdom, and a reformed church will show the world the meaning of true life in community. It will also find an open door that no man can shut in proclaiming Jesus Christ, the Alpha and Omega, the Lord of history and salvation.

"The Politics of the Kingdom" (1979)

# 15

# Into the Future: To Discern Without Dichotomizing

## Ted Ward

*T*oday's academic world emphasizes bits and pieces. In much of the scholarship of our time, "crisp thinking" has replaced "clear thinking" just as reasoning has supplanted wisdom as the major motive. The metaphors of human mind and thought are now commonly based on electronic computers; we talk fluently of bits and bytes, data bases and domains, input and output. The result is a simplistic model of the universe and a demeaning vision of the nature of humankind. Nevertheless, it is comfortable. Perhaps because it plays into so many of the characteristics of fallenness, it is easy for people to fall into mechanistic habits of thought and action.

## A SMALL VIEW OF THE CREATION

Computer metaphors and experiences with computers tend to increase a black-or-white view of things. The rudimentary component of the computer's capability of "remembering" is as dichotomistic as a light switch: within the computer a bit of information is either on or off, a yes or a no. Binary, they call it. For the Christian and for the future of Christian theology, the dichotomistic habit is a menace. In the dichotomistic mind there is no gray, no in between, no maybe. If you can pose the issue just so, you can reduce it to bits of information, each of which represents a clear-cut binary position. It may be fun to be so certain of everything, but it tends to close off further inquiry and the reexamination of faulty conclusions.

Given the concern for ultimate truth—God's truth—it is only natural for theological scholarship to seek a convergence on specific propositions. Add the fondness for words and for writing that is carefully inbred among scholars and the result can be elaborate word-games that ultimately evade the difficult issues of the confused and complex social environment. Surely theological scholarship among Christians has not fallen to such a level of impotence, but to discount the possibility is a disservice to the church.

Within the scholarly traditions we learn to reduce the boundaries of our intellectual territory to some manageable scope so that we can possess it and defend it. Never mind that many important ideas and great concerns are distorted in the process. The tendency to split things along arbitrary lines and to deal with the slivers of important issues that lie on my side of these arbitrary lines assures my claim on the comfort zone of my own narrow expertise.

This pattern within modern science and scholarship in general has even older roots in other aspects of human society. Hierarchical government and management, for example, are based on the fact that power can be derived and maintained by segmenting an organization or even a nation into rudimentary blocks of narrowly defined responsibility and controllable slices of subordinated authority. Bureaucracy gets its bad name from the contrast between autocratic idealism and the inevitable bungling that accompanies top-down management.

The church was never meant to be managed in such a manner. The New Testament images of vine, family, and body are sometimes misunderstood as divisions of labor and commitment to narrowly defined and isolated specialization. Rather, the metaphors represent intense interdependence and community participation. One way to account for the relative impotence of many churches today is to understand the damage done by an image of the pastor as a hierarchical delegator whose narrow expertise in theological and spiritual matters is conceded by "the people." If the pastor is the head of the church in terms of ultimate authority, what happens to Christ? If the church concedes to the pastor the responsibility for initiating and managing spiritual growth, what happens to the spiritual vitality of the people?

## NURTURANT LEADERSHIP

So much depends on the pastor's acceptance of a role within the faith community that is altogether nurturant but nevertheless results in a minimum of dependency on such a figure. The misunderstandings that produce congregational lethargy and stalemated spiritual development can sometimes be traced to poor theological education of the pastor, but even more often they result from poor theological education of the congregation. Pastors must deal with the fact that many natural factors in our society work against people's willingness to accept their rightful responsibilites within the church. Part of the pastor's mission is to teach and guide in such a way as to help the people of God emerge into a co-laboring interdependency. Sometimes it is easier, far easier, for the pastor simply to do what the people want him to do—doing for them, carrying the whole spiritual load, allowing the people of God to become a passive audience—fulfilling roles painfully characteristic of to-day's society.

Even for those of us who ought to know better, the dichotomizing habit is insidious. Especially if it has resulted in a narrowing of our attention so as to exclude what are rightfully the tasks of all Christians, the value of our ministry, especially within the general society outside the church, can be less than God intends.

## CONSCIENTIZATION OF A DICHOTOMIZING CHRISTIAN

Almost twenty years ago a worldwide group of younger leaders of the church met with some of the elder statesmen in a memorable experience called Seminar 70. Of the hundreds of seminars, workshops, and conferences in which I have participated across my forty years as an educator, this event stands out for two reasons. Seminar 70 was unusual in that the line between those who were giving and those who were receiving was almost invisible; indeed, my memories of Francis Schaeffer, Joe Bayly, and many other saints now departed who were with us in Seminar 70 focus on their listening and interacting with younger people—not hiding behind their own proclamations but acknowledging openly the concerns and puzzlement we all felt in that troubled era. I had been part of the group that planned the event, encouraged and pushed as we had been by Joe Coughlin, but my "up front" responsibility during the more formal part of the program was minor. Seminar 70 was intended to facilitate a variety of spontaneous interactions and small-group discussions. The people who came together were all prepared to give and to receive; it was not just to be a round of speeches and sermons. We planned the gathering that way and, by the grace of God, it worked.

We had purposed to note major issues and particular interests that would arise during plenary discussions and move them into follow-up seminars. The role of the seminar leaders was to encourage informal gatherings in order to draw out understandings and insights from the participants. But because some of us were professors, we fell into the academic discourse model from time to time. In one such moment something happened that changed my life.

After a plenary session on the second day of Seminar 70, I was asked to convene an informal group of about fifteen men and women whose concerns about the implications of communication research had emerged during plenary discussions. We retreated to a circle of oddly assorted chairs in the ample lobby of an old lodge there in the Pocono Mountains of northeastern Pennsylvania. I recall vividly the group around me as I sat on the floor with a sprawl of newsprint sheets and several marking pens. We were intensely engaged in my favorite professional activity, erasing the line between theory and practice.

By that time in my career as an educator I had become something of a crusader against the human tendency to create false dichotomies. In terms of social science and the helping professions I was working against the tendency to separate theory and practice, convinced along with Kurt Lewin that nothing is more practical than sound theory. And as a Christian I was vigorously campaigning for the "priesthood of all believers." This latter concern had grown out of my odd history: Presbyterian, Baptist lay ministry, and marriage to a Wesleyan who took Wesley seriously. Nothing distressed me more within the church than pompous pastors who placed themselves above the rest of God's people by virtue of their education and pastoral status.

These predispositions in science and in matters of the faith were brought to focus in one memorable moment. Sitting cross-legged on the floor at the center of this little circle of younger and older brothers and sisters in Christ, just after I had drawn a diagram detailing some findings of recent research on the use of audience feedback to reshape messages, I leaned back, hands spread wide on the floor behind me, and asked, "What does this suggest to you?"

Our group was "on a roll," and I was eager to see the momentum continue and increase. It all seemed so worthwhile—so important. My mind was racing ahead. Then it happened.

"I wonder . . . I wonder . . ." It sounded more like a reflection of the soul than a preface for profound proclamation, but every eye in the group turned toward Ed Clowney. His only contributions to the lively discussion up to this moment had been active eye contact with each contributor in turn, accompanied by an occasional warm smile. He was among a group of people who loved him and valued his ideas, but he hadn't said much, so the attention he received was as to an overdue sage.

Ed slid forward from his almost trapped position in the soft lounge chair, brought his hands together in a gesture that intensified his warm but intensely fixed stare, and fervently asked, "I wonder, Ted, what are the theological implications of feedback theory?"

Until that moment I had always enjoyed my conversations with Ed Clowney. But just then it seemed that he was fulfilling some of the worst characteristics of my stereotype of the theologian. His question seemed trite, irrelevant, and given the gist of the discussion, nonsense. Surely its only purpose was to derail the substance of the discussion and capture the attention of the group for some sort of diversionary homily. Theologians were good at it: taking a conversation in their own direction, ignoring the purposes and agenda of the people around them, finding ways to pull others into topics and experiences that were unreal.

Through careful examination of the dialogues recorded in the gospels, I had become convinced that Jesus never behaved this way; His remarkable capacity to begin where others were concerned and to stick with their agenda had become my model. And now in this moment of intense dialogue no less a person than this brilliant professor-administrator was deviating from the example provided by our Lord. From my viewpoint, Clowney's feet of clay were crumbling. My reaction was disappointment tinged with anger. Theological implications of feedback theory? What a question!

Some part of the momentary frustration was due to a pastor during my youth who used his knowledge of Greek and Hebrew to impress and amaze our little congregation with his scholarship and, at the same time, to remind us of our own inadequacy in matters of the Bible. He was a sincere man of God, of that there could be no doubt; but in my emerging consciousness of the importance of the Bible in my life there was something offensive about being told, on the one hand, that reading the Bible is important but, on the other hand, I could not really trust what I was reading without his corrections from the Greek.

Since 1963, I had been increasingly involved in consultative ministry overseas among missionaries and other ventures of Western assistance. Through these experiences I had discovered something of the bad name that academic theology had created for itself among the emerging churches of the postcolonial nations. These were people who said they wanted Bible schools, yes, but theological schools, no—less because of their awareness of the differences of approach and curriculum but more out of a passionate preference for the practical simplicity of the Bible over against the convoluted and arcane abstractions of academic theology. It was during this period that some of the Christians of other nations became brave enough to urge irrelevant missionaries to go home; no small part of that controversy raged around the issues of a theology more concerned with Western history than with the hurts and hearts of contemporary people.

The matrix of my sense of frustration at Dr. Clowney's question seems reasonable even today. But the anger of that moment was only a flash. I knew better than to let it show. So far, at least, this had been a voluntary gathering of people to deal with a subject in which I had reasonable expertise. It was my audience and my agenda, and it would take more than a diversionary interruption by an academic theologian to derail it—if I could just keep my cool. So I pulled a trick from the professor's handy bag of tried-and-trusted tactics. I kept myself aloof from his question by reason of academic domain and returned his question unanswered.

"Dr. Clowney, I am a social scientist. You are a theologian. You have asked a theological question. Thus I propose that *you* provide us the answer. What, indeed, are the theological implications of feedback theory?" I must confess to a tone of sarcasm; I recall my slowly articulated "DOC-tor Clowney . . ." as I sought to belittle what I saw then as his attempted diversion from the "real stuff" of science. During that period of my own development I was rather hard on people who "spiritualized" problems rather than trying to deal with them more concretely.

Feeling a bit smug and more than a bit superior, I awaited his reply. But the wait was short. Homing in like a torpedo, his simple reply exploded in my mind with devastating accuracy.

"Ted," he began slowly with a disarming sense of personal intensity that I came to realize was totally sincere, "I am a Christian. You are a Christian. Therefore I propose that it is *our* question. What, indeed, are the theological implications of feedback theory?"

It is *our* question! This learned theologian had invited me into what heretofore I had seen only as being *his* domain. Suddenly the inconsistency of my own complaint rose up in judgment against me. The ground upon which we stood in this conversation—indeed in life itself—is not and never had been legitimately divided by scholarly qualifications and categories of disciplines. As Christians we all should wrestle with theological questions. The quality and substance of that wrestling will depend to a great extent on our responsible handling of the Word, but to engage theological questions is reserved neither to the educated clergy nor to theological scholars. Like it or not, their domain of expertise belongs to all of us. Ed Clowney had just invited me in.

## ONE LAYMAN'S AWARENESS

His invitation changed my life. Biblical and theological studies, formerly an avocational hobby and side-interest, became central to my scholarly pursuits. Theological literature and theological dialogue were no longer optional; they were necessary. I have invented more and more ways to involve my own students in Ed Clowney's question: "What are the theological implications?" More to the point, I began to reason with a specific concern for the centrality of God in all matters. My worldview shifted. Formerly my walk with Christ and my care for the Word of God had raised such questions as, What is the spiritual aspect . . . ? and But what does a biblical view add . . . ? My questions, in personal terms and in my leading of classes and seminars, began to shift toward God as the starting point and toward spiritual realities as being more than merely an "aspect." Reflections on truth now required theological underpinnings. And through it all I came to confess that I had been trapped in the worst dichotomy of all: the presumption that spiritual matters and natural matters can be considered separately.

## HEALING THE ULTIMATE DICHOTOMY

The major danger in the lives of Christians is theological-philosophical dualism: the tendency to separate things spiritual from things natural. The misguided attempt to separate life into sacred and secular leads into a downward spiral of intellectual and moral inconsistencies. The line between sacred and secular may serve as a convenient basis for compartmentalization, but the line is not consistent with the way God has created His universe. The practical effect of imposing unnatural distinctions that are inconsistent with reality is deception—self-deception in this case. Because of sin the universe is divided in ways God did not intend, but to hold such distinctions as absolute belittles

God's redemptive purposes. It ultimately results in the compartmentalizing of one's life and consciousness into contrasting sectors wherein separate sets of values and personality characteristics are played out. Thus even a relatively small tendency toward this dualism constitutes a serious threat to integrated spirituality.

Drawing lines where they are not appropriate also provides spurious justification for extrabiblical and nonbiblical contrasts; for example, consider the hierarchial line drawn between clergy and laity. Although a sound biblical case for this distinction is hard to make, it seems pragmatically valuable. It justifies passivity and dependency among the nonordained while keeping high the ego-image and the distinctive authority of those who have been granted the privilege of status.

In my second career as a member of a theological faculty, I see even more clearly the destructive effects of needless dichotomies. My old nemesis, theoretical versus practical, rears its ugly head time and again in the rhetoric and logic of theological professors. They busily draw lines between one another; some are concerned with practical theology, others are concerned with theology. The implication of the latter is never that it is mere theology but, instead, that it is *real* theology.

Surely discrimination is an important aspect of scholarship, but I have encountered few fields where compulsive line drawing seems less valid than in theology. One must come to wonder at this willing acquiescence to categorical distinctions in which some parts of a field are not held to be accountable for their practical effects. The fractioned fields of academic theology are a reflection of intellectual and scholarly reasoning in which the needs of the church are hardly reflected. A revolt of the churches could lead to substantial relocation and transformation of academic theology into forms more appropriate for the twenty-first century. As I read the signals, more and more churches are asking for those qualities in the leadership and human relationship skills of their pastors which the seminaries have long undervalued. They are asking for the whole people of God to participate actively, not just the theological intellectuals. They want to move out of their passivity as sermon audience into renewal and substantial impact on the communities, society, and the world. And if the needed competencies are not substantially more forthcoming from theological schools, churches themselves will take on the job, becoming part of the new trend toward pastoral training within the churches.

By now many a layman has heard the insistent voice of Edmund Clowney and others who have echoed his concern for a whole effort of the whole people of God to grasp the whole of human experience in light of the whole counsel of God: "I am a Christian. You are a Christian. Therefore the theological questions are *our* questions." This declaration is revolutionary. Its timeliness is now clear. Changes are on the way. Institutional realignment, curriculum reform, and even certain kinds of institutional decline and replacement are well begun. If it works toward bringing alive the zeal of the people of God, it will be worth the pain.


## DISCERNMENT AS WISDOM

Ed Clowney's question "What are the theological implications of feedback theory?" represents the master paradigm of biblical wisdom: discriminating between the merely mechanical and the essentially godly meanings of human knowledge. This sort of drawing of lines is theologically enlightening and spiritually fulfilling for a Christian in a scholarly profession. Without it, in reference to feedback theory in the study of communication, for example, we see merely the mechanistic and manipulative possibilities for more expeditiously getting a message across. For some purposes this application has merit, for others it is hellish. How much more important it is to contemplate the motives and the marks of the Creator in the feedback process: His image-bearing creature is designed to be an active partner in the shaping of meaning, not just an automaton receiving declarations in "high fidelity." The natural person asks of science, "What can we use it for?" The godly man asks, "What does it tell us about God and His work?"

It is ironic that within certain traditions, the formal study of theology has fallen into the grip of the scientific presuppositions. Cultural shift itself may offer adequate explanation. Ours is the age of science and thus the age of empirical rationalism; all human inquiry is motivated by the quest for closure on the practical. This observation would explain a theology more concerned with unified conclusions and proofs for current biases.

Modern science is unified by its fervent commitment to a singular view of human inquiry, disciplined by empiricism, rationalism, and experimentalism. Not only are the so-called hard sciences devoted to this narrow core of presuppositions, which discourages intuitive and revelatory sources of truth; even the study of human experience and performance is delimited by this composite of naturalism and objectivism. The social sciences have emerged full-blown as an extension of this unifying scientific method. Especially in the study of the individual person through modern psychology one finds the presumptions of prediction based on the assumption of an essentially deterministic view of man. In other words, the major reason for science of this sort is less a matter of enjoying the majesty of the infinite Creator than it is a quest for knowledge as a source of power. Thus the bottom line has become "What can we use it for?" Even among Christian scholars this self-centered and manipulative question has become a more common motive.

Perhaps the explanation for an intensively closure-oriented academic theology lies deeper. Could it be that the craving for instrumental power, so commonly offered as the engineering validations of today's sciences, may have infected the motives of Christian theology? Is it possible that *knowing how*—how to handle Scripture, how to tell people what they need to know, how to evangelize, how to grow in numbers, how to avoid sin, how to maintain an image of godliness, and, in sum, how to please God—has become the new reason for theology? This compulsion to know how seems an evident motivation underlying the technical emphasis evident in the procedures and much of the graphic and conceptual material in the conservative sector's parachurch activities in youth ministry, evangelism, and missions.

The qualitative gain that comes from discerning in non-dichotomizing ways came back to me again in Malawi. In that relatively small country where David Livingstone so long ago broke into the Dark Continent, there lives a traditional story dismissed by historians but kept alive because the Malawian Christians want to believe it. Whether or not it was true of Livingstone, it is surely true today in the attitude and behavior of many evangelizing Christians. In fact, it seems to be at the heart of their outreach to Muslims. They claim that the secret of Livingstone's success was his style of entry into the predominantly Muslim communities of what was then called Nyassaland: he held high his Bible and proclaimed in a loud voice, "I come to bring you the Book—the Book that tells you of the God you know!" His dislike and fear of Islam was of the sort that the apostle Paul felt for the idolatry of Athens. But well aware of the value of bridges across which the gospel can move into a needy society, Livingstone chose to seize upon the tenuous link between the professed worship of "the one true God" as revealed through Mohammed and the triune God as revealed in the truth of Jesus Christ. There is more to be gained by keeping the drawn lines low than from raising them into impassible dichotomistic barriers.

## DISCERNMENT FOR THE TWENTY-FIRST CENTURY

Some of God's people see the future through the image of the so-called superchurch. Others still see a great hope in the "electronic church." For these sets of Christians the future of the church seems to depend on being able to reflect point by point the common culture of the times and thus to compete for the attention of today's viewers. Given this outlook, the church must be a place of superior entertainment and lifestyle-gratifying experiences. Quality is thus measured in the aesthetics of a gourmet plastic culture and in the attunement to felt needs of people more than to the voice of God. Whereas it can be asserted responsibly that God is capable of using mass media and entertainment-style worship to bring glory to Himself, the risk of the church's becoming centered on persons rather than centered on Christ seems formidable. If the church drifts off its Christological centerpoint, theology becomes of concern only for the select few, and the clergy-laity gap becomes acceptable. In such a situation it is an easy step to the assumption that God doesn't expect us all to take our spiritual sustenance firsthand.

Other Christians note the vitality of little clusters of the faithful here and there—house churches and informal networks of the fellowships and assemblies spreading everywhere. Their image of the church reflects an awareness of Christianity as a distinctive counterculture. From this viewpoint the future of the church is less a matter of passivity than of active outreach spiraling outward from intense centers of spiritual commitment.

One should not compare a good example of one of these manifestations of the church with a bad example of the other. We still live in a fallen world, and the perfect church is yet to come. There are good superchurches and poor superchurches, good small-group fellowships and poor small-group fellowships. The task is discernment, not dichotomization.

Regardless of one's image of the church in the future—whether large groups or small groups, big buildings or no buildings—the vitality of the church will be related to the following factors:

1. The people of God as co-laborers in interdependent, sharing communities—not as private clubs of independent, self-centered, competitive individuals ("carry each other's burdens" [Gal. 6:2]).

2. A Christ-centered fulfillment of the gospel—not a separated sector within society, isolated because of social status and self-righteousness ("good news to the poor" [Luke 4:18]).

3. Worship of God in word and deed, intellectually informed by the Bible and emotionally responsive to the works of the Spirit ("in spirit and in truth" [John 4:24]).

4. Humility before God as undeserving sinners—not prideful in our erudite wisdom and effective works ("through the grace of our Lord Jesus . . . we are saved" [Acts 15:11]).

5. Relating and reaching, bringing people to Jesus Christ—not drawing lines but drawing people! ("I have become all things to all men so that by all possible means I might save some" [1 Cor. 9:22]).

# 16

# In Writing: The Works of Edmund P. Clowney

## Arthur W. Kuschke, Jr.

The following is not a complete bibliography but an illustrative gathering of Dr. Edmund P. Clowney's writings. Works are listed under three headings: "Books, Articles, and Miscellanea"; "Book Reviews"; and "Sunday School and Vacation Bible School Materials." Not included are cassettes, Westminster Seminary papers, and General Assembly reports. It has not been possible to locate a complete file of his Sunday school contributions; some of the smaller items in *The Presbyterian Guardian*, for example, have been omitted.

Publishers and publications frequently cited have been identified by the following abbreviations:

GCP  Great Commission Publications
OPC  Orthodox Presbyterian Church
PG   *The Presbyterian Guardian*
WTJ  *Westminster Theological Journal*
WTS  Westminster Theological Seminary

## BOOKS, ARTICLES, AND MISCELLANEA

1942. "A Critical Estimate of Søren Kierkegaard's Notion of the Individual." *WTJ* 5:29–61.

1944. "The Doctrine of the Self in the Philosophical Works of Søren Kierkegaard." S.T.M. thesis, Yale University Divinity School.

1946. "Consolidated Churches." PG 15:247, 254–55.

1946. "Dr. Stonehouse to Edit International Commentary." PG 15:243–44.

1946. "For the Faith by Faith: New Chapel Marks Victories of Faith for Covenant Church, Pittsburgh." PG 15:227-28, 240.

1946. "Missionary in Tongues: Dr. Welmers Tests Modern Language Methods in Central Liberian Jungle." PG 15:229–30.

1946. "Need in the Netherlands." PG 15:148, 160.

1946. "On the Highest Level." PG 15:247.

1946. "One Decade: A Memorandum on the Anniversary of the Orthodox Presbyterian Church." PG 15:163–64.

1946. "Protestant Panorama: News of the Annual Assemblies of American Denominations." PG 15:194, 203–6.

1946. "Sunday Schools for Salvation." PG 15:35–36.

1946. "The Thirteenth General Assembly for the Orthodox Presbyterian Church." PG 15:169–72.

1946. "Tolerance." PG 15:263.

1947. "The Guardian Youth Center (A Young People's Page)." PG 16:2, 18, 34, 66, 98, 111, 162.

1948. "Training for the Ministry at Westminster Theological Seminary." PG 17:102–4.

1953. "Wanted—Better Preaching." PG 22:46–47, 56–57.

1954. "The Christian School Movement." PG 23:166, 177–78.

1954. "God-centered Unity in Christian Education." PG 23:125–26, 135.

1955. "Ministers and Psychiatrists." PG 24:61–63.

1955. "The Song of the Angels." PG 24:165–66, 171–72.

1956. "The Relation of Ministers to Ruling Elders." PG 25:53–54, 62–63.

1957. "The Office of Ruling Elder." PG 26:55–56.

1958. "Secularism and Christian Mission." WTJ 21:19–57.

1959. "The Place of the Layman in the Church." PG 28:179–80.

1959. "Understanding Christian Schools." PG 28:230–31.

1959. "The Zeal of Thine House." PG 28:148–51.

1960. *Eutychus (and His Pin).* Grand Rapids: Eerdmans.

1961. *Preaching and Biblical Theology.* Grand Rapids: Eerdmans.

1961. "Russian Church Applies for WCC Membership." PG 30:91.

1962. "When the Tie Binds." PG 31:97.

1964. *Called to the Ministry.* Philadelphia: WTS.

1964. *Discovering Biblical Theology: A Project Workbook.* Philadelphia: WTS.

1965. *Another Foundation: The Presbyterian Confessional Crisis.* Philadelphia: Presbyterian and Reformed.

1965. "Preaching Christ." *Christianity Today* 9 (12 March):5–7.

1966. "Literature: The Perpetuation of an Idea." *Christian Life* 27 (January):42–44.

1966. "The Ministry of Hope," Inaugural address as president of WTS. PG 35:131–35.

1966. "The Theology of Evangelism." *Christianity Today* 10 (29 April):5–8.

1966. "What's in a Name? That by Which God Calls You Establishes Your Person and Assigns Your Work." Philadelphia: WTS. Reprinted from *Christian Life Magazine.*

1967. "A Critique of the 'Political' Gospel." *Christianity Today* 11 (28 April):7–11.

1967. "Distinctive Emphases in Presbyterian Church Polity." In *Church Order and Church Union: Conference Papers of the Reformed Ecumenical Synod Conference on Church Order* (Glenside, Pa., Dec. 5–6). Grand Rapids: Reformed Ecumenical Synod.

1967. Letter concerning the apologetics of Francis Schaeffer. PG 36: 41–42.

1968. "Man's Fight with Lostness." *Evangelical Missions Quarterly* 4 (Summer):217–26.

1968. "Toward a Biblical Doctrine of the Church." *WTS* 31:22–81.

1969. *The Doctrine of the Church.* Philadelphia: Presbyterian and Reformed.

1969. "Lord of the Manger." *Christianity Today* 14 (5 December):3–5.

1969. "Molded by the Gospel." Address delivered at the fortieth anniversary of WTS. PG 30:55–58.

1970. "The Christian College and the Transformation of Culture." *Christian Scholar's Review* 1:5–18.

1970. "Resource of Divine Guidance: The Bible and Management Principles." Typescript.

1970. "The Tie that Binds: What Unity Does Christ Require in His Church?" Presentation paper given at IFMA Cooperation and Comity Workshop, Missionary Internship, Farmington, Mich., May 11–13. Typescript.

1971. "The Biblical Doctrine of the Ministry of the Church (Biblical Ecclesiology and the Crisis in Missions)." In *Missions in Creative Tension*, edited by Vergil Gerber, 231–92. South Pasadena: William Carey Library.

1971. "By God's Grace . . . the Church." Paper delivered to the National and Reformed Fellowship in April. Philadelphia: WTS.

1971. "The Final Temple." In *Prophecy in the Making: Messages Prepared for Jerusalem Conference on Biblical Prophecy*, 69–88. Carol Stream: Creation House.

1971. "Prophecy in Jerusalem." Report on the Jerusalem Conference on Biblical Prophecy. PG 40:93.

1972. "A Brief for Church Governors in Church Government." Mimeo.

1973. "The Broken Bands: Constitutional Revolution in American Presbyterianism." On the Confession of 1967. In *Scripture and Confession: A Book About the Confessions Old and New*, edited by John H. Skilton, 158–216. Nutley, N.J.: Presbyterian and Reformed.

1973. "The Final Temple." *WTJ* 35:156–89.

1974. "Jesus Christ and the Lostness of Man." In *Jesus Christ: Lord of the Universe, Hope of the World*, edited by David M. Howard, 53–68. Downers Grove: InterVarsity Press.

1975. "Man's Dilemma of Sin and Suffering." In *Let the Earth Hear His Voice*, edited by J. D. Douglas, 1022–36. Minneapolis: World Wide Publications.

1976. "The Biblical Doctrine of the Christian Church." Philadelphia, WTS. Class syllabus.

1976. "The Missionary Flame of Reformed Theology." In *Theological Perspectives on Church Growth*, edited by Harvie M. Conn, 127–49. Phillipsburg, N.J.: Presbyterian and Reformed.

1977. "The Biblical Pattern of Leadership." In *Issues for Christian Leaders: Briefs from Westminster Theological Seminary* (March, May 1977), 1–7.

1977. "The New Israel." In *Dreams, Visions, and Oracles: The Layman's Guide to Biblical Prophecy*, edited by Carl E. Armerding and W. Ward Gasque, 207–20. Grand Rapids: Baker.

1977. "The Song of the New Mankind." *Decision* 18 (December):5.

1978. "Church Policy and Scripture: United Presbyterians and the Homosexual Issue." PG 47:9,14.

1978. "Church, World, Kingdom (a Response to Herman Ridderbos)." In *Justice in the International Economic Order: Proceedings of the Second International Conference of Reformed Institutions for Christian Higher Education*, 34–42. Grand Rapids: Calvin College.

1978. "God on Trial." *Christianity Today* 22 (24 February):16–17.

1978. "NAPARC '78" PG 47 (July-August):14–15.

1978. "The Unchanging Christ." *The Gospel Magazine* (March-April), 51–56, and (May-June), 103–8, 139. For a different article by the same title, see 1980.

1978. "The Worship God Wants." *Moody Monthly* 79 (September): 49–50.

1979. CM: *Christian Meditation.* Nutley, N.J.: Craig Press.

1979. "How Christ Interprets the Scriptures." In *Can We Trust the Bible?* edited by Earl D. Radmacher, 33–53. Wheaton: Tyndale.

1979. "The NPRF and the Church: A Response." *PG* 48 (May): 4–5, 16.

1979. "The Politics of the Kingdom." *WTJ* 41:291–310.

1979. "The Singing Saviour." *Moody Monthly* 79 (July):40–42.

1979. "Toward the Future of the Presbyterian Church." *PG* 48 (October): 3–4, 11.

1979. "Westminster's Jubilee Celebration." *PG* 48 (September):3–4.

1980. "If You Liked Jesus Christ in the New Testament, You'll Love Him in the Old." *Moody Monthly* 80 (January):38–40.

1980. "Is the Old Testament an Antique?" *Moody Monthly* 80 (May):58–60.

1980. "The Unchanging Christ." In *Our Savior God: Man, Christ, and the Atonement: Addresses, Philadelphia Conference on Reformed Theology, 1977–79,* edited by James M. Boice, 71–81. Grand Rapids: Baker. For a different article by the same title, see 1978.

1980. " 'Who Do Men Say that I Am?' Beliefs of the Clergy." *Christianity Today* 24 (6 June):696–99.

1981. "The Parachurch Fallout: Seminary Students." *Christianity Today* 25 (6 November):36–37.

1981. "The Singing Christ." Philadelphia: WTS. A message from a radio series presented by WTS.

1984. "Interpreting the Biblical Models of the Church: A Hermeneutical Deepening of Ecclesiology." In *Biblical Interpretation and the Church,* edited by D. A. Carson, 64–109. Nashville: Nelson.

1984. "Preaching the Word of the Lord: Cornelius Van Til, V.D.M." *WTJ* 46:233–53.

1986. "Distinctive Emphases in Presbyterian Church Polity." In *Pressing Toward the Mark: Essays Commemorating Fifty Years of the Orthodox Presbyterian Church,* edited by Charles G. Dennison and Richard G. Gamble, 99–110. Philadelphia: The Committee for the Historian of the OPC.

1986. "Finding Christ in the Old Testament." A four-part series. *Evangelicals Now:* "I: Redemption Revealed" 1 (September):10–12; "II: Symbols and Types: The Focus on Christ" 1 (October): 10–14; "III: Christ in the Psalms" 1 (November): 4–5; "IV: Christ Our Wisdom" 1 (December):4–5.

1986. *Living in Christ's Church.* Philadelphia: Great Commission Publications.

1986. "Preaching Christ from All the Scriptures," In *The Preacher and Preaching,* edited by Samuel T. Logan, Jr., 163–91. Phillipsburg, N.J.: Presbyterian and Reformed.

1987. "The Biblical Theology of the Church." In *The Church in the Bible and the World,* edited by D. A. Carson, 13–87. Grand Rapids: Baker.

1987. "The Church and Its Mission." In *Applying the Scriptures,* edited by Kenneth S. Kantzer, 97–122. Grand Rapids: Zondervan.

1988. *The Message of 1 Peter: The Way of the Cross.* Downers Grove: InterVarsity Press.

1988. *The Unfolding Mystery: Discovering Christ in the Old Testament.* Colorado Springs: Navpress.


## BOOK REVIEWS

1942. *Walter Rauschenbusch,* by Dores Robinson Sharp. *WTJ* 5:120–25.

1943. *Our Eternal Contemporary. A Study of the Present-Day Significance of Jesus,* by Walter Marshall Horton. *WTJ* 5:209–15.

1944. *Interpreters of Man. A Review of Scholar and Religious Thought from Hegel to Barth,* by Gwilym O. Griffith. *WTJ* 7:41–43.

1945. *An Essay on Man. An Introduction to a Philosophy of Human Culture,* by Ernst Cassirer. *WTJ* 7:174–79.

1947. *The Abolition of Man,* by C. S. Lewis. *WTJ* 10:79–81.

1949. *Our Christian Heritage,* by Jan Karel van Baalen. *WTJ* 12:105–9.

1949. *Riches of Divine Grace,* by Louis Berkhof. *WTJ* 11:192–93.

1949. *Secular Illusion or Christian Realism?* by D. R. Davies. *WTJ* 12:92–95.

1950. *Dogmatics in Outline,* by Karl Barth. *WTJ* 12:155–62.

1951. *That Ye May Believe,* by Peter H. Eldersveld. *WTJ* 14:97–98.

1952. *Christian Education in a Democracy,* by Frank E. Gaebelein, and *God in Education,* by Henry P. Van Dusen. *WTJ* 14:173–77.

1954. *A Faith to Proclaim,* by James S. Stewart. *WTJ* 16:234–37.

1954. *Fundamentals in Christian Education,* by Cornelius Jaarsma. *WTJ* 17:45–49.

1955. *Basic Concepts in Christian Pedagogy,* by Jan Waterink, and *The Pattern of God's Truth,* by Frank E. Gaebelein. *WTJ* 17:201–8.

1955. *Inleiding in de Zendingswetenschap,* by J. H. Bavinck. *WTJ* 18: 78–85.

1957. *Christ and His Church,* by Anders Nygren. *WTJ* 19:242–47.

1958. *Religion and the Christian Faith,* by Hendrik Kraemer. *WTJ* 20: 218–22.

1959. *The Reality of the Church,* by Claude Welch. *WTJ* 22:77–84.

1961. *A Theology of the Laity,* by Hendrik Kraemer. *WTJ* 23:187–90.

1963. *The Missionary Nature of the Church: A Survey of the Biblical Theology of Mission,* by Johannes Blauw, and *Upon the Earth: The Mission of God and the Missionary Enterprise of the Churches,* by Daniel T. Niles. *WTJ* 26:55–65.

## SUNDAY SCHOOL AND VACATION BIBLE SCHOOL MATERIALS

1950. *The Exodus and Wilderness Wanderings of the Israelites.* Flan-l-map manual. Grove City: Visuals.

1951. *Paul's Missionary Journeys.* Teacher's manual for flannel-map. Grove City: Visuals.

1952. *The Children's Saviour.* Vacation Bible school beginner teacher's manual (with Betty Colburn). Philadelphia: GCP.

1952. *The Gospel of John.* Vacation Bible school intermediate teacher's manual. Philadelphia: GCP.

1952. *Kings.* Vacation Bible school primary teacher's manual. Philadelphia: GCP.

1952. *The Lord in the Land.* Vacation Bible school junior teacher's manual. Philadelphia: GCP.

1952. *New Testament Lessons:* "The Miracles of Calvary" (6 April), 1–6; "Jesus Appears to Doubting Disciples" (13 April), 7–11; "Jesus Goes to Heaven" (18 May), 41–46; "The Holy Spirit Comes from Heaven" (1 June), 54–59; "The Coming of the Wise Men" (28 December), 81–87. Philadelphia: GCP.

1952. *New Testament Lessons.* October-November-December. (with Robley J. Johnston). Philadelphia: GCP.

1952. *Old Testament Lessons.* July 6-November 28 (with some commentaries by Meredith G. Kline). Philadelphia: GCP.

1953. *The Exodus.* Vacation Bible school course for the intermediate department. Philadelphia: GCP.

1953. *Fathers and Sons.* Vacation Bible school course for the primary department. Philadelphia: GCP.

1953. *The Life of Christ.* Flan-l-map manual. Grove City: Visuals.

1953. *Old Testament Lessons.* January 4-March 22. Philadelphia: GCP.

1953. *The Ten Commandments.* Vacation Bible school junior teacher's manual (with Dorothy Partington). Philadelphia: GCP.

1954. *New Testament Lessons:* April-May-June; October-November-December (with Robley J. Johnston). Philadelphia: GCP.

1954. *Our Bible.* Vacation Bible school junior teacher's manual (with Dorothy Partington Anderson). Philadelphia: GCP.

1960. *Missionaries.* Vacation Bible school primary teacher's manual (with Audrey D. Hall). Philadelphia: GCP.

1960. *Paul, an Apostle of Jesus Christ.* Vacation Bible school intermediate teacher's manual. Philadelphia: GCP.

# Index of Persons

# Index of Subjects

Abortion, 73, 165

Africa, 64, 97, 125, 232, 284

[American] Association of Theological Schools, 15, 91, 92, 96, 99, 112, 124, 126

American Council of Christian Churches, 4

American Scientific Affiliation, 5, 16

Amyraldianism, 157

Anabaptism. *See* Mennonite Church

Andover [Newton] Theological Seminary, 110–11

Anglican [Episcopal] Church, 51, 58–59, 73–74, 75, 131, 135, 137, 154–55, 235, 257

Apartheid, 73, 260

Apologetics, 39, 50, 51, 55–59, 63–64, 65, 120, 212, 237

Art, 47, 53, 55–56, 57, 58, 60, 62–63

Asia, 34, 97, 106, 222, 236, 238, 257, 259, 270

Assemblies of God, 190

Australia, 34, 244

Bangladesh, 257

Baptist churches, 135, 142, 160, 211, 257

Bible, xi, xiii, 2, 22, 24–44, 113, 132, 133, 134–38, 281

  analogy of Scripture, 29–30, 34

  authority of, 5, 24, 28, 31, 70, 120, 153, 157, 163, 176, 235

  Christian education and, 186, 188, 189, 190, 193

  counseling and, 205–6, 209, 211, 213, 214

  evangelism and, 227–28, 284

  higher criticism, 27, 208

  humanity of, 39–40

  inerrancy of, 8, 28–29, 31, 43, 64, 158, 160

  infallibility, 27, 43, 157, 266

  mythology and, 41–42, 167

  "phenomena" of, 30, 43

  preaching and, 162, 163, 176, 182

  revelation, 30, 36–38, 166–67, 182, 267

  translations, 16, 136

Bible colleges, 13, 213

Bible institutes, 4, 13

Bible study, 6, 8, 23, 81, 187, 236

Biblical theology, xi, 34, 36–38, 181–83, 204, 263

Billy Graham Center, Wheaton College, 9

Bio-ethics, 65

Biola University, 13, 211

Black churches, 19–20, 126, 164, 237

Black theology, 18, 126

*Book of Confessions*, 158–59

Bread for the World, 17

Britain, 25, 33, 34, 51–52, 56, 69, 73–74, 134, 139, 232

Buddhism, 255, 256, 264, 270

Calvinism, xi, xii, 2, 7, 30, 53–55, 84, 113, 119, 120, 146, 160–61, 180, 189, 219, 220, 224, 226–28, 236, 249

Campus Crusade for Christ, 5, 11, 132

Canada, 224, 238

Center for Urban Theological Studies, 105

# Index of Scripture